FRAMES OF MIND

REFLECTIONS ON INDIAN CINEMA

FRAMES OF MIND

REFLECTIONS ON INDIAN CINEMA

EDITED BY
ARUNA VASUDEV

UBSPD

UBS Publishers' Distributors Ltd.
5 Ansari Road, New Delhi-110 002
Bombay Bangalore Madras Calcutta Patna Kanpur London

Cover Design : Dushyant Prashar

Lasertypeset in 11 pt. Times Roman at Alphabets, New Delhi
Printed at Rajkamal Electric Press, Delhi

Preface

It is possible that some may wonder as to why the Indian Council for Cultural Relations (ICCR) is bringing out a book on Indian Cinema, although those who know about ICCR's activities, and its mandate, will not see any contradiction. Indians are great cinema-lovers. Cinema is very much part of our culture, and has been so for almost a hundred years. It is not a coincidence that the film industry in India is the largest in the world. Whether it is the 'formula' Bollywood film, or the films produced in different languages in the states of India, or the so-called 'art' films — all these provide a mirror in one way or another into the way in which we think, and how our mind works.

It is the projection of the whole tapestry of Indian culture which is the task of ICCR, and in doing this the publications programme of ICCR plays a most important part. These publications represent a wealth of knowledge and scholarship, on different aspects of Indian culture. They have a permanent value which goes beyond that of a single cultural event, no matter how beautiful and moving that event may be.

And so, at a time when India is on the threshold of celebrating a hundred years of the existence of cinema in this country, it is natural that ICCR should bring out a book that is aptly called 'Reflections on Indian Cinema'. Aruna Vasudev who, apart from being a cinema connoisseur, has played such a major role through *Cinemaya* in bringing to us the films of Asia, agreed to guest-edit this issue. And is, to my mind, an ideal choice. She has put together not a history of Indian cinema but rather a canopic overview, which at once informs and excites as it delves into the panorama and romance of the screen.

The future of cinema has always been a subject of debate, as technology moves faster and faster and takes the science of audio-visual communication into levels of sophistication which just a few years ago would have been in the realm of science fiction. First television, then the video revolution, and now the opening up of the skies through satellite television. Surprisingly, while there have been many funeral orations delivered on the future of the cinema, the medium somehow continues to thrive and even find new audiences. Who thought that *Aladdin* would be playing to packed houses in India not only in Hindi but in Telugu, and that *Jurrassic Park* would be such a success also in Hindi.

This book does not pretend to be an encyclopaedia of cinema in India nor a comprehensive exercise in crystal gazing into the future. But we have a lively and scholarly account of how cinema has evolved in India over the last (almost) hundred years, and we do hope our readers will find the same pleasure in going through this book as all of us had in bringing it out.

New Delhi

— Shiv Shankar Mukherjee
Director-General
ICCR

Contents

Preface
Introduction xi

Part I

1. In the Age of Silence 3
   – *P.K. Nair*

2. The Turbulent Thirties 17
   – *B.D.Garga*

3. The Great Four of the Golden Fifties 29
   – *Iqbal Masud*

4. Indian Film Directors in Malaya 43
   – *Tamaki Matsuoka-Kanda*

5. When Melody Ruled the Day 51
   – *Partha Chatterjee*

Part II

6. Bengal in the Forefront 69
   – *Kironmoy Raha*

7. Enter the Government 79
   – *Vinod Bhardwaj*

8. A Showcase for the New Cinema: Indian Panorama 89
   – *Sudhir Bose*

9. Form and Content 103
   – *Chidananda Das Gupta*

10. The Technicians 117
– *Amrit Gangar*

11. Ideologies of Underdevelopment 137
– *Aruna Vasudev*

12. The Space of Encounter: 145
A Re-reading of *Sant Tukaram*
– *Madan Gopal Singh*

PART III

13. Documentary Cinema: A Visual 157
Metaphor for Cultural Pluralism
– *Shoma A. Chatterjee*

14. Hindi Commercial Cinema: 171
Changing Narrative Strategies
– *Rashmi Doraiswamy*

15. Who is the Bad Guy? 191
Commercial Cinema in the South
- *K. Hariharan*

16. A Bit of Song and Dance 197
– *Partha Chatterjee*

17. When Stars Become Tsars 219
– *Dr. S.Krishnaswamy*

18. The Stars Call the Shots 229
– *Deepa Gehlot*

19. To Be a Woman 241
– *Maithili Rao*

Contents

20. Narrativity 257
– Kumar Shahani

PART IV

21. Directors' Perspective: 267

Subhash Ghai 268
Gulzar 269
Saeed Mirza 270
Ketan Mehta 271
Govind Nihalani 272
Yash Chopra 274
Ramesh Sippy 275
Shyam Benegal 276
Jahnu Barua 278
Adoor Gopalakrishnan 280
Buddhadeb Dasgupta 281
B.Narsing Rao 282
Aribam Syam Sharma 282
Mani Kaul 282
Kumar Shahani 283
Sai Paranjpye 284

Contributors 285
Landmarks (Compiled by Rafique Baghdadi) 289
Indian Panorama Films (1978-95) 305
Index 319

Introduction

Contradictions abound in Indian cinema as much as they do in India. And like the country, the cinema absorbs them all, offering a pot-pourri that has its own passionate adherents. To be able to grasp this cinema an awareness of deeply entrenched values, traditions, contemporary events in this complex and multi-faceted society is essential.

From the glitziest of entertainment to the sparest of intellectual abstraction, from lavish spectacle to minimalist poetry, issues of gender, of politics, of poverty and plenty, India's cinema encompasses them all. It is not one national cinema, as is common in other, more homogeneous countries: its range covers many styles, themes, approaches, treatment and language, both spoken and cinematic.

It does not offer the known genres of comedy, tragedy, musical, thriller, romance.... Rather, for several decades, its single category was a musical melodrama which included a dash of comedy, initially thwarted love, a bit of suspense, plenty of songs and dances and a happy ending. Now, in the '90s, that mix has turned more to violence and sex, the melodious songs and dances into sexually explicit gyrations set to raucous sounds. Vanished has the once-clear division between villain and hero, heroine and vamp. The villain provides comic relief, the hero verges on the world of the villain, the heroine absorbs the qualities of the old-time vamp. The world has undergone a radical change.

The parallel movement of 'art' cinema emerged in the early

’70s to challenge this mainstream cinema. It made an immediate appeal to the urban intelligentsia and was dismissed as irrelevant and anaemic by the dream manufacturers. But it has survived and it is this cinema that has brought international attention to India’s cinema. Subdivided into social realism and creative self-expression, the directors of these films, most of them trained at the Film and Television Institute of India, Pune, show a greater awareness of cinema as a vehicle for ideas. In today’s chaotic media world, with minds mediated by images, the documentary as cultural resistance and as political activism has assumed greater significance.

The government has played a key role, both positive and negative, in shaping the face of Indian cinema: the institutes that were established for training and funding and promotion, film festivals and national awards on the one hand, excessive taxation and confused policy decisions on the other.

Today, the cinema lies in disarray. What does the future hold? There are many possible answers but to foresee the future, there are lessons to be learnt from the past.

I am grateful to the Indian Council for Cultural Relations for having initiated the book and to the generous help I received from friends and colleagues: Partha Chartterjee not only contributed two essays but was always ready to act as a sounding board and a fount of factual knowledge; Pramod Gupta was most generous with photographs; colleagues at *Cinemaya* gave of time and laughter, both equally essential in a period of stress, and my family provided a cushion against the odds. To the cinema itself, which has filled so many hours of my life with pleasure and stimulation, this is a small homage on the centenary of its birth.

— Aruna Vasudev

New Delhi

Part I

1

In the Age of Silence

— *P.K. Nair*

NEARLY EIGHT DECADES ago, in a small town, about one hundred kilometres from Pune, a devout man, brought up in a traditional Hindu family, to take over the family profession of priesthood, sold his wife's ornaments, pledged his life insurance policies, and made the first Indian film. The man — Dhundiraj Govind Phalke — popularly known as Dada Saheb Phalke — the place — Nasik and the film — *Raja Harishchandra* (1913), a silent four-reeler with intertitles in Hindi and English — the story of a benevolent king, who sacrificed his kingdom, family and material wealth, to uphold the ideals of "truth", which he cherished most. The dream of a visionary to see Indian images in a "Swadeshi film", thus became a reality. And so began the long march of Indian cinema. The Phalke venture was by no means an accident. It was the result of long years of untiring struggle and perseverance by a great genius and his illustrious predecessors.

Pre-Cinema Efforts

Telling stories from the puranas using hand-drawn tableaux images in pat/scroll paintings, with accompanying live sounds, mostly emanating from human vocal chords and musical instruments has been an age-old Indian tradition. The narrative depicts a tale, brought alive by a singer/performer as portions of the painting are selectively lift, with an oil lamp, and unravelled by the Shaman — the familiar stories of gods and goddesses and episodes from mythology and folklore are revealed slowly through choreographic movements. The successive projection of glass slide images in a magic lantern created the illusions of movement. And so when the Lumière brothers' representatives held the first public showing at Bombay's Watson's Hotel on July 7, 1896, the new phenomenon did not create much of a stir here and no one in the audience ran out at the image of the train speeding towards them, as it did elsewhere. The Indian viewer took the cinematic experience in his stride as something already familiar to him.

Bhatwadekar, who happened to be present for the Lumière presentation, was more keen on getting hold of the Lumière Cinematograph— the three-in-one gadget i.e. camera — projector and processing machine all combined into one, and trying it out himself rather than show the Lumière films to a wider audience. The public reception accorded to Wrangler Paranjpye at Chowpatty on his return from England with the coveted distinction he got at Cambridge was covered by Harischandra Sakharam Bhatwadekar (Save Dada) in December 1901 —and the first Indian topical or the actuality film was born. Bhatwadekar also recorded on film, interesting snippets of life of ordinary people caught in the midst of their daily routine activities. The 1903 Durbar that celebrated the coronation of Edward VII with oriental and occidental splendour was another event photographed and shown by Bhatwadekar.

In Calcutta, Hiralal Sen photographed scenes from some of the plays at the Classic Theatre. Such films were shown as added attractions after the stage performances or taken to distant venues where the stage performers could not reach. The possibility of reaching a large audience through recorded images which could be projected several times through mechanical gadgets caught the fancy of people in the performing arts and the stage and entertainment business. The first decade of the century saw live and recorded performances being clubbed together in the same programme. As the popularity of the film caught on, all forms of live shows were pushed out and film dominated the entertainment scene. However, the early films were in the form of photographed stage plays from a fixed viewing position in the auditorium. *Bhakta Pundalik* of Chithale and Dada Torne, exhibited in 1912, was one such attempt at recording on film a live play performed on stage.

A Pioneer Gets Inspired

It is said the inspiration for Phalke came when he was watching the imported film — *Life of Christ* — on Easter Saturday of 1911. Phalke started mentally visualising the images of Indian gods and goddesses. What really obsessed him was the desire to see Indian images on the screen in a purely *Swadeshi* venture. While struggling to familiarise himself with the intricacies of the operation of his imported camera, Phalke exposed single frames of a seed sprouting, to a growing plant, shot once a day, over a month — thus inadvertently introducing the concept of "time-lapse photography", which resulted in the first indigenous "instructional film" — *The Birth of a Pea Plant* (1912) — a capsule history of the growth of a pea into a pea-laden plant. This Swadeshi instructional film came very handy in getting the financial backing for his first film venture. Postponing his favourite Krishna project, Phalke decided on a comparatively easier subject — *Raja Harishchandra* — also based on Indian mythology and which, according to him, had enough potential to have a powerful appeal. He fixed up a studio in Dadar Main Road, wrote the scenario, erected the sets and started actual shooting in the summer of 1912. In an interview to *Mouj* magazine in 1939 Phalke had declared, "if I had not possessed the artistic and technical faculties required for filmmaking, namely — drawing, painting, architecture, photography, theatre and magic and had not shown the courage and daring, the film industry would never have been established in India in 1912".

The first full-length story film of Phalke was completed in 1912 and released at the Coronation cinema on April 21, 1913, for special invitees and members of the Press. The film was widely acclaimed by one and all and proved to be a great success. The Ravi Varma-inspired opening tableaux presents a scene of royal family harmony — with a space "outside" the frame from where the people emerge, and to which space the king when banished seeks shelter. Phalke's narrative is abbreviated into little more than a sequence of such defined spaces in which the logic of movement is effected via the viewer's gaze. The film's treatment is episodic, following the style of the Indian folk theatre and the primitive novel. The film has title cards in Hindi and English — English as the language of the elite and Hindi that of the common man. Most of the camera set-ups are static, with plenty of movements within the frame. However, one notices an instinctive pan movement in unison with the movement of the characters, beautifully reflected in the river below in the first outdoor sequence when Harishchandra goes out hunting with his retinue. The palace sets are so well designed and mounted that the visual impact is as striking and pleasing as the sets seen in latter-day films. The bathtub sequence where Harishchandra comes to call his wife Taramati, who is in the tub, with her fully drenched attendants, (a couple of whom playfully trying to stop the sprouting fountain in the middle) is indeed the first bath-tub scene in Indian cinema. And when we realise all the females in their wet sarees and blouses clinging to their bodies are in fact all males in female garb, we keep wondering at the extent of eroticism Phalke has managed to bring out in this well-composed scene. Only a fertile mind as that of Phalke could have incorporated such a sensuous scene in what is primarily a 'religious' subject.

Who could ever have conceived the idea to make a film on the 'making of the first Indian film'? Phalke's one-reel short — *How Films are Prepared* (1913) — a film record on the making of Raja Harishchandra — a study film primarily designed to inform the audiences the various technical aspects of filmmaking, is an eloquent testimony to the vision of a man, a creative genius, who believed the role of cinema even at that infant stage is not only to entertain but to inform and educate also.

Why Mythological?

It is not just an accident that the first Indian film happened to be a 'mythological'. Phalke, we know, came from an orthodox Hindu household — a family of priests with strong religious roots. So, when technology made it possible to tell stories through moving images, it was but natural that the Indian film pioneer turned to his own ancient epics and puranas for source material. Moreover, the characters, incidents and plot outlines were very much part of our rich tradition and thereby close to the heart of each and every Indian. As such their presentation through the new medium of cinema did not pose much problem of communication and acceptance. Another factor could well be the intense religious ethos inherent in the performing arts in the country. Through the performance in the precincts of a religious atmosphere, the performer reached out for a spiritual experience. And since cinema took off as an extension of the performing arts, the same binding relationship existed between the author/creator and the work in the initial stages, especially in the works of Phalke. It was, therefore, but logical and natural that Indian cinema had to commence its long and historic journey with the 'mythological' genre.

The phenomenal success of *Raja Harishchandra* was kept up by

Phalke with a series of mythologicals that followed — *Mohini Bhasmasur* (1914), significant for introducing the first woman to act before the cameras — Kamalabai Gokhale (Reena Mohan's recent hour-long documentary film *Kamalabai* is a fitting tribute to this great octogenarian artiste of Indian cinema and theatre). The significant titles that followed include — *Satyawan Savitri* (1914), *Satyavadi Raja Harishchandra* (1917) — a remake of the 1913 Phalke film, *Lanka Dahan* (1917), *Shri Krishna Janma* (1918) and *Kaliya Mardan* (1919).

Phalke does not wind up *Shri Krishna Janma* (1918) with the killing of the devil king Kamsa by the child Krishna played by his own daughter — Mandakini Phalke. He goes beyond the framework of his mythological narration to show he is as much a committed social activist as a story-teller. This is evident in the title card prologues and epilogues in which he sandwiches his mythological narration, as well as his down-to-earth treatment of gods and goddesses. His tableaux presentation of devotees of different castes — from the Brahmin to the Shudra — offering their obeisance to the Lord may appear naive to our present-day viewers. But, a closer look at the organisation of space and movement within the frame, the entry of characters, their movements, looks and exits and the props they carry, the clothes they wear, reveals the rationale behind the filmmaker's ideological concepts. The need to impress upon the unity of all religions and the equality of man in a highly caste-ridden society must have been uppermost in Phalke's mind, when he conceived this sequence. Being a true nationalist, he was contributing to the patriotic cause by using an entertainment medium like the cinema to motivate people to higher values and positive action.

The opening section of *Kaliya Mardan* (1919) gives one the impressions that the screen test Phalke took of his daughter Mandakini has been inadvertently added to the main film. Judging from what he did earlier on the making of *Raja Harishchandra*, this seems to be in order and a very conscious decision. He could very well have made another short film explaining the do's and dont's of acting before a movie camera, to accompany the main feature. But he preferred not to repeat himself and devised a novel method of introducing his daughter to the audience.

Neo-Realism in a Mythological

Isn't it rather ironic to look for 'neo-realism' in a traditional Indian mythological? To Phalke, God's land is no different from man's. He transposes Gokul, Mathura and Brindaban to his familiar Nasik back-drops, river banks and alleys and Yashoda and the Gopis to local Maharashtrian rustic women in their nine-yard sarees. They are more like ordinary people, picturised against familiar backdrops, behaving in a natural manner, rather than imaginary, heavily made-up characters, coming out of fantasy world. There is no attempt to deify them or make them supernatural or larger than life. The scene where mother Yashoda and father Nanda face an irate crowd of belligerent women complainers — some with broken pots, others with twisted knots — all wanting the naughty Krishna to be banished from their midst, brings out this aspect rather convincingly. The image of the cow which Krishna draws on the inside wall of his living room, when the complaint drama is going on outside, in a sense is a premonition of the next phase of his life i.e. — Krishna the cow-herd. Later, the haunting music of his flute sends waves of raptures to the Gopis of the village, who rush out of their houses, leaving their household chores, and come flocking around the Lord to dance in ecstasy to the melody of his magical flute. This is one of the most haunting sequences of the film. A sensitive viewer may even experience the musical sound of the flute after some time, though the film is silent.

The Phalke Trail

'Phalke Films' — is the name of the company which Phalke started initially to realise his ambition of turning filmmaker. It was more of a cottage enterprise with borrowed money and personal mortgages and helped by well-wishers and family friends like Trymbak B. Telang, whom he trained in the operation of the Williamson camera. The first five films were made under this banner. However, by that time, he found his home enterprise too inadequate to handle the problems of administration, keeping track of returns from distribution, raising capital and planning more ambitious productions. In keeping with the times, he had to start a purely indigenous outfit — Hindusthan Film Company in 1918 as a corporate partnership between M/s Vaman, Shridhar Apte, Laxman Balwant Phatak, Mayashankar Bhatt, Gokuldas Damodar

D. G. Phalke

and Madhavji Jessing. Phalke himself resigned as its partner in 1919, returning to it as Chief Producer and Technical Adviser and, of course, its artistic creator in 1923. Out of the 93 films made under the 'Hindusthan' banner, Phalke contributed to over 40 films — the most significant ones being — *Shri Krishna Janma* (1918), *Kaliya Mardan* (1919), *Sant Tukaram* (1921), *Sant Namdev* (1922), *Sant Eknath* (1926) and *Bhakta Prahlad* (1926) — all silent.

Film as Business

When Jamshedji Framji Madan (1856-1926) launched his bioscope show in a tent on Calcutta Maidan, he heralded the public exhibition of films in the country. By 1907 the tent cinema had developed into a Picture Palace, and film exhibition became a big, glamorous business, and cinema theatres had sprung up all over the country. By the end of the second decade, Madan himself had a chain of thirty-seven theatres and had built up an exhibition-distribution and production empire, on the lines of Hollywood. Side by side with importing films for showing in his vast chain of theatres, he also imported foreign actresses (Ermeline, Patience Cooper and others) to act in Indian mythologicals and folk tales as Indian females were hesitant to expose themselves to the gaze of the film camera. S.N. Patankar of Patankar Friends & Co., a contemporary and close associate of Phalke, came up with a four-part serial — *Ram Banvas* (Exile of Lord Rama) in 1918. Well, the 'serial' is not something introduced by television! The format was then very much part of cinema experience both in our country as well as abroad, especially during the silent era. The interest did not survive the introduction of sound and filmmakers switched on to what is known as 'sequels' whenever a particular subject turned out to be a phenomenal success, beyond their normal expectations.

Regional expansion

The credit for making the first feature film in southern India — *Kecchaka Vadham* (1916) — goes to R. Nataraja Mudaliar, an automobile spare parts dealer-turned filmmaker. As the title indicates the subject is again mythological from the Mahabharata. Another film made in Madras — *Valli Thiru-Manam* (1921) by Whittaker — drew critical acclaim and box-office success. Hollywood-returned Ananthanarayanan Narayanan founded General Pictures Corporation in 1929 and established filmmaking as an industry in South India and became the single largest producer of silent films. Kolhapur in Western Maharashtra was another centre of active film production in the twenties, and the man who spearheaded the film scene in this city was Baburao K. Mistry — popularly known as Baburao Painter. He came originally from the stage with experience in set design, painting and art direction. His long apprenticeship in the cinema gave him valuable experience and first-hand knowledge. In 1919 he formed the Maharashtra Film Co. with the blessings of the Maharaja of Kolhapur and released the first significant historical — *Sairandhari* — in 1920 with Balasaheb Yadav (another veteran of Kolhapur), Kamala Devi and Zunzarrao Pawar in stellar roles. Because of his special interest in sets, costumes, design and painting, he chose episodes from Maratha history for interpreting in the new medium and specialised in the historical genre. The exploits of Shivaji and his contemporaries and their patriotic encounters with their opponents formed the recurring themes of his 'historicals' which invariably had a contemporary relevance to the people of a nation, who were fighting for liberation from a colonial oppressor. The attack against the false values associated with the Western way of life and their blind imitation by some Indians was humorously brought out by Dhiren Ganguly (popularly known as D.G.) in his brilliant satirical comedy — *England Returned* (1921) — presumably the first

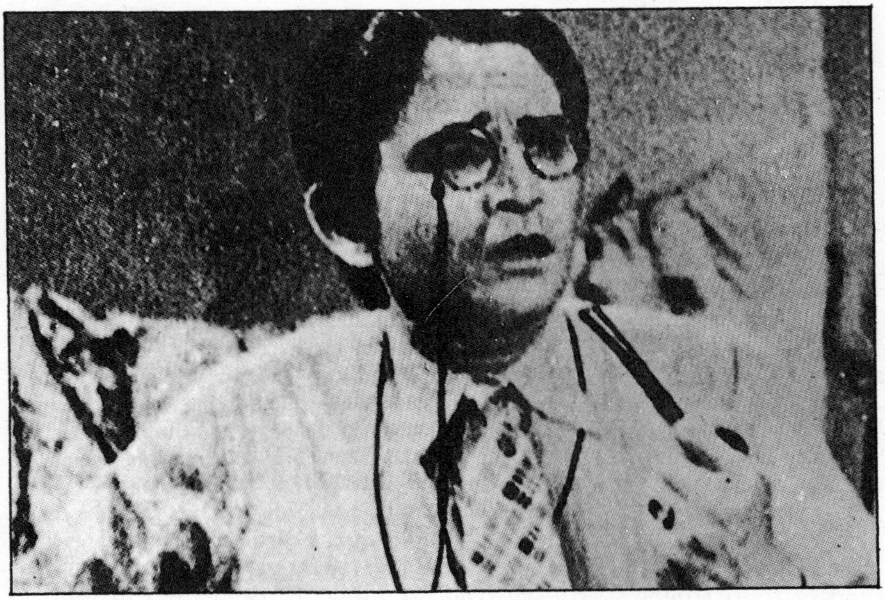

England Returned, 1921, Dhiren Ganguly

"social satire" on Indians obsessed with Western values. And with that another genre of Indian cinema known as "the contemporary social" slowly emerged. Baburao Painter followed it up with another significant film in 1925 — *Savkari Pash* (The Indian Shylock) — an attempt at realistic treatment of the Indian peasant, exploited by the greedy money-lender. V. Shantaram, who started his career as an understudy to Painter, got his acting break as the young village peasant in this film. Painter remade the film as a talkie version eleven years later. Writing about the film, director J.B.H. Wadia says in his memoirs : "I go into a trance even today when I recollect the long shot of a dreary hut photographed in low key, highlighted only by the howl of a dog to symbolise and intensify the stark tragedy inside...."

Co-productions

Bengal-born Himansu Rai came from a large family of theatre enthusiasts. Rai's initiation to theatre and later cinema started in London in the early twenties when pursuing his legal education at the Inner Temple, he came into contact with playwright Niranjan Pal — who showed him a script he had written based on Edwin Arnold's poem — "Light of Asia". The two set up a partnership, Pal got Peter Ostenmeyr's German company, Emelka, to pre-buy the European distribution rights and to contribute the technical crew consisting of Director Franz Osten (Ostenmeyr's brother), cameraman Joseph Wirsching, production designer Karl Von Spretti and assistants and all technical equipments, while Rai got the Delhi-based Great Eastern Film Corporation owned by Moti and Prem Sagar to invest in one-third of the production. And thus took shape — *Light of Asia* (1925) — the first significant international co-production. The unique film was shot entirely in India in actual locales without aid of studio sets, artificial lights, faked-up properties or make-up. The Maharaja of Jaipur placed the whole of the resources of his State for the making of the picture. Designed primarily for an international audience, the film opens with an introduction to "the wonder that was Ind" with a five-to-six-minute travelogue footage of India, covering places of religious worship and of tourist interest, till we land up along with the English tourists in Bodh Gaya and the story is unfolded through a flashback, being narrated by an old sadhu. Despite the best intentions of the filmmakers, and fine technical accomplishments in terms of camera work, use of locales and competent performances, the film did not create much of a stir in the international scene — possibly due to the deliberate effort to project the conventional romantic image of India with all its exotica — as a land of tigers, elephants, snake-charmers, maharajas, princely weddings, processions, hunting expeditions and royal tournaments. The Himansu Rai-Franz Osten team repeated the co-production exercise in two more films — *Shiraz*, the loves of a Moghul prince (1928), based on the story of the Taj Mahal, and *Throw of Dice* (1930) — inspired by an incidents from the great Mahabharata epic. All the three titles had more or less the same approach resulting in the film having a lukewarm reception, both nationally and internationally and remained an interesting though unsuccessful attempt to capture an international market.

Marthandavarma (1931) produced by R. Sunder Raj under Shri Rajeswari Film, Nagercoil, banner and directed by P.V. Rao, got into a legal tangle and was withdrawn after the premiere. Based on the celebrated novel by Shri C.V. Raman Pillai the film recounts the adventures of the crown prince and how he eliminates the arch-villains to become the unquestioned ruler of erstwhile Travancore State. He has also been remembered by many as the builder of modern Travancore. The film has title cards in English and Malayalam, some of which are taken from the original text. A few of the title cards and action make obvious reference to the Swadeshi movement of the time. This film also opens with a seven-minute actuality footage — a newsreel coverage of the famous temple procession of the late Travancore Maharaja, Shri Chithira Thirunal. We see the caparisoned elephants, the State cavalry, the Nair brigade, the barefoot officers and the maharaja being carried in a decorated palanquin in a ceremonial parade. Had it not been for the legal embargo, the film would have had a great impact on the regional cinema of the South.

Government and Cinema

Government's first intervention of the cinema industry took place in 1918 when, appalled by the deplorable conditions in which the public were watching films and also the indiscriminate growth of crime and sex especially in imported films, it passed the Indian Cinematograph Act, which made compulsory the licensing of cinemas and introduced censorship of films. Soon a bureaucrat in West Bengal came up with a brilliant idea to impose an education cess on the tickets sold at the box-office counter: the venom of 'entertainment tax' was injected into the system. Starting with a negligible percentage in 1922, the entertainment tax has now grown to such monstrous proportions in several States that the film industry is reeling under its burden.

In 1928 the Indian Cinematograph Committee was set up under the chairmanship of Dewan Bahadur T. Rangachariar, with the primary brief of improving the status of "Dominion Empire" films which, according to the British, included both British and Indian. Rangachariar neatly undermined the basic premise that had prompted the British Government to set up the I.C.C. According to him, there was no case for discriminating against American films or for offering special privileges to British productions. Being a true nationalist, he used the opportunity to study the condition of the Indian film industry and suggest ways and means for its improvement. To arrive at its decision, the Committee launched a major investigation, travelling the length and breadth of the country and questioning over 300 witnesses including all those who mattered in the film scene of the country then. The resulting material — the one volume *Report of the Indian Cinematograph Committee* and five volumes of *Evidence* — form a rich storehouse of information on the first two decades of Indian cinema.

Giving his evidence before the Committee, Phalke stated: "I am interested in the production of educational, motivational, instructive and travel films. Even, if the Government were to undertake the production of such films, they would not come into conflict with my venture, *as the field is quite vast and exhibitors are ready to have my short films as side attractions*." He cited the example of *Talegaon Glass Factory*, an industrial short, which he made in the early '20s and which was quite popular with moviegoers. Thereafter, theatre proprietors were eager to screen short subjects made by Phalke. Phalke and his contemporaries were conscious of the immense potentialities of the new medium of cinema, not only as a vehicle for escapist entertainment, but also for purposes of education, information and motivation. Practically every film company of the silent era engaged in the production of indigenous entertainment films saw the necessity of diverting part of their resources for recording the Indian actuality of people, events and places and deemed it their moral responsibility to show this to paying audiences side by side with their pictorial entertainments. It is rather ironic that a fimmaking process which grew out of such enlightened consciousness came to be looked down upon with suspicion when the national Government got installed, so much so that they took it for granted that only a Government agency could fulfil the onerous task of production and distribution (though compulsorily!) of newsreels and documentaries. We must have made a terrible mistake somewhere along the way and the sooner we correct ourselves, the better for short filmmaking in the country.

The Devolution Act of 1920 had regularised transfer of certain powers to the then Provincial Governments. The items transferred included, among other things, the power to license theatres, to censor films and develop industries. The Rangachariar Committee had concluded "every characteristic of the cinema industry makes it *unsuitable* for provincialisation...our view is both control and production ought to be made Central subjects....The Committee, therefore, recommends a Central Cinema Department for the overall supervision and control of the film industry."

For the development of the film industry in India, Rangachariar made several recommendations which, more than half a century later, seem far ahead of their times and challenge any Government to implement them. Apart from creating a Central Cinema Department consisting of experts 'to advise, guide and assist the trade and industry', he suggested the building of more permanent cinemas and encouraging the growth of travelling cinemas, the grant of institutional loans to producers for setting up of a national film library, instituting awards and prizes to meritorious films, the production of documentary and educational films by the Government, since the trade cannot be expected (to do that) from motives of philanthropy and, most of all, 'that the raw materials of an industry should be free of duty is almost axiomatic.'

The Rangachariar report was completed in 1928 with a note of dissent from the British members of the Committee. The I.C.C. report disappeared into the dusty corridors of bureaucracy. The industry that Rangachariar had so meticulously studied and shrewdly analysed was itself poised for a revolutionary change with the technological innovation of sound. The world of silent cinema was soon to come to an end with a whimper.

Balance Sheet

According to the Censor records available with National Film Archives of India (NFAI) since 1918 a total of 1268 silent features have been made in this country. Unfortunately most of them vanished long, long ago. Despite its best efforts, the NFAI could preserve only ten

Throw of Dice (1930), Franz Osten with Sita Devi and Charu Roy

or twelve titles so far and the majority of them are incomplete. The complete ones are the three co-productions — *Light of Asia* (1925), *Shiraz* (1928) and *Throw of Dice* (1930) which were obtained from abroad. It is a pity neither the filmmakers nor the authorities concerned took the trouble of preserving the country's silent cinema heritage. However, an archivist keeps on hoping these mute treasures, at least some of them, may turn up somewhere, some day!

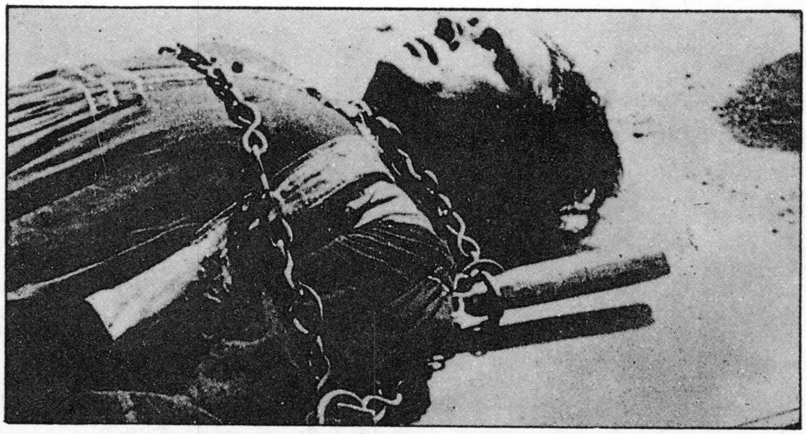

Himanshu Roy in *Shiraz*, 1928, Franz Osten

2

The Turbulent Thirties

— B. D. Garga

QUITE COINCIDENTALLY, WHEN Jawaharlal Nehru, the President of the Indian National Congress, gave a call for 'Purna Swarajya' (complete independence) to end colonial rule, the British architect, Edwin Lutyens, was busy in the new Imperial capital — New Delhi — giving finishing touches to the splendorous Viceregal palace, a palace larger than Louis XIV's at Versailles, as if the empire would last forever. Gandhi had set off on his famous Dandi march in defiance of Government's monopoly and the hated salt tax. The colonial government retaliated the only way it knew: repression — police firings, arrests, confiscation of property and suppression of the media. In the midst of the imperial show of might and national resistance, the silent Indian film began to talk.

Master Vithal and Zubeida in *Alam Ara*, 1931, Ardeshir M. Irani, the first Indian sound film.

Not only talk, but sing and dance as well. That is what *Alam Ara* did to the delirious delight of the audience. Produced by Ardeshir Irani (Imperial Film Company) and released in his own theatre, the Majestic cinema, on March 14, 1931, the film drew crowded houses, notwithstanding what the *Times of India* described, "its patchy voice reproduction due to the inexperience of the players in facing the microphone and a consequent tendency to talk too loudly". Although Indian audiences were familiar with talkies, Universal's *The Melody of Love* having been shown in 1929 followed by some others, to see a film in one's own language was a different experience. *Alam Ara* triggered a revolution. Also, a crisis. Sceptics held on to the view that the novelty would soon wear off, but the huge crowds outside any theatre showing a sound film belied any such expectation. In the war of the survival of the fittest many just disappeared. So did the stars who lacked mike-friendly voices.

Zebunissa, glamorous star of the '30s

The Rise and Dominance of Bombay

As now, so also then, Bombay was the hub of the film industry having a number of self-contained production units. Till the mid-thirties, Irani's Imperial Film Company led the way with its well-regulated production (6-8 films a year), seasoned directors (R.S. Chowdhury, Moti Gidwani, Mohan Bhavnani, Nandlal Jaswantlal, Ezra Mir) and a large stable of stars (Sulochana, Zubeida, Zebunissa, Jillobai, Jal Merchant, Mazhar Khan, Yaqub, Prithviraj). Sulochana was the studio's "hottest" property, advertised as "The Fawn-eyed Beauty", "The One and Only Sulochana" and "The Star of Stars" and cast in a myriad roles including such runaway successes as *Madhuri* (1932 — her first talkie), *Indira, M.A.* (1934) and *Anarkali* (1935). Imperial's formidable rival was Ranjit Movietone founded by Chandulal Shah and Goharbai, a reigning star of the thirties who, though no match to Sulochana in looks, was a far better performer. Prolific in output, Ranjit produced every genre of film — mythological, historical, ruritarian romances, action, musicals, social and family drama — and kept the country's theatres well-supplied all through the thirties. On an average, the studio maintained a production staff of 600 that included artistes, technicians and directors. It also ran a house magazine to promote its products and stars.

Wadia Movietone was the only company that earned a sizeable following from a particular genre — the stunt film — which had its lineage in the Hollywood serial of the twenties — films of Pearl White and Ruth Roland. It all started with a film called *Hunterwali* (the Lady with the Whip in1934) which became a sensational success and made its heroine, Nadia, a household name. There were male actors who could perform all manner of stunts but no women who could match Nadia. Carrying a man on her shoulder, she could run the length of a moving train, leap from a tree onto a horse and outchase her adversary, float down the dangerous rapids or enter a lion's cage bare-handed. All this earned her the sobriquet "Fearless Nadia" for she never used a double for her thrilling stunts. *Miss Frontier Mail* (1936), *Punjab Mail* (1939) and *Diamond Queen* (1940) were some of her popular films, all directed by Homi Wadia, whom she later married. From stunts to serious filmmaking. Among the leading filmmakers operating within the Bombay/Maharashtra region were V. Shantaram, Master Vinayak, Mehboob Khan, Sohrab Modi, Franz Osten and a few others. Of them all, Shantaram was arguably the most innovative and ambitious. From his first talkie *Ayodhya ka Raja* (1932) to *Admi* (1939), it was clear that here was a filmmaker with a distinct style and social concern whose films generated wide discussion and debate. If his films appeared at times didactic (but never dull) he was only

V. Shantaram's *Ayodhya ka Raja*, 1932

responding to the mood of the times which was reformist — issues like caste system, religious bigotry and women's rights. Even when Shantaram took up stories from the past, he used these as parables to highlight contemporary situations. *Amirt Manthan* (1934) opposed the senseless violence of Hindu rituals — a priest unable to find someone for sacrificial offering cuts off his own head to propitiate the deity. A critic who saw the film recently found it "more relevant today as fundamentalism has grown to be more dangerously powerful than it was in 1934." *Dharmatama* (1935) which concerned Brahmanical orthodoxy and caste system would appear to be no less topical today in the context of a strong Dalit movement. Originally titled *Mahatma* the film was entirely banned by the colonial censor on the ground that it treated a sacred subject irreverently and dealt with controversial politics. *Amarjyoti* (1936) was an allegory on the oppression of women in which the protagonist seeks revenge. It could perhaps be called the first women's lib film.

Duniya Na Mane (1937) was again about a young woman's courageous resistance to a much older husband whom she had been tricked into marrying. It was in this film that Shantaram made an effective and highly imaginative use of sound, controlling and

Duniya na Mane, 1937, V. Shantaram

manipulating it much the same way as his visuals. Throughout the film, he used no background music, only atmospheric sounds and voices; nor was there any musical accompaniment to the few songs in the film. Devoid of all mandatory box office ingredients, the film was a box office success to the surprise of the industry. Shantaram's major work was *Admi* (1939) which even now, over half a century later, retains much of its earlier power and angst. The film opened in Bombay on September 9, 1939, a week after Lord Linlithgow, the Viceroy of India, took India to war with Germany. At a time when every column inch of a newspaper was given over to the coverage of Hitler's lightning sweep through Europe and political strife within the country (cinema, understandably, had a low priority), the *Bombay Chronicle* columnist K.A. Abbas was so moved by *Admi* that he ran a seven-column review of the film with a headline that screamed: HATS OFF TO A GREAT ADMI.

Apart from Shantaram, Prabhat had other highly skilled and sensitive filmmakers like the Damle-Fatehlal duo who made one of the most beautiful biographicals ever on the 17th century saint-poet *Tukaram* (1935). He belonged to a movement similar to Bhakti/ Sufism — the rise of which diminished the hegemony of the priestly class who wrote in Sanskrit. Poets like Tukaram, Ramdas, Eknath, Vidyapati and Chandidas wrote in the language of the people, which accounts for their ever-increasing popularity. The press hailed the film as "a human document of great value" and with a continuous run of 57 weeks at one theatre (Central, Bombay), it set a new box office record. In the years that followed, its popularity has continued, especially in the villages of Maharashtra, where groups of people travel long distances to watch it.

Not all the films of the period were sombre and sermonising. There were any number of comedy films, though not always of a high order, which punctured pomposity and lampooned hypocrisy. Master Vinayak, who started his career as an actor with Prabhat Film Company in Kolhapur, had an uncommon flair for social satire. He directed a number of films for his own company, Huns Pictures. Of these, *Brahmachari* (1938) was delightful spoof on celibacy as practised in an ashram, and *Brandi Ki Botal* (1939), a tongue-in-cheek propaganda for prohibition, introduced by the Congress Ministry formed during colonial rule.

Few men have the grit and determination Mehboob Khan had. He started his career as a face in the crowd in innumerable Imperial films and went on to become Sagar Film Company's most acclaimed director. Making his debut with a film called *Al Hilal* (1935), he directed a string of successful films like *Watan*, *Jagirdar* and *Ek Hi Raasta*, all of which confirmed his extraordinary talent. It was with *Aurat*, a film he would remake 17 years later in colour as *Mother India*, that he came to be regarded as a front-rank filmmaker. Shot in black and white and much of it in his childhood village, Mehboob brought alive the very heart of rural India — its beauty and its beastliness. When drought hits the land, the parched earth, the sunken, shrivelled faces of men and beasts, and vultures hovering over carcasses had the gritty quality of a documentary. In many ways, *Aurat* was a better film than his much acclaimed *Mother India*.

Working in an entirely different genre was Sohrab Modi who came to films from his brother's Arya Subodh Theatrical Company. It is not surprising then that the company he started initially was called the Stage Film Company and its two early films were adaptations of Shakespeare's *Hamlet* (*Khoon ka Khoon*) and *King John* (*Said-e-Havas*). However, Modi was to soon discover that film and theatre ill consorted with each other and public taste was rapidly changing after the release of Barua's *Devdas* and Shantaram's *Duniya-na-Mane*. He too turned to more pertinent contemporary themes in *Meetha Zaher* (1938), a film on alcoholism and *Talaq* (1938) on Hindu women's right to divorce that was being agitated for by All-India Women's Conference at the time. Though both films earned him enough acclaim, Modi's strength lay elsewhere: the historical genre. Focussing on the persona of the Mughal emperor Jehangir, whose great sense of justice it sought to celebrate, *Pukar* (1939) was Sohrab Modi's first highly ambitious film. Legend has it that Jehangir had bells installed in the royal palace which an appellant, whatever his rank, could toll to seek redress personally from the king. Released on the eve of World War II, the film had an unprecedented triple theatre premiere in Bombay. The public and press response was unexpectedly enthusiastic.

It is important to mention that at the time *Pukar* was made, communal riots raged in many parts of the country. Filmmakers usually shied away from subjects that involved Hindu-Muslim characters in conflict, fearing it might spark off communal passions. Modi showed courage in taking up a story in which a proud Rajput father, who had given the best years of his life in the service of the king, begs mercy for his guilty son — and is denied it. Modi credibly builds the character of a just king who is unsparing when his own queen is found guilty of a murder. Of the chief players, Chandramohan (as Jehangir) and Modi (as the Rajput father) gave sterling performances. Modi's assets were his stately bearing and a rich and resonant voice.

Another filmmaker who made significant contributions to the raising of standards of filmmaking in India was Franz Osten, a German director from Emelka of Munich. Osten had collaborated with Himansu Rai in producing three silent films — *The Light of Asia, Shiraz* and *A Throw of Dice* and when Rai founded Bombay Talkies in 1934, many of his earlier colleagues joined him; among them were Osten as director, Josef Wirsching as cameraman and Carl von Spreti as art director.

Primarily these men were brought in to train Indian technicians, which they did (Sashadhar Mukherjee, Savak Vacha, R.D. Pareenja, R.D. Mathur, Amiya Chakravarty, N.R. Acharya, Najam Naqvi to name a few). Osten directed all the 16 films produced by Bombay Talkies starting with *Jawani Ki Hawa* (1935, starring Devika Rani and Najamul Hussain) to *Kangan* (1939, starring Leela Chitnis and Ashok Kumar). *Achhut Kanya* (1936) was one of his most successful films, the work of a seasoned craftsman. The film established Bombay Talkies as a major studio and Devika Rani as a hugely popular star. It is well to recall that the film's music, particularly the duet sung by Ashok Kumar and Devika Rani, 'Main ban ki chidya ban ban dolun re' remained popular long after the film was forgotten. Bombay Talkies provided clean, wholesome entertainment with commendable taste and skill.

Calcutta

Notwithstanding its material and technical resources, the glitz and glamour of its stars, the opulence of its productions, Bombay's hegemony was under serious threat from an unexpected rival — the Calcutta studios.

Though *Alam Ara's* one song 'De de khuda ke nam par pyaare' sung by W.M. Khan had become very popular, generally the film's music was a patchwork affair without a proper lyricist or music director. It was left to Madan Theatres of Calcutta to present in *Shirin Farhad* and *Laila Majnu* (1931) a well-composed and recorded (R.C.A. Photophone system as against Irani's single system Tanar) musical score. Featuring two of Hindustani stage's accomplished singers Miss Jahanara Kajjan and Master Nissar, the lyrics were written by Agha Hashr Kashmiri and music composed by Vrijlal Varma. Both films replete with songs had a tremendous impact on the audience and can be said to have established the unshakeable hold of songs on our films which continues till today. Kajjan, who played the female lead in both films, and several more to follow in quick succession, had the looks, talent and voice. I, particularly, remember the balcony scene in *Laila Majnu* where she sings of her undying love for Majnu who stood below to steal a glimpse of her.

In Bengal, the trend was to produce bi-lingual versions — Bengali and Hindi, most often using the same cast. This lowered the costs and raised revenues. Madan Theatres with its unrivalled financial resources, large production unit and widespread theatrical network had played a key role in the Indian film industry. By the mid-thirties, however, its fortunes had begun to decline. It was then that New Theatres founded by B.N. Sircar came to the fore. A highly cultured man, Sircar created a vortex of creativity, drawing the young and talented around him. Among them were film directors: Debaki Bose, P.C. Barua, Nitin Bose; music composers: R.C. Boral, Pankaj Mullick, Timir Baran; and technicians: Mukul Bose, Bimal Roy, Yusuf Mulji, Subodh Mitra. The work of these men has become a reference point in the history of the Indian cinema.

Chandidas (1932, Bengali), the story of a Vaishnavite poet-priest who falls in love with a low caste washerwoman and defies convention, was New Theatre's first superhit, which ran for a whole year in Sircar's own theatre Chitra. Directed by Debaki Bose in a meditative style, which was to become the hallmark of all his work, the film was marked by sincere emotion and sensitivity. This was also the first film to effectively use background music to enhance dramatic impact. That it was not a flash in the pan was proved by the success of *Puran Bhakta* (1933, Hindi), the film that followed. The story being well-known, Bose used a minimum of dialogue, complementing the visuals with sound effects and music. Even the selection of musical instruments was judiciously made. Both these films perished in the fire that broke out in the New Theatres studio laboratories in 1940.

Debaki Bose's only work extant is *Vidyapati* (1937) on the 14th century Maithili poet. In the opinion of musicologist Vanraj Bhatia (who saw the film 11 times), *Vidyapati* "altered the conception of the quality and function of music in films". This was, in the true sense, the first film that showed that a song could take over the function of the dialogue and manage an intenser communication. The two singers, K.C. Dey and Kananbala, who between them rendered most of the songs, became highly successful. Dey had already added to his fame in *Puran Bhakta* and Barua's *Devdas* but in *Vidyapati* he excelled himself in songs like 'Panghat pe Kanahiya aata hai'. For Kanan, this was her first major role. As Anuradha, the poet's silent worshipper, her songs cast a hypnotic spell — they still do — whenever played on All India Radio.

If Debaki Bose looked to the past for his filmic material, Pramathes

Chandra Barua (better known as P.C. Barua) impressed contemporary themes firmly in the minds of his audience. With *Devdas* (1935) he not only raised the expectations of the viewers but also spawned a host of imitators. One can hardly over-stress the impact and influence of the film at the time which affected a whole generation of viewers and filmmakers. Saratchandra Chatterjee's famous story of frustrated love had been filmed a few times earlier, but never with quite the same emotional intensity as Barua was able to inject in his film. Other features which set it apart were Barua's handling of actors, an eye for detail, the subtly created milieu, the simple, colloquial dialogue, and the superb musical score of Timir Baran made immortal by K.L. Saigal who became something of a cult figure. Barua's shooting of the train journey depicting Devdas' agony, mingled with the sounds of the train was a *tour de force*. A fastidious craftsman, he displayed a similar sense of movement and rhythm in his next film (*Manzil/ Grihadaha* (1936) — about the confused emotions of two friends, one of whom falls in love with the other's wife and deceitfully abducts her during a train journey. Unable to win her love and driven by a sense of guilt, he courts death.

Death, as the inevitable final solution, is a recurrent theme in many of Barua's films. In *Mukti* (1937), the protagonist played by Barua in both the Bengali and Hindi versions, disillusioned by the rich but philistine set to which his wife belongs, goes to live with the aborigines in the jungles of Assam. When his wife arrives with a hunting party, he is killed. Barua shot a good part of the film on location in Assam. Rabindranath Tagore who allowed him the use of some of his songs in the Bengali version had also suggested the title of the film. In style and approach, Barua was unlike any of his contemporaries. Gentle irony, deep pain and unrelieved pessimism marked his films. The cant and hypocrisy he saw around him revolted him. He knew that he couldn't and did not try to change the world. In the end, like one of his characters in his films, he died a broken man. There is no other filmmaker who evokes so much admiration and nostalgia.

An acknowledged cameraman, Nitin Bose came to direction by default. When Debaki Bose suddenly left New Theatres to make *Seeta* for a rival company, Nitin was offered a film to direct. He chose to remake a Hindi version of *Chandidas* (1934) with Saigal as the poet-priest and Umashashi as the washerwoman. Briskly paced and expertly photographed (by Nitin himself), the film was a winner at the box office. But the film that marked him out as a superb craftsman was *President* (1937), the story of two sisters, the elder one, tough, autocratic, president of the family's textile mill, the younger an easy-going college dropout, both in love with the same man. Nitin wove his triangle into a terse, compelling narrative. The elder sister played by Kamlesh Kumari was an extremely well-formed character unlike the usual stereo-type of a rich, wilful woman. Her transformation from a stern disciplinarian whose world revolved around her textile mill to a woman in love was subtly made manifest.

Among the other talented filmmakers working at New Theatres were Hem Chandra (*Crorepati, Anath Ashram*), Phani Mazumdar (*Street Singer, Kapal Kundala*) and Amar Mullick (*Bara Didi*) who tried, and often lived up to the standards set by B.N. Sircar. The thirties marked the heyday of the studio system. Like any other major studio in the country — Ranjit, Bombay Talkies — New Theatres produced on an average 5-6 films a year, but unlike others, they were not standardised assembly-line products. Each New Theatres' film managed to bear an individual's stamp. There was no mistaking, a Debaki Bose or Barua film for someone else's. Sircar ensured that his directors had complete freedom to choose and shape their material. In 1972, on receiving the prestigious Dadasaheb Phalke award, I asked him, what in his opinion was the way out of the industry's increasing problems? With a twinkle in his eyes, he said, "Perhaps a return to the old studio system". He genuinely believed that the studio system not only guaranteed discipline and organised growth of the industry, it also created conditions for better films.

In Madras

At the time, film activity in the south was sparse and sporadic. Not until mid-thirties did Madras acquire a studio with sound recording facilities. All early Tamil and Telugu films were produced either in Bombay or Calcutta to which pioneer producers like H.M. Reddy (he made the first Tamil film *Kalidas* in 1931 at the Imperial Studios), A. Narayanan and K. Subramanyam took their artistes and writers to. Sometimes it was the entire dramatic troupe which performed in front of the camera. Frontally photographed, these films were, to borrow Rene Clair's words, "canned theatre". Mythology and quasi-historicals filled the screens. Loaded with songs and dances, the presence of well-known singers like M.K. Thygaraja Bhagavatar, Dandapani Desikar, K.B. Sundarambal (much later she would appear in the lead role of S.S. Vasan's hugely popular *Avvaiyar*) and M.S. Subhalakshmi, ensured the success of these films. Cinema, thus, became an integral part of South Indian life, much like folklore and mythology which it had taken over from other performing arts. In time to come film stars and writers, in the south, would wield uprecedented power and shape the thinking and destiny of its people.

The thirties was a period of challenge and change. All institutions, whether cultural, social or political, stood exposed to it. This was also a period of hope, idealism and great causes. The Indian film did try to reflect some of this mood and momentum, give the constraints of censorship, the literacy level of the audience and the burden of traditional arts. The outbreak of the second world war caused the collapse of the studio system, irreversibly changing the rules of the game.

3

The Great Four of the Golden Fifties

— Iqbal Masud

THESE DAYS THE 'auteur' theory, which attributed the specific quality of a film to its director and placed some directors in the Golden Pantheon, is not as powerful as it was in '60s and '70s. But if we ever set up a Golden Pantheon, directors like Mehboob, Bimal Roy, Guru Dutt and Raj Kapoor are bound to be there.

Some but not all the films of these directors were made in '50s which is called the golden era of cinema. Such phrases can be misleading. You cannot isolate one decade in a continuing cultural process. The root of the '50s cinema lay firmly in the past.

Indian popular cinema, unlike art or parallel cinema, has always been close to the people, divining in its own way the ebb and flow of forces in the sub-continent. The above four directors were formed in '30s and '40s which were traumatic years for the Indian people. The fight for independence, famines, changing social mores, the global fight against fascism, all contributed to the ethos in which the directors grew up.

There are many common traits in the works of these directors. The foremost is that much abused word, humanism. That word in our film criticism has become meaningless due to excessive and inappropriate use. The doctrine itself has been marginalised by neo-fascism and by what has been called 'undialectical materialism' — the triumph of the marketplace in the '80s and '90s. But in the '40s 'humanism' had a specific connotation. It was fuelled by outrage against India's savage poverty and inequalities (exacerbated by the rise of the black market in the Second World War). A second element was its deep awareness of India's past and present cultures — both 'high' and 'popular'. A third was the skill in communicating its outrage and call for change to the masses. This last element has been called 'entertainment'. But in the '40s and '50s this had an aspirational touch about it which has vanished long ago from our cinema.

Mehboob

Mehboob can be called a congenital filmmaker. He sprang from the Gujarat soil and his work generally remained close to the earth. In specific terms this meant a direct vitality, a tendency to portray, conflict in dramatic, even melodramatic, terms. At some level or another confrontation/conflict formed one of the elements in the work of all directors. But it was most obvious in Mehboob's work. Certainly this is a constant theme in western classical and popular works universally from *Paradise Lost* and *Dallas.* But conflict in Indian cinematic terms has its own inimitable intensity, its own type of denouement.

Take a Mehboob film of the early '40s — *Roti* . On the surface this seems a product of German Expressionism — those looming shadows, that exaggerated acting style, those violent changes of moods and fortunes. But it really is a critique of Indian society with prophetic insight. It deals with two models — one of a rags-to-riches millionaire (Chandramohan), the other of a tribal couple (Sheikh Mukhtar and Sitara). Both models are caricatured or idealised. The millionaire is shown as possessed of the lust for money and power in an industrial civilisation. The tribal couple live in a primeval state of nature. The millionaire is saved by the couple after an air crash, the tribals emigrate to the city, do not find happiness and return. The millionaire is ruined in the city, tries futilely to find salvation among the tribals.

It's a simple tale but has its moments of power and insight. Sitara, after her first night in a Bombay chawl, dances down the steps of her building. Tribal sensuality is set against urban dehumanisation.

Mehboob will be remembered for his classic *Mother India.* But *Mother India* cannot be viewed in isolation. It has to be 'read' with its progenitor, *Aurat* (1941). In fact, the difference between the two films furnished a key to the 'essential' *Mother India.*

The first and foremost difference is of course 'colour'. *Mother India* is obviously not only a 'social' film, it is an entertainer, shot in colour, full of song, dance and melodrama. Mehboob thinks too consciously of a woman's role in *Mother India*: Beloved, housewife, mother. Nargis is another 'difference' between the two versions. She

Mehboob's *Mother India*, 1957 with Nargis and Raj Kumar

throws herself into the role, becomes the entire focus of the film so that the overarching meaning of the original film is lost. Finally, Nehruism in a crude and obvious sense is espoused by the film towards its end with its reference to the Community Block Development Movement. This brings to the film a bogus ambience of 'resolution' and 'harmony'.

The earlier story, *Aurat*, was a study of conflict in Indian rural society. It was a multifaceted conflict — an economic one, a gender one — but the struggle was about power. In fact Mehboob's version is startlingly Foucaultian. There are two protagonists. Birju, the younger son, and the mother. A film critic trying to fit *Mother India* into the Ramayana/Mahabharata, found counterparts for the mother — Durga/Kali, and for the good elder brother — Ram. But he could find no counterpart for Birju — a total 'outsider' — a mocker and destroyer of the system. Durga/Kali is the upholder of dharma which is of the system but much bigger than it. Birju breaks dharma; Kali destroys him.

I do not say Mehboob thought through all the ramifications of the borderland of mythology and current sociology. But he was a 'genius' and he lived these contradictions. He created the picture of an impossibly unjust society tolerated by its victims; he created a Rejector — Birju. Yacub plays him as a totally negative hero — he rejects all blandishments of society — including its 'knowledge'. When he tears up the account books of the money-lender, he says: "This is the knowledge that has destroyed us".

At its deepest level *Mother India* is a study of culture in conflict with itself. Birju and Mother represent headlong, near-suicidal rush to change an impossible situation, and the inner force of the system fighting back, trying to alter the system 'peacefully'. These are archetypal creations in Indian cinema. Mehboob made many other films but none viewed lived Indian life in such 'essential', stark terms.

Bimal Roy

Bimal Roy, on the other hand, was basically a reformist. This is not to be read in a dead, passive sense. For him 'change' was essential but he did not quite see it in Birju's terms — or more precisely refused to consider the Birju option.

To take two of his most notable creations: *Do Bigha Zamin* and *Sujata*. These two set Roy firmly on the side of humanist liberals. But

Bimal Roy's *Do Bigha Zamin*, 1953,
with Balraj Sahni and Nirupa Roy

there are humanist and humanists. Roy's humanism is capable of showing stark suffering caused by economic exploitation. The conflict is evoked in melodramatic, early Eisenstein terms. But melodrama alternates with the quite reflective performance of Balraj Sahni. This gives a resonance to the film which takes it out of a narrow realistic framework.

Do Bigha Zamin (DBZ) was one of the first films to chart mass migration of rural people to the cities and their degradation in urban slums. The process is still going on. DBZ set the archetypes and even the cliches of films dealing with the process through the following decades.

One archetype or cliché was the 'poetry and music' of the slums. Though ultimately the situation was tragic, Roy sought to relieve the starkness by brave and hopeful songs and dances. In one sense it was a cop-out, but it also carried the film to the masses; it was part of the song and dance in Indian popular cinema tradition. Another archetype was the street-smart kid played by Jagdeep. DBZ was a seminal film. The urban slum — womb and inferno — became part of popular cinema.

Sujata was a different cup of tea. A lost soul from the nether world of untouchable underclass had escaped by accident to the genteel world of the urban middle class. The disturbance such escapades cause was the theme of *Sujata.* One can look down on this film as a soft surrender to commercial demands, as glossing over a real, conflict situation. These criticisms are valid. Still, *Sujata* survives because it shows the dilemmas of its cloistered conflict in a sensitive fashion. In fact 'sensitivity' is the key word and it is shown in the performances of Sunil Dutt and Nutan. A middle class fairy tale with a happy ending? Maybe. But it is more than a fairy tale and surprisingly it does touch some chords within.

Guru Dutt

The next great directors — Guru Dutt and Raj Kapoor — are set apart in a distinctive fashion from Mehboob and Bimal Roy. They were younger, they belonged to a troubled, introspective generation. But were children of the '40s — not 'Midnight's Children' but 'Sunrise Children', with something of the initial zest of India's freedom as also the later disillusionment. The 'heroic age' of Indian cinema — the '50s owed a great deal to this mix.

Guru Dutt began as an artist-entertainer, meaning that he had been trained at Uday Shankar's Almora Dance Institute and later at Prabhat Talkies, his 'trainers' being the directors Santoshi, Amiya Chakraborthy, and Gyan Mukherjee. You see the influence of all this in three of his early classic entertainers *Aar Paar* (1954), *Mr. and Mrs. 55* (1955) and *C.I.D.* (1956). There are certain distinctive elements of these films. First, there is a 'design', a certain elegance and care for detail. This comes from Dutt's artistic and professional training. Secondly, the scripts are crisp and lively. Abrar Alvi (dialogue writer) came to be associated with him in nearly all his films. There was fresh wit here, warmth and touch which was both common and rare. Next, there was

Guru Dutt and Madhubala in Guru Dutt's
Mr & Mrs 55, 1955

a superior sitcom touch in the best of the films — *Mr. and Mrs. 55*. The three films took you back to *Kismet* of the '40s. These films constitute the peaks of cinematic 'thriller'.

The *Kismet* connection also highlights another aspect of the films. Their urbanness and depiction of the urban underworld. It was virgin territory then and Dutt exploited it with a light touch.

Guru Dutt used the tradition of music, song and dance too in a fresh fashion. He married cinematography to verse and performance. The 'garage' song in *Aar Paar* - 'Sun sun sun zalima'...(Listen, you heartless girl), 'Aankhon hi sankhon mein ishaara ho gaya' (Your eyes passed on the message) in *C.I.D.*, the office romancing between Johnny Walker and partner in *Mr. & Mrs. 55*, 'Jaane kahan mera jigar gaya ji'... (Good gracious! I've lost my heart).

Why did Guru Dutt turn sombre after *C.I.D.?* That question has puzzled many including his friend Dev Anand. Whatever the reason, *Pyaasa* burst on an amazed audience with its celebration of a kind of a 'life-in-death wish' — later to appear in full panoply in *Kaagaz ke Phool*. There's such a noticeable similarity of tone and theme in the two films that they can be discussed together.

Both are basically portraits of an artist — not 'as a young man' but as a man battered by philistines and conventional morality. Unwittingly, Dutt also conveys a basic weakness in the artist himself — his self-doubt, his fatal self-divisions.

Pyaasa is the more abstract, the more metaphorical of the two, setting love against money, art against philistinism. This ought to weaken the film but strangely it does not. I can only attribute it to the heady dose of Persian romanticism administered in Sahir's verse, the intensely felt conflict situations and the performances of Waheeda Rehman and Guru Dutt himself.

Both in *Kaagaz* and *Pyaasa* two themes merged — the radicalism of the artist and of the 'outsider'. This was a common assumption of the 'progressives' in '40s and '50s — that art was inevitably committed to a subversion of accepted social and cultural values. There is an inner conflict in *Pyaasa* — between the visions of dialogue writer, Abrar Alvi, and Sahir, the lyricist. This was disclosed by Alvi in a long interview with me, almost glancingly. "I was fascinated by the character of Gulabo, the prostitute", said Alvi. "I had known a similar character in real life with the same name". Alvi was taken up with the emotional side of the artist-prostitute — society girl triangle (A touch of

Waheeda Rehman and Mala Sinha
in Guru Dutt's *Pyaasa*, 1957

Baudelaire). Then came Sahir with his 'Yeh mehlon, yeh takhton yeh tajon ki dunia' (What is it worth, this world of thrones and crowns...) raising the banner of revolution which simply confounded Alvi. At the Festival of Three Continents in Nantes, I was closely questioned about this 'merger' by French critics. "Isn't it self-indulgent to fuse personal disappointment in love with establishment hatred?"

Absolutely right. But here a third element entered. What is crudely called Dutt's 'death wish' and I call his 'poetry of defeat'. Like Webster, Dutt was strongly possessed by death, but it was a lyrical attachment to grace in defeat, going down with a dying fall. This comes out in the sequences showing a beggar killed in an accident and being mistaken for the poet because he was wearing his coat (the death on the tracks in *Apur Sansar*). The poet is honoured in death and comes back like Christ resurrected to denounce the philistines.

It is this mix of personal sense of loss, romantic revolt and lyrical surrender to defeat that make *Pyaasa* a quintessential — indeed heartbreakingly so — 'Indian' film.

In *Kaagaz ke Phool* Dutt leaves obvious radicalism behind and focuses on the theme of artist and celebrity. Here another side of Dutt's personality comes out — the love of success, combined with a razor-edge sense of vulnerability. Sometimes the artist hits the victory trail but in that triumph lie the seeds of his downfall. The theme has been played out in many Hollywood films and in American real life. Dutt has framed the tragedy of rising and falling stars in a transitional Indian cultural frame. Romance, angst, the sudden fever and fret of love between the brilliant film director (Dutt) and the rising actress (Waheeda) become increasingly marginalised in a world half governed by custom (Dutt's marital/family bonds) and half by the new corporate lust for success which deliberately strokes the anarchy of celebrity. There is a money fame struggle (not a narrow class struggle) and a struggle to preserve personal relationships. The defeat of the latter is a deep resonating defeat, vaster than the defeat in *Pyaasa.* The death of the director at the end of the film is not a facile, rhetorical metaphor. It is the culmination of over-arching tragedy in which in a very real sense there are no winners and losers. In the growing alienation caused by urban/industrial/commercial culture the victims are all of us — the celebrities and the celebrators.

Compared to the above films *Chaudhvi ka Chand* and *Sahib, Bibi aur Ghulam* are less ambitious. *Chaudhvi* is a calculated 'Muslim social' but the dark vision is there — see the way the splendid qawwali 'Meri duniha lut rahi thi aur main khamosh tha' is shot.

Sahib... is, in fact, credited to Abrar Alvi though Dutt's presence colours the film. It is a little masterpiece with brilliant islands of pleasure but somehow the performances of Dutt and Wahed are too neat and ordered.

The honours go to the set piece music song and dance sequences. And of course to Meena Kumari and Rahman who have etched a marvellous portrait of barren marriage. It is an underestimated achievement and the preset explorers of middle class sexual angst should look at it again.

Guru Dutt is one of the most adventurous artists in the history of our cinema. He tried everything. Most of his tries came off.

Raj Kapoor

Raj Kapoor was no less adventurous but his was a buoyant adventurism with a streak of neuroticism almost invisibly undercutting the surface optimism. There were three other elements which gradually came to the surface. His egoism, his sensualism and his showmanship.

Let us look at three of his films *Aag* (1948), *Awara* (1951) and *Shree 420* (1955).

Aag is a young man's film. There is longing for a 'lost love' who comes and goes out of the hero's (a stage artist and director) life in a mysterious even surrealistic fashion. The message seems to be that a completely satisfying love is impossible, though this is spoilt by a contrived 'happy' ending.

The striking feature about *Aag* is the vitality of the hero Kewal (Raj Kapoor himself). He is in revolt against his father's static ethos, in a sense he represents the restless post-independence youth. As in Guru Dutt's films, there is the strong thrust of an artist in search of a vocation. The nostalgia for a lost 'perfect' love is the motivation for the artist in his work! This is clearly visible when Nargis as the lost love, Nimmi, dances down a few steps in a rehearsal. In its mix of love, sensuality and romance, this brief sequence reminds one of Sitara dancing down the chawl steps in *Roti*. The 'sacred face' theme (Kewal practically sets himself on fire when he learns his friend is in love; with Nimmi) surfaces again in *Satyam, Shivam, Sundaram*. An implicit question is posed: "What is the test of true love? Can it survive the loss of beauty?" There is a metaphysical questioning side of Kapoor's vision from the beginning and it should not be undervalued because it became routine and theatrical towards the end of his life.

Awara continues the spirit of youth and revolt though in a more elaborate setting. Here again the obvious theme is theatrical: are criminals born or made? But today *Awara* is seen to have a myriad nuances and significations, some of which have been explored by Gayatri Chatterjee in her book *Awara*.

Awara introduced a self-conscious element of 'modernity' into Indian cinema. First, the title itself with its echoes of rootlessness, 'lost generation' and a free-floating, amoral consciousness. It recalls Walter Benjamin's analysis of the Baudlerian city with its twin archetypes of the Dandy and the Apache (Raj and K. N. Singh). The element of romance and nostalgia is summed up in the figure of Nargis — unattainable/attainable society girl. Nargis here is both social metaphor and physical reality. Part of her charm is social status and money. "There's money in her voice", says Gatsby of millionairess Daisy in Scott Fitzgerald's *Great Gatsby*. That's Nargis' attraction too. But there's also Nargis' physical desirability brought home in a direct fashion hitherto unmatched in Indian cinema. Both elements are fused in that seminal song-dance number 'Ghar aaya mera pardesi' (home returns the beloved stranger). Urban life as a snakes and ladders game is strikingly summed up in that sequence.

Where *Awara* is a many-sided achievement, *Shree 420* is a more reflective, anguished statement in the same genre. In a way, Raj Kapoor continues on his *Awara* journey in *Shree 420*. But while *Awara* was about individual alienation in the city, *Shree 420* is about urban class war. Raj and Nargis are castaways in the city but both represent a traditional, 'value-bound' India. Raj, however, is tempted by the new, cynical rising middle-class — ancestor of the present liberalisation's products. The song number where Raj is seduced into the class 'Murh murh ke na dekh' (Don't look back! don't look back !!) — is a kind of watershed sequence if its significance is truly understood. The understated, tragic performance of Nargis signifying 'traditional' India going down in defeat before the ruthless march of capitalism is greater even than her magnificent melodrama in *Mother India*. Recall the 'O janewale, murh ke zara dekhte jaana' (Wait o! wayfarer...turn around and see the havoc you have wrought) sequence where two Nargises — one a judgemental figure and the other a supplicating one — fail to win back Raj.

Shree 420 ends in a flight away from the city — as much a cop-out as Raj going to jail in *Awara* or Dutt's flight in *Pyaasa* and death in *Kaagaz*. There's an important point here. Dutt and Kapoor could not really face up to the ruthless logic of the industrialized brutal city. That is why Dutt retreated to the inanities of 'Chandhivi... and the sterile perfection of *Sahib*. Kapoor went on to the melodramatic triange of *Sangam*, to the mediocre metaphor of *Satyam*...and the crudities of *Ram Teri Ganga Maili*. *Mera Naam Joker* was a confessional film; moving in places, yet self-indulgently egoistic towards the end.

When people call the '50s 'golden' there are many nuances. The

'50s themselves have become a 'lost Eden'. There was a self-assurance among the filmmakers even in their most tortured moments, there was a response from an unfissured audience. The ethos was both 'whole' and 'wholesome'. Today that ethos, that audience are gone. That is why it is not possible to 'churn out a Guru Dutt', to use Shabana Azmi's words at a seminar.

For the present generation, the '50s cinema is still unexplored territory. That is a patrimony we can ill afford to neglect. Even in our fissured, anarchic condition the '50s are capable of furnishing example, insight, and a motivation to a relevant heroism.

Bringing
Laughter
and Joy to
Every One !
Shree
420
Starring
NARGIS · RAJ KAPOOR
NADIRA · NEMO · KUMAR
and LALITA PAWAR
Music
SHANKAR JAIKISHEN
Written by
K. A. ABBAS
Directed by Raj Kapoor

4

Indian Film Directors in Malaya

– *Tamaki Matsuoka Kanda*

NOT ONLY IN INDIA but also in other Asian countries, very few people are interested in the culture of neighbouring Asian countries. But in the '50s and '60s Asian countries carried out active cultural exchange through films. One of the centres was Singapore. Chinese bosses, Malay stars, and the staff from all over Asia — Indian, Filipino, Chinese, Malay, Indonesian and Japanese also — made films together. As S. Ramanathan said, "It was a really cosmopolitan atmosphere."

In a list of Malay films made after World War II, the names of many of the directors are Indian. P. Ramlee, for example, was the most famous actor, director, singer and composer the Malay film industry has ever had. He became a popular star actor with *Hang Tuah*, a story of a loyal vassal of the Sultan of the Malacca kingdom in the 15th century. The film was directed by another Indian, Phani Majumdar.

The first Malay film, *Laila Majnun*, made in 1933, was the first production of producer Chisty and director B. S. Rajhans, two Indian nationals from Bombay.

It was the days of big studios when a number of Indian directors were invited to make Malay films in Singapore. In 1947 the Shaw Brothers film Mogul Sir Run Run Shaw and his elder brother, the late Dato (Sir) Runme Shaw set up Malay Film Production Ltd. (MFP) in Singapore and started to make Malay films. Their studio was built on Jalan (Street) Ampas in Singapore. In their earliest five years they appointed only Indian directors and made many successful films. Under the stimulus of their success another filmmaking company was set up by two big distribution companies in 1951. One of them was Cathay

Production owned by late Dato Loke Wan-tho and the other was Keris Film Productions owned by late Ho Ah-loke. Their new company was named Cathay-Keris Productions and their studio was built on East Coast Road in Singapore. Thus the curtain was raised on the age of strong competition.

Cathay-Keris enticed some Indian directors from Shaw Brothers and started filmmaking. But later on Ho Ah-loke parted company with Cathay and entered into partnership with Shaw Brothers. They opened Merdeka Studio in Kuala Lumpur in 1960. Again they appointed Indian directors to start filmmaking. But in the middle of the '60s those big studios had to face many problems, for example, increase of production costs and artists' pay, drop in the box office and profit margin. Moreover, Run Run Shaw moved his base to Hong Kong in 1959 and Loke Wan-tho was killed in a plane crash in Taipei in 1964. So those studios gradually lost their power and finally MFP of Shaw Brothers closed down its studio in 1967 and Cathay in 1972. Those were the last days of filmmaking in Singapore which became independent of the Malay Federation in 1965. After that the centre of Malay filmmaking shifted to Kuala Lumpur and the era changed from studios to independent productions. P. Ramlee also passed away in 1973 and the heyday of the Malay film industry was over.

Looking back on those days, we find that Indian directors contributed much to establish the golden days of Malay film industry. They directed many films and trained many Malay filmmakers, as well as actors and actresses. What brought those Indian directors to Singapore? Why did the Shaw Brothers invite them to make Malay films? At the same time Shaw Brothers invited some Filipino directors too. So it was, so to say, an international film making that occurred in Singapore in the '50s and '60s.

S. Ramanathan was born in Kuala Lumpur in 1919. His father was an Indian citizen from Tamil sent to Malaya to join the railway service around 1912. He was educated in Kuala Lumpur and later entered college in Colombo where his family had shifted from Kuala Lumpur after his father's retirement. He was a fanatic cine-goer from his childhood and dreamt of becoming an actor. After seeing the Tamil film *Chintamani* (1937) in Colombo the charm of Tamil cinema captured him and he went to Madras to see Y.V. Rao, the director of the film. But on that occasion fortune didn't smile upon him.

In 1942, S. Ramanathan joined the British Admiralty and later was shifted to Bombay. There again the enthusiasm for the cinema caught him and he resigned his job to join a film company in Coimbatore as a studio assistant. As a studio assistant and also an actor for a small role in three films, *My Son* (1945), *Krishna Bhakti* (1948) and *Kanniyin Kathali* (1949). Then one of his friends brought him the news that Shaw Brothers studio in Singapore was looking for a director of Malay films. His friend encouraged him to apply as he knew the Malay language. He wrote a letter to Shaw Brothers and finally got the job.

He set out for Singapore in 1949. Almost at the same time L. Krishnan also arrived there from Madras. When S. Ramanathan saw the Shaw Brothers studio for the first time, he was disappointed by the old and poor equipment. He hesitated to make films there. He wrote one film story and asked L. Krishnan to direct it. He wanted to wait and see how things went. That film *Bhakti* (devotion) was released in 1950. Then he decided to start filmmaking himself. His first film *Kembar* (Twins) was relased in the same year and had a good response though the heroine was played by a new face.

After that S. Ramanathan made three films a year and became a popular director in the Malay film industry. At the studio he was known as a quick filmmaker full of new ideas. His first film was made in 20 days (and saved a great deal of production costs). Run Run Shaw liked his smartness and always praised him. So whenever he asked for new equipment, Shaw said, "Go ahead!". Shaw never interfered with his filmmaking, but checked only the progress. Thus he made eighteen films in eight years. 1n 1953 he cast P. Ramlee who was still struggling to become a big-name actor, as a hero in his film *Ibu* (Mother). He encouraged P. Ramlee and they became very good friends. This friendship lasted till he went back to India in 1957 with the hope of doing other activities.

Actually P. Ramlee first appeared in B.S. Rajhans's film *Cinta* (Love) in 1948 as a villain. As to B.S. Rajhans, who was the first director of Malay film industry and directed eighteen films for Shaw Brothers and five films for Cathay-Keris, there is only a little information about him at the National Film Archive in Pune. His full name was Baldev Singh Rajhans, a Punjabi, and he made a Hindi film *Imam Farosh* for Saroj Movietone, Bombay, in 1937 and a Punjabi film, *Jagga Daku,* for Indian Movietone, Calcutta, in 1940.

After B.S. Rajhans, P. Ramlee got his first chance to play a hero in L. Krishnan's film *Takdir Ilahi* (Will of God) in 1950. S. Ramanathan told me L. Krishnan was still in Kuala Lumpur. When I arrived in Kuala Lumpur after travelling in India and Thailand, I was ready to search for him even if it was difficult. But, to my surprise, I found his contact address very easily at FINAS which is NFDC in Malaysia, as he is one of the famous film persons with the title Dato and the owner of Gaya Film.

L. Krishnan was born in Madras in 1922. He moved to Penang, Malaya, in 1928 as his father had started a garment business there. After finishing his education he came to Singapore and got a job at Raffles Hotel. During war time he served as an interpreter of Japanese and also joined the Indian National Army. After the war he was repatriated to Madras by the British Military Administration. There he formed the Youth Movement of the Indian Congress and later joined the film industry in 1947. It was a Tamil film director K. Subramaniam who liked him during the activities of the Congress and took him into the film industry. In 1948 he directed a Sinhalese film *Amma* for Sri Lankan production.

At that time Menon, the agent of Shaw Brothers, came to Madras to recruit a director. Menon found out that L. Krishnan had once been in Singapore. Menon contacted him and Krishnan accepted his proposal. He left for Singapore in 1949 where he first directed *Bhakti* based on S. Ramanathan's story, and became a director in great demand. He directed three films in 1950 and 1951, four in 1952. Originally his contract with Shaw Brothers was for three years. When the contract was renewed Shaw Brothers refused to raise his wages even by ten per cent. So he left Shaw Brothers and joined Cathay-Keris which offered him much higher wages.

At the time L. Krishnan left his friend K.M. Basker at Shaw Brothers; K.M. Basker had been his comrade both in Indian National Army in Singapore and in the Congress movement in Madras. When L. Krishnan asked him to come to Singapore in 1952, K.M.Basker was an assistant director of Malayalam films in India. After making fourteen films for Shaw Brothers in six years, K.M. Basker also moved to Cathay-Keris in 1958 and made five films there.

L. Krishnan made fifteen films for Cathay-Keris and he was again enticed by Ho Ah-loke to his new Merdeka Studio in Kuala Lumpur.

As Merdeka Studio was in collaboration with Shaw Brothers, he was comfortable. He made five of the earliest films and resigned from there in 1963. As he felt he had taken root in Malaysia by then, he decided to stay there.

The same case of changing studios was B.N. Rao, who was invited by Shaw Brothers through the agent Menon, too. Shaw Brothers were eager to get him, because he was "one of the successful filmmakers of early Tamil cinema" (Randor Guy, *History of Tamil Cinema*) at that time. He was born in 1909 in a Malayali family and joined films in 1926 as an actor. He directed his first film in Hindi *Kimti Qurbani* in 1933. He had worked in Bombay, Calcutta, Coimbatore and Madras and directed several popular films including *Gumasthavin Penn* (Clerk's Daughter, 1941) in Tamil. This film was shown in Singapore during the war time and a Japanese film writer Hideo Koide mentioned this film in his book *Nampo-engei-ki* (Theatres and Films in Southeast Asia) published in 1943.

B. N. Rao

When B.N. Rao was offered the proposal by Shaw Brothers, Tamil film industry was very dull and that situation made him to decide to go to Singapore. In 1953 he arrived in Singapore and made a contract for three years. He found the studio followed the Hollywood system and he liked it very much. Those days Indian studios had no discipline, so he was particularly grateful for the opportunity to work in Singapore. The filmmaking schedule — three months' shooting and one month of post-production with regular work every day — was his favourite. He made nine films in those three years.

But to renew the contract Shaw Brothers offered him only the same amount of wages. So he decided to return to India and arranged the ticket for the passage. It was then that Cathay-Keris offered him three times as much as Shaw Brothers'. He refused this offer as he had already bought his ticket home, but Cathay-Keris did not give up and asked him to return from India in 20 days. Finally he joined Cathay-Keris and made eleven films in seven years. His first film *Pontianak* (1957) was a great success and later turned into a series. Whenever his film succeeded, Loke Wan-tho praised him highly. It was Loke Wan-tho's sudden death which made him leave Singapore.

In the same way, Phani Majumdar and Kidar Sharma were also invited by Shaw Brothers because of their fame at home. Phani Majumdar, who was born in 1912, was invited to make *Hang Tuah*, the big project film on Malay national hero. It was Indian film distributor Babulal Patel who recommended him to Run Run Shaw. When he arrived in Singapore in 1956, Run Run Shaw asked him not only to make *Hang Tuah*, but also to establish the studio system, the system of filmmaking at MFP studio.

Kwek Chit Jain, the studio manager of that time, recalls that Phani Majumdar was really a great director who had his own theory and discipline of film making. He was a hard working director and completed *Hang Tuah* in only 28 days. The unit had to work till 1 or 2 o'clock in the morning almost every day. One day, the cameraman Vaudev fell asleep while he was looking into camera eye.

Hang Tuah with numerous songs and dance scenes was a great hit and even now this film is considered one of the best Malay films ever made. Phani Majumdar was going back to India after completing this film, but Shaw Brothers begged him to stay on. He stayed in Singapore for five years and made seven films. Some of them were bilingual so he himself counts films made in Singapore were eleven.

Finally Phani Majumdar left Singapore in 1959, though he had been offered citizenship by the government. It was just after the independence of the Malay Federation within the Commonwealth, and he felt the rise of Malay nationalism and did not want to stay there as an Indian immigrant.

Like Phani Majumdar, Kidar Sharma, who was born in 1910, was also invited to direct only one film. He remembers someone in the account section of Shaw Brothers recommended his name to Run Run Shaw. In 1958, after arriving in Singapore he attended the first meeting at Shaw's office. But at that time he felt an unfriendly atmosphere. The attitude of the Malay staff made him realise that he was unwelcome there. When he went back to his huge flat in Capitol building (which still exists in the heart of Singapore as the government has preserved this beautiful building), he felt very lonely. That loneliness, however, was blown away when the next morning Run Run Shaw sent his Rolls Royce to invite him for lunch at home. He was treated with the highest and warmest hospitality by Run Run Shaw. He enjoyed making the Malay film *Kaki Kuda* (Race Horse) and his filmmaking satisfied Run Run Shaw. If he had not promised Bombay producers to come back soon, he may have stayed longer in Singapore.

In the same year when Kidar Sharma worked in Singapore, another Indian director reached Singapore and joined Shaw Brothers. His name was Dhiresh Ghosh and he was the last one to have stayed with Shaw Brothers. According to L. Krishnan, Dhiresh Ghosh first went to Indonesia at the invitation of an Indonesian producer. But as the film flopped he came to Singapore with some other Indians and asked L. Krishnan for help. At that time L. Krishnan was working for Cathay-Keris, which had no vacancy for a director. So Krishnan recommended him to Shaw Brothers. Thus Dhiresh Ghosh got the position at MFP studio and there he made eleven films in six years.

At the National Library in Singapore they keep some issues of Shaw Brothers film magazine *Majallah* (Magazine) *Film* of the 60s. In the 1962 New Year issue, *Majallah Film* introduced the staff and stars of Shaw Brothers and we can find Dhiresh Ghosh as one of the four biggest directors of the company. The other three were P. Ramlee, Jamil Sulong, and Omar Rojik who are all praised as great masters of Malay film history. In almost every issue of this magazine Dhiresh Ghosh of MFP and L. Krishnan of Merdeka Studio made a regular appearance. Later Dhiresh Ghosh also shifted to Merdeka Studio and worked there to make three films till 1966. He came last, and left last.

After going back to India, Dhiresh Ghosh joined the Film and TV Institute in Pune. But, according to Satish Bahadur, his colleague at that time, he didn't seem happy at FTII. Because while other professors spoke up about Eiensteins and Kurosawas, he could tell only about the filmmaking in India and Malaysia. Who cares about the filmmaking of Asian developing countries?

There were several reasons why those studios invited so many Indian directors. Firstly, the Indian film industry had already developed so much. Secondly, Indian directors were cheaper comparing with Hollywood directors. Thirdly, Indians could understand English so well that they could communicate with other staff. Fourthly, Indians were familiar with Malay Peninsula because there were already a large number of Indian immigrants. The former three reasons also apply to Filipino directors.

Thus, Shaw Brothers invited young Indian directors first, and then they invited veteran famous directors. Cathay-Keris later took young directors away from Shaw Brothers by offering higher wages. This fact suggests the economic growth of Malay film industry. Indian directors laid the foundation of Malay film industry and led it to the prosperity. Among their assistant directors many great Malay directors were born. But now in Malaysia their contribution to Malay films is hardly told by people, because they are not Malay. And in Singapore people seem to have forgotten that there were once great film studios. Maybe it is because modern nation states have been established firmly. But as an Asian, one should not forget the heritage of such wonderful film making era in Asia forever.

5

When Melody Ruled the Day

— Partha Chatterjee

THE HINDUSTANI FILM SONG is a twentieth century musical phenomenon. No other modern musical form from any part of the globe, including jazz, can boast of such diversity, richness, subtlety and reach. It is the Hindustani or Hindwi (inclusive of dialects like Avadhi, Bundelkhandi, Bhojpuri, Deccani, amongst others, that have enriched the Urdu language) film song that has cut through all the language barriers in India to engage in lively communication with a nation where more than twenty languages are spoken and, despite the havoc wrought by the forces of progress, scores of dialects still exist.

What makes the Hindwi film song unique is that it exists solely because it has been commissioned to fulfil certain demands made by the script and the finished film. The song has myriad functions in a commercial film especially those produced in Bombay. Indeed in a cinema that has had scant regard for script-writing since its inception, the spoken word (dialogue) — and especially the song — are the two devices available to make the film come alive memorably if only for a few minutes, thus giving credence to the observation made in another context by the great Dadaist Man Ray that even the dullest of films has five very interesting minutes in it!

This snide digression notwithstanding, it would be safe to say that the song had played a pivotal role in Indian cinema in general and the Hindustani or Hindwi cinema in particular since the talkies came to India in 1931. How is it that only Indian films had many songs in them regardless of the genre they belonged to? It did not matter whether a social drama, historical adventure, comedy or mythological was being produced, songs were bound to be an organic part of the finished film. No other cinema in the world had this peculiar characteristic.

In Hollywood, with the coming of sound the musical was discovered — partly from looking back upon the spectacular song and dance stage entertainments produced by such mughals as Florence Zeigfield and Erroll White and adapting many aesthetic ideas from them, including those related to choreography. However, the American musical was an autonomous cinematic form which, in the hands of a master, could achieve or uncover the truth despite the patently artificial means used in the search. This was one of the many genres of filmmaking in vogue in Hollywood through the '30s into the early '60s. The average film there did not have songs in them. The Chinese also produced musicals as an independent genre and based their productions on the triumphs of the Peking Opera. On the other hand the Japanese drew inspiration from American films and the full-tonal scale of European music to augment their own five-tone system and produced musicals with a distinctly local flavour. But in Japan too, other genres of filmmaking flourished without songs. Only in India did vocal music wield such overwhelming power in every kind of film. The western-educated *Wogs* (Westernised Oriental Gentlemen) regarded this influence as pernicious without even understanding the phenomenon.

Long before the cinema came to India an active musical theatre had come into being. The plots during the British rule in the second half of the last century dealt mainly with mythological tales or historical ones. The message, so to say, a patriotic one of overcoming the foreign oppressers, was concealed in the medium! Since India already had such a vast, varied and rich musical tradition, songs based on classical ragas and folk melodies became the energising force of such theatrical forays into the world of socio-political reality. By the time sound came to Indian films, musical-theatre was a very popular source of entertainment in Maharashtra, Gujarat, Bengal, Karnataka, the Madras Presidency (Tamilnadu) and Northern India stretching from undivided Punjab to United Provinces (Uttar Pradesh) and Bihar. Vocal music had become a part of the Indian psyche. It would not be an exaggeration to say that the Indian genius expressed itself best through song. Are not the lyrics of Vidyapati, Kabir, Meera and hundreds of other anonymous bards proof enough? It was, therefore, only natural that the song becomes an integral part of the Indian sound film and the Hindustani or Hindwi productions from Calcutta, Lahore, Bombay and Pune immediately accepted it much to their benefit.

The Second World War was still a few years away, as was the technological revolution that came in its wake, especially in communications, that once and for all robbed protected cultures like ours of all privacy and made them prey to all kinds of socio-political influences from the Occidental world and not necessarily for the best. The radio and the newspaper made this possible.

First Phase

In its first phase (1931-45) the Hindwi film song, like its counterpart throughout the country, was a judicious mixture of well-known classical ragas and folk tunes of overtly religious and directly spiritual overtones. Sometimes a composer used either form of music independently to great effect — most of them came from a classical background. In Calcutta, Raichand Boral and Timir Baran Bhattacharya were established Hindustani musicians. Boral was an accomplished tabla player and Bhattacharya a sarod player of immense promise. Pankaj Mullick too was not unfamiliar with ragas although he won fame for his more eclectic song compositions and his orchestral adaptations of English military bands as backgrounds to them.

In far-off Bombay a court musician Ustad Jhande Khan, bypassed by history and science, was trying to earn an honourable living as a composer of film songs. A master of khayal singing, Ustad Mushtaq Hussain Khan Bariellywale, was making similar efforts in Calcutta and Bombay. Madhu Master, Anil Biswas and Sajjad Hussain were accepting the emerging film song as a new form of expression and contributing to its evolution. In nearby Pune, Master Krishna Rao and Keshav Rao Bhole, not to forget the cherubic boy wonder Vasant Desai, were trying to create lovely new melodies out of the old repertoire of Marathi Natya Sangeet or music of the (now urban) folk theatre that was so successful in small towns and cities. But none of the Bombay-Pune composers could fully realise their dreams for they never had really versatile singers at their disposal. True that in Bombay artists like Master Nissar, Jahanara Kajjan and Farhad Jahan Bibbo (who later married one of the late Pakistani President Zulfiqar Ali Bhutto's uncles) were there and in Pune was the gifted Shanta Apte. But they were by training and temperament classical singers.

Only in Calcutta was there a voice capable of rendering everything the composer wanted and it belonged to Kundan Lal Saigal, a young man from Jammu, a troubadour with hidden mystical reserves who could, as if by a divine decree, lay bare both the mystery and the soul of a song. Though not trained in classical music he knew the structure and nuances of ragas by instinct and could render complex forms of light-classical music like ghazal, thumri and bhajan with an unequalled sense of truth. Rarely since the advent of sound-recording has song been sung with such a gracious awareness of the temporal and the eternal. The singular English metaphysical poet William Blake would have found a soul brother in Kundan Lal Saigal, who was to die at forty-two in 1946 of acute diabetes (before insulin became easily available) and not alcoholism as is popularly believed. He was and continues to be the most enduring star of the Hindwi film song and his baritone voice that could both roar and coo, transcends the lack of technical finesse in the recording and establishes a permanent rapport with the seeker. Songs like 'Kidhar haye tu aye meri tamanna' (Where are you o! elusive desire) sung towards the end of life with almost both feet in the grave!; 'Tada pata beete din rain' (In torment went the day and night); 'Sojaa Raaj Kumari' (Sleep well my little princess); 'Do naina matware' (Thine twin eyes, drunk with mischief); 'Babul mora' (a thumri rendered as a young bride's lament at parting from her parents) are but a tiny part of a fairly large and unforgettable repertoire.

End of the Age of Innocence

With the passing of Saigal the age of innocence came to an end. Even able colleagues like Pankaj Mullick (despite the military bandmaster's phrasing in his singing), the slightly coy but very capable Kanan Bala and, of course, the consistently competent Uma Shashi, had to concede ground to new artists who were more in tune with the times. The Second World War had made some major changes in people's perceptions of the world around them and with that the music that was emerging from major social and psychological changes that were coming about.

The film song which had till then been a vehicle of tempered, civilised emotions in a distinctly literary garb, suddenly found itself accommodating the needs of the times. The musings of Wali Saheb, Dr. Safdar Aah, Pandit Indra, Arzoo Lucknawi, D.N. Madhok and Zia Sarhady (to become within the next few years the torch-bearer of the left-wing tradition of filmmaking with works like *Hum Log, Foot Path*) were per force making way for a more open appraisal of life. In a 1950 film called *Samadhi*, the dual nature of Nalini Jaywant's screen personality suddenly became evident. Her innocence came through very naturally, laced with potent sexuality as she sang (to the young Lata Mangeshkar's playback) 'Gore gore o banke chore, kabhi meri gali ayaa karo' (Do come by where I live, fair and sprightly boy).

Nine years earlier in 1941 Dalsukh M. Pancholi produced a serio-comedy in Lahore called *Khazanchi*. It became a huge hit because of the music composed by a former dentist called Master Ghulam Haider, who came from a family of traditional musicians called Mirasis who had in earlier times sung raga-based shabadh kirtans from Guru Granth Sahib as ragis in Gurdwaras. Haider had sung a duet in the film with a young singer he had discovered — Shamshad Begum. She had a voice that was strong, transparent, melodious and earthy. The song *Sawan ke nazaren hain* (Behold! The scene of the monsoon) became a rage, as did others like 'Diwali phir aa gayi sajni' (Diwali is here again, beloved!); 'Man dhire dhire rona' (Cry slowly dear heart).

In a career that lasted less than ten years in India (he left a year after the partition in 1947) he changed the conception of the Hindustani film song. He wedded strong assertive melodic lines with an articulate beat usually derived from the store-house of pulsating, Punjabi rhythms. A lesson that was so profitably imbibed by a young Lahori prodigy called O.P. (Onkar Prasad) Nayyar who came into the limelight with his very first film *Aasmaan* in 1952.

Haider had, without intending to, become the leader of the Lahore school of film composers. Apart from his star pupil Shyam Sundar (who died so young), there were talented musicians like Husanlal-Bhagatram, their elder brother Pandit Govindram, Rafiq Ghaznavi, Salim Iqbal, Feroze Nizami, and Jnan Dutt. They, like their master, employed a wholly indigenous technique of composition with tricky and sinuous melodies and captivating background scoring even when they used Western instruments and orchestral colouring they did it with freshness and originality. There are many who believe that the Lahore school created a body of work that would stand the test of time more readily than the efforts of composers who came after them. Another great service that Ghulam Haider had rendered to the film song was to discover Noorjahan, arguably the most expressive and most powerful female voice in the history of Hindwi film music. Those who remember 'Ankh micholi khelenge' (Hide and seek! We shall play), 'Umange dil ki machli' (Heart's desires soared), 'Awaz de kahan hai' (Call out to me, beloved), 'Kya ye tera pyaar thaa' (So this was your love, was it?) will heartily agree.

The holocaust that resulted in the partition also brought about a need for chastity and purity in people's lives. This view was reinforced by the proponents of the Arya Samaj who had migrated to India from East Punjab. Many of them had found employment in the Bombay film industry and soon made a name there. Among them were Ramanand Sagar, B.R. Chopra, Devendra Goyal, Raj Kapoor, and others. They very quietly and effectively launched the cult of virgin worship. The heroine, regardless of her outer trappings of sensuality, had to convey to the viewer her virginal purity; there was no question of her asserting her sexuality. In its most open and healthy form sex in films was taboo and could only be smuggled in as a necessary evil — like the hot water bottle. Seen in this context the phenomenal rise of Lata Mangeshkar must also be attributed an extra-musical reason.

The Phenomenal Lata

The daughter of Master Dinanath Mangeshkar, one of the really fine exponents of Marathi Natya Sangeet, Lata had to begin very early (at thirteen) in order to support a large family impoverished by the sudden demise of her father. Despite many hardships she learnt classical music from such stalwarts as Anjani Bai Malpekar, and Professor Amanat Khan (brilliant pupil of the venerable master Rajab Ali Khan Saheb of Dewas) while pursuing a career as a playback singer in films. Her voice retained its exquisite sweetness and malleability over a period of ten years — from 1948 to 1958 and had such tonal purity that you could tune an instrument by it.

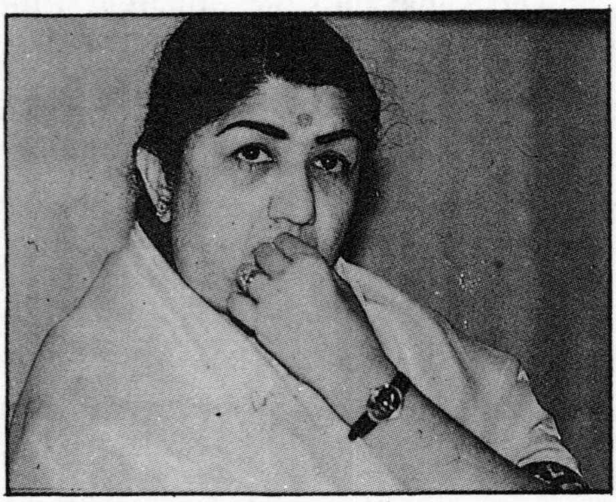

Lata Mangeshkar

Perhaps an early exposure to the duplicity and moral degradation within the film industry made her turn away from worldliness and seek emotional sustenance in a less troubled private world. The result of this experience was startling: her singing had an innocence and naivété that was completely at odds with the trying world she had lived in. Thus when she sang (playback) for adult heroines in films her songs, in retrospect, were a surreal counterpoint to the amorous desires of the actresses concerned. This Hegelian accident of intention and execution involuntarily helped perpetuate the myth of the screen heroine as a snow-white virgin — made necessary by people who had lived through (and in many cases taken part in) the carnage of the partition and needed all the hope in the world to face life again and seek expiation for their real and imagined sins.

Lata Mangeshkar became the richest and most popular playback singer in the history of Indian films and also an extremely influential figure within the Bombay film industry. Her rendering, despite astonishing technical skill, lacked for most part a sense of (adult) truth. But once in a while when this gap was bridged then the results were truly remarkable. Examples are her rendering of 'Bedard tere dard ko seene se laga ke' (Heartless one! I cling to your memory) for her mentor Ghulam Haider; 'Chanda re jaare jaare'... (Keep my secret, dear moon) composed with great delicacy by Khemchand Prakash; 'Tum naa jaane kis jahan mein kho gaye' (Where did you lose yourself, love), a cry from the heart by Sachin Dev Burman; 'Mitti se khelte ho baar baar kis liye' (Why must you play incessantly with mortal clay?); The duo Shankar-Jaikishan's tribute to her musicality and 'Muhabbat aisi dhadkan hai' (Love is a heart beat...) by the exceptionally gifted C. Ramchandra.

Heroines and Singers

The song, to state the obvious, was the most important component of the Bombay film. In its kernel was hidden the film's message: the director's true intentions. Since the stories had a monotonous sameness about them, without the élan or creative vitality evident in the folk theatre, it was left to the director to bring a measure of elegance, sophistication and artistic integrity to his work through the songs. A lot of attention was paid to the lyrics, the tune, the singing and finally the picturisation so that it appeared to be a film within a film, a testimony to the filmmaker's artistic credo. The singer was chosen with great care in most productions regardless of the budget available.

The women singers in the pre-Lata era were from the professional singing classes. Most of them were classically trained and sang their songs in a full-blooded manner highlighting the emotional content of the song including the sexual and sensual elements. Amongst them were Khursheed and Noorjahan who, despite their youth, had wide knowledge of the emotions that actually rule the thoughts and actions of men who run the world....with such perverseness and lack of sensitivity and intelligence. These two singers projected this awareness in their song with great ease. But the one singer who could not shrug off the injustices of the world with irony and insouciance was Raj Kumari whose songs had an overpowering intensity that could neither be confronted nor ignored. A case in point is 'Ghabra ke jo hum sar ko' (In utter despite I bang my head) composed by Khemchand Prakash and written by Naqshab. Director Kamal Amrohi and composer Khemchand Prakash used her voice to underline the eternally tragic in the film *Mahal* and Lata Mangeshkar's to express the sad longing of youth. Both sang for the young heroine Madhubala whose screen persona simultaneously projected girlish innocence and womanly maturity.

The heroine was in reality a more important person in Bombay films than the hero, despite the fact the latter got paid more and hogged the best lines in the script and the marquee. What after all was a leading man like Raj Kapoor without Nargis, or for that matter Dilip Kumar without Nalini Jaywant or most of his heroines including Madhubala, Nargis, Meena Kumari and Vyjayanthimala. How effective would Dev Anand be without Geeta Bali in his early films or Nutan, Vyjayanthimala and Waheeda Rehman later on? The woman was never a foil to the man in Hindustani films, quite the contrary. Hence the role of the female playback singer was significant since song was given so much importance in the very conception of the film. The heroines willed life into a film and their playback voices into them. The men, in keeping with the contrariness of the coding systems of this cinema, only appeared to be the keys to the scripts when in reality they were the locks!

Songs sung for the leading lady and occasionally other female characters in the film were vehicles for multi-layered thoughts and feelings. The one singer who could do this with exemplary emotional integrity was Geeta Dutt whose voice, sometimes under strain because of her physically demanding life-style and high-strung personality, could render a very wide range of emotions and had an inner fire that vindicated the song's existence. She could spiritualise a lyric and make it sensuous at one and the same time. A torch song like 'Suno gajar kya gaye...' (My how time flies!) also becomes a perceptive comment on the passage of time; the pastoral 'Thandi hawa kali ghata...' (Dark clouds and cool winds have arrived in a trance); 'Nanhi kali sone chali' (The little bud is going to sleep), a lullaby worthy of Brahms, and 'Jaane kya tune kahi' (What was it that you said....) an eternally feminine tease, speak volumes for her artistic range as a singer and make us mourn in memory of her life so sadly cut short through emotional damage.

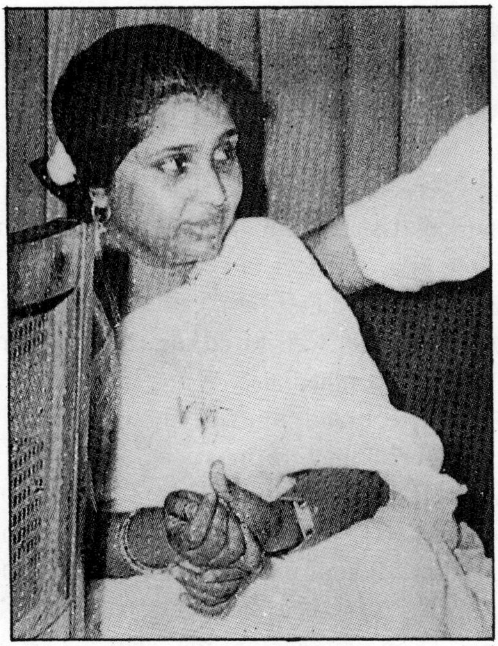

Asha Bhonsle

The one singer who benefited the most from Geeta Dutt's erratic life-style was Lata Mangeshkar's younger sister Asha Bhonsle. Gifted with amazing vocal flexibility and complete professionalism she had at the insistence of her Svengali O.P. Nayyar, modelled her singing style on Geeta Dutt's. Nayyar had been responsible for some of her

(Dutt's) finest achievements; a credit he shared with the ebullient Sachin Dev (S.D.) Burman. Asha stopped copying her celebrated older sister and absorbed the outer raiments of Geeta's style. The result was a Nabokovian paradox! She began to sing with the abandon of a twelve-year-old who has discovered the delights of sex on the sly!! This trait became so much a part of Asha Bhonsle's style that it stayed with her throughout her long and exceptionally successful career. This claim is substantiated by listening to some of her greatest hits like 'Chota sa balama' (My little darling) 'Yeh hai reshmi...' (Come into the silken darkness of my tresses); 'Beete din yaad dilate ho' (You make me recall those forgotten days); 'Saba se ye kehdo' (Tell the gentle breeze...) 'Such hue sapne mere' (My dreams have come true!). Never has she sung as a fully integrated woman as she did under Khayyam's guidance for Zia Sarhady's *Footpath* at the outset of her career. Those three songs, now forgotten, are truly marvellous achievements.

The Men: Rafi, Talat, Mukesh

Among the male playback singers the most popular, versatile and happy-go-lucky was the classically trained Mohammad Rafi. Under the loving tutelage of the famous Ustad Behre Waheed Khan of Kirana he quickly became a very able khayal singer but like Lata Mangeshkar, he had to give it up because of demanding family responsibilities. His generous, easy going nature made him well-loved; he could only respond fully to farcical songs sung for comedians. With other material his attitude was scrupulously correct and tuneful, though not always inspired. Despite enormous success in film music he seemed to secretly mourn the loss of a career in classical music. He could when pushed be heard to advantage in songs like 'Suhani raat dhal chuki' (The velvety night has descended); 'Hum bekhudi mein tumko...' (In a trance I call out to you); 'Aye na baalam...' (The beloved comes not...) and 'Isharon isharon mein dil lene wale' (You who capture my heart with a glance).

Since the lyric was all important as it carried vital information about characters and situations in the story it had to be interpreted with the greatest care. Two of the best exponents were the Urdu-speaking representatives of the Gung-O-Jaman civilisation — Talat Mehmood from Lucknow's Marris College of Music, and Mukesh Chand Mathur from Old Delhi. Both were detectives-of-the-soul. If Talat worked with a Sherlock Holmes-like precision in uncovering the mysteries of the human heart in song, Mukesh went a step further and probed even more lucidly in the manner of Holmes' almost clairvoyant elder brother Mycroft! Both had problems with their voices, but of a different nature.

Talat in the beginning had a powerful melodious tenor voice; evidence of which is still available on tape and disc. That voice, however, disappeared by 1951-52. When Amiya Chakravarti's *Daag* was made in 1953, Talat sang for it in his new avatar. His voice now was soft, sweet... pianissimo. His silken legato enabled him to go up and down the vocal register with unbelievable ease. But such a voice needed a great deal of looking after and Talat the gourmet and heavy smoker ignored the possibility of disaster. Over a period of fifteen years his voice gradually grew darker and by degrees disappeared. He sang hundreds of memorable songs in his prime and after. How can one forget 'Sham-e-gham ki kasam' (I think of you in the palpable sadness of the evening), 'Aye mere dil kahin...' (Let's go elsewhere restless heart), 'Jayen to jayen kahan' (Where does one go from here), 'Ana hi parega' (You'll have to come dearest), 'Pyar par bus to nahin haye...' (I know not my fate in love). Talat's singing like his personality was mellifluous and changing trends in cinema and society finally by-passed him as singers were phased out in favour of howlers!

Mukesh

Mukesh was a survivor. Without making too many compromises he tailored his songs to suit the times. Fond as he was of the good things of life he did not abuse his highly expressive but not too flexible light baritone voice that needed a couple of hours to warm up and get into tune. As an interpreter of song he was supreme. Like a seismographer alert to the slightest tremor in the bowels of the earth so was Mukesh sensitive to the hidden nuances in the lyric. Amongst a host of masterpieces are pieces like 'Dil, jalta hai, to jalne de', 'Awaara hoon...', 'Choti si yeh zindagani re' (The small woeful tale that is life), 'Hamein aye dil kahin le chal' (Take me dear heart far far away), 'Mera juta hai Japani, woh subah kabhi to aye gi' (The dawn shall come yet!), 'Phir na kije meri gustakh nigahi ka gila' (Don't chide me then for my bold glances). Not all singers were lucky in finding the right composers or producers to put their talents to use. A prime example was and is Manna Dey, nephew of the legendary Krishna Chandra (K.C.) Dey, the blind kirtan singer and character actor from New Theatres, Calcutta. Probably because of his classical training, Manna Dey was slotted for a particular type of song. He was never allowed to show his versatility, despite being gainfully employed. His soul-stirring kirtan-like 'Chale Radhe Rani' (In tears goes Radha, away from her beloved Krishna) will continue to move listeners over time.

The Composers

No song can come into being without a composer or lyricist. In Bombay the laws of creativity have followed a peculiar path. While the song writers were known Urdu or Hindwi poets, composers were from many parts of India, including Bengal. Three of the finest — Anil Biswas, S.D. Burman and Salil Choudhury — were from there and only Biswas knew the subtleties of the Hindustani language and its accompanying dialects. Yet all the three composed haunting melodies set to words that were not a part of their childhood psyche.

In the '40s and '50s Bombay was teeming with music directors. Amongst them were the scintillating duo of Shanker-Jaikishan, Madan Mohan (Kohli), Roshanlal (Nagar), both introspective artists, the underrated N. Dutta (Treya) and the dark horse from Patna, Chitragupta; not to forget Ghulam Mohammad, a talented *tabla* player of the Delhi gharana who also composed flowing film melodies. Between them they composed a body of work that was both varied and rich and could stand up in any company.

Sajjad Husain made his debut in Bombay in the middle thirties but really came into his own about a decade later. He had by then developed a taste for intricate melody inspired by ragas and folk music coupled with a flair for western rhythms, particularly the beat of the waltz. That he managed to combine the two and create a new aesthetic in the film song is in itself a considerable achievement. With Noorjahan he created 'Badnam muhabbat kaun kare' (Who wishes to bring ill upon himself?) that had a most beguiling quality of sadness and defiance. Structurally it was novel, with the *taans*, *murkis* and *khatkas* in Noorjahan's resonant voice blending miraculously with the two/four rhythm, the flowing melody rendered even more exquisite by the staccato piano accompaniment. He took note of this musical adventure and used it later in a Lata-Talat duet in *Sangdil* — 'Dil mein sama gaye sajan' (You've merged in my heart, beloved). This song, while deriving its outer structure from the older song, employed sparking, new harmonics and became a dynamic, fresh creation. One does not know if Sajjad had heard recordings of pre-18th century European orchestral music but he had somehow imbibed it. It is quite possible that he, and later O.P. Nayyar, heard them from their Goan arrangers, many of whom were schooled in Western classical music.

Sajjad used these valuable lessons with great tact in his own compositions, for instance, in the Geeta Dutt-Asha Bhonsle duet in *Sangdil* — 'Aja basane naya sansar, aja' (Come with me to a new world) he uses the call and response technique of old European (Spanish/ Moorish?) music in a song with metaphysical resonances. In *Sangdil* again is his completely original treatment of Mirabai's timeless bhajan — 'Darshan pyaasi aayee daasi' (Your slave's eyes thirst for a glimpse of you, lord). The voice and the instrumentation merge into a crystalline whole, imbuing the song with tremendous pathos. His career was relatively short because of his perfectionism and mercurial nature. He never had any intentions of adapting to changing market trends and rather regally wanted the market to accept him as he was and celebrate his music. Had that been so then masterpieces like 'Loota dil mera haay abaad to kar' (Having ruined me), 'Aaj mere naseeb ne mujhko rula rula diya' (My fate made me cry...), from *Hulchul* and the *Sangdi*l gems: 'Kahan ho kahan ho' (Where art thou, maker of this universe?), 'Woh to chale gaye aye dil' (The loved one has gone, dear heart), would have become a part of our national musical heritage instead of fuel for conversation amongst connoisseurs.

O.P. Nayyar, like Sajjad Husain, was/is acutely aware of melodic structures and rhythmic patterns. His compositions, the best of them (and there are many examples) for all their spontaneity are mathematically precise. He too is secretly obsessed with correctness although his own life has been, to put it euphemistically, volatile and lacking in logic. His knowledge of Punjabi folk music, organic structures of certain elemental ragas and openness to outside influences, particularly to that of Latin American music, has made him at his best a scintillating composer and at his worst a fair one. He has been accused of being too versatile for his own good and a purveyor of formula music. Both the charges have some truth in them, but Nayyar at his best is something else altogether!

Compositions like 'Main soya ankhiyan meeche' (In a reverie I lay); 'Chota saa baalama' (My little darling) ... 'Jaaeye aap kahan jayenge' (Go where you will), 'Piya mein hun patang tu dore' (I am your kite sweetie and you are my string); 'Mujhe dekhiye hasrat ki tasveer hun main' (Look at me I am the very picture of hope); 'Isharon, isharon mein...', (Beckoning with your eyes); 'Yeh lo mein hari saiyyan' (You win, sweetheart); 'Puchho na hamein hum unke liya...' (A present for you — Don't ask me what 'Bekasi hadh se gar guzar jaye' (when the cup of sorrow spills over); 'Jaaeye aap kahan jayenge' (Go where you will) speak for his stature as a composer; his ability to unite all the elements in his song and fuse them into a thing of musical beauty put him in the same league as Jelly Roll Morton and Sidney Bechet — great men of classical jazz and masters of form.

Ever since the late forties the song-writer or lyricist has been the most harried man in the film business. He has had to come up with the goods against all odds, often to the detriment of his health. Shailendra, one of the two lyricists of genius (Majrooh Sultanpuri being the other) was an early casualty further burdened by the debts of *Teesri Kasam*, a surprisingly fine film that he had produced.

Lyricists were either poets like Majrooh, Jan Nissar Akhtar, Sahir Ludhianvi and Shakeel Badayuni, Raja Mehdi Ali Khan, Kaifi Azmi, or just song-writers like Rajendra Krishan, P.L. Santoshi and Shailendra. More often than not they had to write words to an already composed tune, relying on their native talent to fathom the necessary poetic, psychological, social insights into the character or characters singing the song. Since it was also to be picturised the lyricist had to work a shade harder than the director or cameraman to ensure that his words actually worked visually as well as musically.

Usually song writers worked in tandem with the composer: Shakeel and Naushad, Shailendra and Hasrat with Shankar-Jaikishan, Majrooh with S.D. Burman and O.P. Nayyar in mid-career, then, as in the beginning, with a host of music directors. The two giants of this profession are no doubt Majrooh and the late Shailendra. Majrooh, a major Urdu/Hindwi poet and also a prolific song-writer who has written to order four thousand songs for three hundred and thirty films over the last fifty years, is difficult to approach for consistency and quality. Four hundred of his songs shall surely live and in their range and scope equal the surpassing efforts of Hugo Wolfe, the great German song (Lieder) writer. It is all the more remarkable that his songs have all been written at the behest of others.

Shailendra, who died in 1966, had an exceptional ear for turns of everyday speech and the poetry of the Hindwi dialects. He could with seeming lack of effort turn a simile, proverb or figure of speech into a song. His 'Dil ka haal sune dilwala sedhe si baat na mirch masala' or 'Ramaiyya vasta vaiyya meine dil tukhko diya' can never be translated into any western language because of their indigenous rootedness. Majrooh's 'hum hain rahi pyar ke, hum se kuch na boliye' and 'Hum aaj kahin dil kho baithe too', cannot be translated for identical reasons. The best works of these two masters are models for would-be lyricists who wish to achieve a perfect blend of clarity and economy in their work.

The Hindustani film song in its golden period embraced vast areas of human emotions and experiences and became an independent art form that enriched while it entertained. Its mesmeric pull can still be experienced after nearly thirty years. It is quite likely that it may well survive into the next century and later.

Part II

6

Bengal in the Forefront

— Kironmoy Raha

EARLY IN THE HISTORY of cinema in India Bengal had earned a reputation of being in the forefront among other regional cinemas. Not on the count of numbers of films made but for its artistic good taste and narrative appeal.

Both were the products of the upsurge in literature, arts, education, social reform and scientific enquiry that Bengal experienced in the nineteenth century. The inheritance of this so-called Renaissance rubbed off on the new craft of filmmaking, which by the twenties of this century had improved sufficiently to make story-based films. Even in those early years many educated persons, some of renown among them, became actively associated with the making of films or took a thoughtful interest in it. Persons like Pramathes Barua, Nitin Bose, B.N. Sircar and others gave up the callings and vocations their background and training prepared them for, to devote their time and skills to film-making. How keen was the interest taken by the intelligentsia in cinema can be gauged by an illustrative example. As early as 1929 Tagore saw its possibilities as an art form and communicator, and deplored in a widely quoted letter its crippling dependence on literary and other supports.

The Bengali middle class had grown and prospered because of various socio-economic and historical reasons. It became the natural leader of Bengali life and thought in the period of efflorescence referred to earlier. Its decline had not set in when in the thirties, sound and talkies put an end to the period of silent films. The interest and spirit of enquiry which the middle class had shown in cinema became keener, its involvement wider and deeper. Besides providing a major share of spectator patronage it brought to cinema elements of its cultural and intellectual inheritance. But the involvement also meant that it brought to filmmaking its predilections and biases.

Two traits of those were a love of literature and enthusiasm for theatre. Abundance of fictional material afforded filmmakers a wide choice of stories to base their films on. This led to a reliance on and adoption of literary modes of exposition. It is worth noting that well-known writers like Premendra Mitra, Sailajananda Mukhopadhyay and Premankur Atarthy became closely associated with cinema as script writers and directors.

The influence of theatre was even less felicitous. Talkies gave ample scope which was eagerly utilised for theatrical dialogues and dramatic acting styles. The impressive list of stage actors and actresses including the great Sisir Bhaduri who were contracted to act or even direct films shows how Bengali cinema looked to theatre for support.

Add to the crutches of literature and theatre a third one of songs and one can see the pitfalls that lay in the path of Bengali cinema's progress.

If despite them Bengali cinema forged ahead of other commercially bigger regional cinemas, it was because of several factors: technical competence, a growing awareness, dim as it was, that theatre's ways and profusion of songs were impediments instead of aids to cinema, stories by eminent writers, good taste and the support of the middle class were largely responsible for Bengali cinema's progress and reputation in the thirties and forties. However, all these might not have been of much avail if it did not also have the advantage of the model of a well-run and equipped studio built and managed by B.N. Sircar, a person of vision and exceptional managerial abilities.

By the early fifties, however, most of the shine of Bengali cinema had worn off, exposing its weaknesses. The emergence of the matinee idol pair Uttam Kumar and Suchitra Sen, ensured spectator support but could not hide the deficiencies to a growing section of thinking viewers. They had become aware of cinema's expanding horizon and expressive power. They saw that for all its narrative appeal even the above average Bengali film was sentimental, wordy and painfully distanced from psychological and social reality.

The social and economic realities of post-independence partitioned Bengal were too grim not to generate anger and protest, and a search for cinematic ways to express them. In the field of the other arts rejection of established norms and exploration of untrodden paths had taken place yielding fruitful results.

Indications that there indeed were stirrings to break away from set ideas of form and content was seen in such films as Bimal Roy's *Udayer Pathe* (1944), Nemai Ghosh's *Chhinnamul* (1951) and Ritwik Ghatak's *Nagarik* (1952). Ghatak's film was not released but the fact of his making a film depicting the pauperisation of a refugee family is a pointer to the undercurrents of ferment and striving. A few Hindi films like Uday Shankar's *Kalpana* (1948) and Bimal Roy's *Do Bigha Zamin* (1953) caused excitement among viewers in Calcutta. Brief exposure to European and Japanese cinema in the first international film festival in 1952 added to the excitement. The very few off-beat Bengali films made reflected the disquiet and the excitement. They were laudable efforts but they showed that their makers were steps away from fully grasping the authentic language of cinema. When that was seen to have been done, and in a first film at that, a true divide was drawn and a big leap forward taken.

Uma Dasgupta in *Pather Panchali*, 1955, Satyajit Ray

Pather Panchali, released for public viewing in Calcutta in August, 1955, first bewildered and then overwhelmed the public, the average as much as the discerning viewer. Over the years, until his death in 1992, Satyajit Ray created a body of work which has ensured him a secure place among the greats of world cinema. It appears in retrospect that the right person appeared at the right time to make the most important landmark in the history of Indian cinema bestowing in the process incalculable benefits and prestige on Bengali cinema.

Satyajit Ray and his work may appear to some as overwritten subjects. It may occur to others that they have not been written enough about. If all has been written in many languages about his life, his creative output and facets of his personality were to be collected it would fill shelves. Yet the analytic and interpretative studies that continue to engage students and aficionados of cinema would suggest that there are areas and aspects of his work awaiting discovery.

This is not unusual. Works of art are frequently judged and interpreted afresh. For an art form which has evolved in the crucible of many arts, science, technology and commerce, and which continues to grow at a furious pace the gates remain wide open for new approaches. In a short article covering a wider subject it is not possible to discuss, even selectively and summarily, Ray's films. Nor is it possible to try to unravel connecting links and running themes in them in a few paragraphs. However, some observations may be made.

Facts about Satyajit Ray's life and background are more or less known. Even so a few bear repetition if only to underline a point not always remembered. His background for instance. He had the advantage of a singular combination of circumstances to make him the right man at the right time and place to achieve what he did.

Writing on Japanese cinema Ray noted in an article his reaction on seeing *Roshomon* which, incidentally, was the first ever Japanese film screened in Calcutta. He wrote: "It was the kind of film that immediately suggests a culmination, a fruition rather than a beginning. You could not as a filmmaking nation have *Roshomon* and nothing to show before it." It is a thought that *Pather Panchali* seems to refute his observation. Bengali cinema might have been ahead for two decades and more of cinema in other filmmaking regions in India. But did it have much to show? Not really. Thus in a way *Pather Panchali* was a beginning and not a culmination.

How did it happen? There is, of course, the unsolvable mystery of inborn gifts. That apart, the genetic and environmental advantages that Ray had seem to have been designed to nurture and bring them to fruition.

Satyajit Ray's grandfather Upendrakishore Ray and father Sukumar Ray were among the finest products of the nineteenth century resurgence in Bengal. The range of their interest and creativity in literature, graphic arts, printing technology and science were rare even in an era crowded with great names. For a person who would apply in future his faculties to acts of creation in what has been called the dominant art form of this century, the inheritance was of immeasurable value. So was the ambience of his childhood and the congenial atmosphere and opportunities in Calcutta to pursue and develop his interest in Indian and European music, painting, literature and typography. Discovery of and reverence for Indian's artistic heritage in the Santiniketan years ensured that roots in his native soil would never dry up. Work as art designer and illustrator for advertising copy and books, intense love for cinema, fitful viewings of classic films and then the first real exposure to world cinema in London (a hundred films in a five months' stay) — there you have the ingredients for the right mix. Additionally, were the lessons of Bengali cinema which, he once remarked, taught him how *not* to make a film.

After the Apu trilogy his work has been discussed by many critics in Europe and America. Most have elaborated the view that central to his beliefs are humanism, a modern outlook and understanding of the processes of change in traditional societies.

In recent years Ray's films are being studied in supposedly greater depth within a wider framework of reference. In them a noticeable tendency is application and use of criteria and arcane terminology of modern psychology, post-structuralism, social anthropology and semiology, not to mention Marxism, sociology, etc. Doubtless they have their value. But I wish to make two points arising out of them.

The first is that in appraisals of Ray's outlook and his work most European and American critics and students of cinema apply standards of aesthetic judgement developed in the West. There is an apparent lack of interest in analysing and connecting the emotive content and formal structures to Indian theories of art and indices of appreciation. Such an interest would balance to some extent the emphasis given to western role-modelling in Ray's films. When critics in western countries find more of Renoir, De Sica, Mozart and Chekhov in Ray's films they are prone to neglect his Indian, more specifically Bengali, sensibilities as sources of inspiration.

I would refer to two examples to substantiate my point. When Robin Wood in his book *The Apu Trilogy* remarks that "this (in *Charulata)* emotional complexity, the delicate balancing of responses, what one may call the Mozartian aspect of Ray's art, which links him with Renoir, is already characteristic in *Pather Panchali,"* he leaves out Bibhuti Bhusan Bannerji, Indian musical forms and nature's role and significance in lives as lived in a Bengali village.

The second example is from Edwin Gerow's book on Sanskrit drama. He observes there that Ray's films "do not seem to respond to any Indian need at all" and "they are difficult to account for in (Indian) classical terms" and are "therefore in a technical sense tasteless". One wonders if a knowledge of the Bengali mind and milieu is considered unnecessary in appreciating Ray's films and what taste is made up of. Similarly, preoccupation with culture specifics in evaluating films often leads to bizarre misjudgements. Thus, *Sita Kalyanam* is highly praised by western critics and Ginsberg finds *Sampurna Ramayana* more insightful than *Pather Panchali.* Another trend is a search for subtexts and analysis of constructs. They do not necessarily help.

The second point is that there is a misconception that Ray's films have not been popular in India and have been appreciated only by western audiences. This is incorrect, certainly so in Bengal. Viewers went wild over *Pather Panchali* long before it won an award at the Cannes festival without the benefit of analytical studies by western observers. Ray himself never tired of saying that he made films with the audience at home in mind. The targeted audience nearly always responded.

The lead that Satyajit Ray gave to Bengali cinema with *Pather Panchali* instituted courage and confidence to young aspiring filmmakers to make films to express their dissenting mood and ideas. Ray was without question the primary cause of a fresh and feverish burst of creative activity in Bengali cinema.

The most venturesome of those who struck out on their own was also the most original in his outlook and methods. Ritwik Ghatak was not influenced by Ray, not overtly. This first film to be released for public viewing, *Ajantrik* (1958), showed his originality. It was evident that his imagination and concerns were of a different kind from Ray's. If the film he completed just about the time Ray began shooting *Pather Panchali* showed his concern for the disintegration caused by the partition of India in 1947, he projected in *Ajantrik* his discernment that the same process was at work in post-independence India.

Ritwik Ghatak's later films laid bare the compelling drives behind his passion and his pain, as much as his desperate search for abiding roots. The release that he sought from the prison house of memories and the brutal reality he faced found expression in haunting imageries of nature and dramatic situations in his films. They also reveal his faith in the mythic attributes of the supreme mother goddess, which were for him a psychological need to find roots deep and strong enough to withstand the turbulence and ruin he found all around.

The contrary pulls of affirmation and negation were reflected in his films and made them uneven. Stunning sequences depicting the grandeur of nature and the human soul would be jarringly followed by the superficial and the contrived. Ritwik Ghatak's control over the medium evidenced in the riveting outdoor visuals, the melodramatic situations, the use of songs and musical motifs is not in doubt, and yet his films give the impression that he rebelled against the very discipline the use of the tools of the medium necessarily imposed. It was as if he explored the limits of the medium and found them constricting for conveying his passion and the intensity of his feelings.

More than others Ritwik Ghatak personified the Bengali ethos. It is difficult to explain why his films, almost all of them, were box office failures. The only solution to the paradox I can think of is that he was too unconventional and erratic in his technique and style to gain acceptance. The reference points of his films appeared obscure and confusing. He was perhaps ahead of his times, a *Meghe Dhaka Tara* (A Star covered by Clouds) in his lifetime. It is only recently that the extraordinary qualities of his films are being appreciated and his worth as one of the most significant directors of Bengali cinema acknowledged.

If Ritwik Ghatak's films were box office failures, so have been many of Mrinal Sen's. But there the resemblance ends. Mrinal Sen has generally been regarded as the leading proponent of political cinema in India. But in his espousal of causes or depiction of reality he has been free from Ghatak's obsessions and fixations. His Marxist views and penchant for experimentation did not deflect him from his resolve to explore the psychology of individuals nor blunt while doing so his protesting social conscience.

Anil Chatterjee and Supriya Chowdhry in
Megha Dhake Tara, 1960, Ritwik Ghatak

From his third film *Baishey Sravan* (1960) onwards Mrinal Sen's control over the craft of filmmaking was evident. And so was his irrepressible urge to experiment with the ways of cinematic expression. His long career in films has helped in no small degree in enhancing Bengali cinema's reputation and its claim to be counted in world cinema. One does not become internationally the best known Indian film director without sufficient reason and justification.

Mrinal Sen's career graph shows wide fluctuations. It reflects the variety of his films in both thematic content and formal experiments. He has been concerned as much with personal relationships, under-currents of middle class familial tension-ridden existence as with social issues like destitution, decay, struggle and political activism. He has not been afraid to cross linguistic barriers, one fruitful result of which has been *Bhuvan Shome* (1969) in Hindi, generally regarded as the precursor of parallel cinema in that language.

Utpal Dutt in *Bhuvan Shome*, 1969, Mrinal Sen

Many of Mrinal Sen's films can be faulted for their structural imbalance and hasty eagerness to break narrative moulds. Many of them, on the other hand, are memorable creations. There can, in any case, be no question, that his contribution to Bengali cinema has been immense. What is particularly remarkable and welcome is the fact that making films for well over three decades now he shows no sign of tiredness or waning of his innovative imagination.

The primacy Bengali cinema had regained with *Pather Panchali* remained for nearly two decades. Others besides Ray, Ghatak and Sen contributed to its vigour. Tapan Sinha, Rajen Tarafdar, Asit Sen, Barin Saha are some of the names that come to mind in this regard. Their thematic ideas and handling of the craft differed in depth and competence. But collectively they sustained the strength and vitality of what after all was minority cinema.

By the mid-seventies the vigour was gone. Ritwik Ghatak had not made a film for ten years. Many like Rajen Tarafdar and Barin Saha just dried up. Asit Sen migrated to Bombay. Only Tapan Sinha demonstrated his staying power and self-assurance. By charting and consistently following a middle path he ensured a measure of popular support for good cinema at a time when but for Ray's eminence and Sen's courage Bengali cinema might well have been relegated to a minor position.

In the seventies the commercial or mainstream Bengali cinema was in dire straits. Even middle-class viewers, the traditional support base of Bengali cinema, turned away. The expanded class of wage earners showed no desire or inclination to watch Bengali films when entertainment was what they wanted. The fact that more than eighty per cent of cinema houses in West Bengal screen Hindi films tells its own tale.

The loss of leadership status of Bengali cinema in the seventies was symptomatic of the decline the in nearly all spheres of Bengali life. The cultural inheritance of which the middle class was the chief beneficiary was spent and the social and political consciousness which has been an important trait in Bengali character lost in self-destructive ideological strife and loss of direction. What remained were isolated individual talent and endeavour. In such a situation cinema could hardly be expected to prosper. Its decline was brought into sharp relief by the enormous strides taken meanwhile by other regional cinemas of India.

Paradoxically, interest in serious cinema grew. The number of film societies swelled and film festivals, big and small, have become regular events drawing huge crowds. Governments and institutional agencies began providing finance and other facilities.

As a result of these, a few young filmmakers, unburdened of the baggage of the past and anxious to move out of the shadows cast by Ray and Sen made some notable films in the eighties. Aparna Sen, Goutam Ghose, Utpalendu Chakraborty and above all Buddhadeb Dasgupta have refurbished to some extent the faded image of Bengali cinema. They have won critical acclaim in India and abroad and, a few of their films, spectator support in Bengal as well. However, the sobering thought is that they have depended mostly on state institutional patronage. Can they continue to do so without damage to their independence and creative energy?

In 1995 countless functions will be held in filmmaking countries to celebrate one hundred years of cinema, and Bengali cinema will observe its seventy-fifth anniversary. If one ruminates over what it has achieved, its ups and downs, its successes and failures during seventy-five years of its existence one is assailed by mixed feelings of pride and elation, dejection and despair. My personal misgivings arise from the evidence of near-complete erosion of cherished values and coarsening of the Bengali mind and sensibilities.

7

Enter the Government

— *Vinod Bhardwaj*

As a rule writers, artists and playwrights are not overly dependent on government institutions for their creations. But this is not true of those who make films. By its very nature, film is a very expensive art and dependent on all kinds of paraphernalia as well as the vagaries of the box-office and the market place.

About a century ago when film first came into being it proved to be explosive, its presence viewed as magical. Film made free use of various art forms like literature, painting, music and stagecraft but from the very beginning the pressures and constraints of commerce began to be exerted.

The reach and power of film was awe-inspiring. It could hold sway over millions — crossing all boundaries; it could hold viewers spellbound. The rich western nations came to view film as a vehicle of entertainment and trade and the socialist nations saw it as an instrument of mass instruction and propaganda. Two different and even opposing ends were thus served by the same art form.

All over the world since its inception, film has been grappling with the various, usually opposing, forces interacting on it — be they from the world of entertainment, ideas, trade or art. These relationships are very complex. A filmmaker can use the camera like a pen — indeed in the history of film there are many successful examples — but he can never claim that his work has nothing to do with the box-office. Those who do so are either hypocrites or do not understand the very nature of filmmaking.

In the history of the arts there have been examples of painters who have destroyed their own canvases (the British painter Francis Bacon destroyed much of his earlier work himself), writers who have attempted to destroy their own work (remember the Czech writer Franz Kafka) but can there possibly be a film director or producer who can even contemplate taking such a step after giving the finishing touches to his work? There are numerous examples of incomplete films but no filmmaker can ever be happy seeing his film rotting in cans. As film distribution is a business many a film does not see the light of the screen — but that is not a fate easily enjoyed by its creators.

Taking all these factors into account, the role of government bodies in the making of films has been significant and decisive.

All types of governments, democratic, socialist or dictatorships have felt the necessity to impose some form of film censorship. Often battles have been fought between filmmakers and censor boards. However, despite the censor, all kinds of permissive and unimagined things are being shown today on screeens all over the world.

Can societies that dubbed the novels of D.H. Lawrence and James Joyce pornographic, leading to their being banned, ever imagine that the German novelist Gunter Grass' novel, *The Tin Drum*, with its graphic depiction of sex, ever be filmed without disturbing the parameters of art and culture? It was, and successfully too, by German director Volker Schloendorff.

At the end of the '70s the Japanese filmmaker Nagisa Oshima, in his *The Empire of the Senses*, shocked the world with a freedom in the depiction of sex and violence which could not even be imagined in the '60s. On the other hand, the Polish expatriate who settled in the US, Roman Polanski, after having catered to these twin obsessions in his films suddenly made *Tess* (based on Thomas Hardy's novel), a three-hour film which completely eschewed a graphic portrayal of sex and violence.

During this period Poland's Andrez Wajda and other directors managed to achieve another kind of freedom in political expression in films like *The Man of Iron*. Attempts were made to censor this film but by then socialist regimes had learnt that bans tend to generate greater controversy. Hence it was quietly sent to the Cannes film festival to receive laurels and awards.

In 1980 Cuban filmmaker Tomas Gutierrez Alea had said: "In my view the best way to propagate socialism is by making good films. Forget that you have to propagate socialism. It is good films that will prove that socialism is a good thing."

The point is that whereas censors the world over permitted radical changes, during the same period the censor in countries like India became the victim of a peculiar problem. The question was to decide the degree of severity in the depiction of sex and violence.

Those were the days when a commercial Bombay film would show a kiss in the twining of two red roses.

In the '70s, Indian censorship concerned itself with putting a stop to any depiction of sex but after the advent of Prakash Mehra's *Zanjeer*, the Bombay film reached the heights of crudity in its showing of senseless violence. 1973 saw the simultaneous release of Raj Kapoor's *Bobby* and *Zanjeer*, the film that first projected Amitabh Bachchan in an angry image. *Bobby* showed teenage romance and *Zanjeer* focused on the anger of a police officer.

Even twenty years after the release of *Bobby* our cinema has not progressed in its love themes or the depiction of sex but since the release of *Zanjeer* our cinema has ripped off all sanctity and decorum surrounding the law, judges and ministers. Not only this: the films seem to revel in all kinds of obscenities. The dialogue is vulgar and replete with double-meanings while rape has been shown in the crudest form. To illustrate the sad state of things after independence the film *August 15* portrays graphically both violence and rape at their most gory and tasteless.

One should note that after some time a free depiction of sex on the screen leads to a loss of novelty and magic associated with it. But a graphic portrayal of violence serves as an opiate. People tend to view it time and again. This is why sex is shown along with violence in films. In his confession, a killer admitted to having seen Bruce Lee's *Enter the Dragon* more than 20 times. This happens to be among those films that have repeat value and is filled with kung-fu and violence of the martial arts kind.

During the last two decades among the various government institutions, it is the Censor Board that has played a crucial role. Its problems have been compounded by the video and the satellite invasion. In the north during the '60s and '70s it was really difficult to gain membership of a film society. Not because as in Kerala and Bengal, there were more people keen on serious cinema but because this way our shallow and middle classes could easily get to see uncensored films.

During film society screenings in the '70s many a viewer could be seen yawning and becoming alert only when some explicit sex scene came along. Luckily the video wave has given this kind of viewer opportunity to see blue films sitting in their homes. Even then the charm and allure of the big screen eludes them and they flock to the 'hot' films at film festivals.

Our censors have had to face some difficulties too. When a serious and responsible filmmaker shows sex and violence in his film, it is usually passed. This is as it should be. But even a commercial filmmaker tries to take advantage of the censors' broadmindedness. He says: "Why can't I show all this?"

The freedom given to Stanley Kubrick in *Clockwork Orange* in 1973 in depicting sex and violence will have different results if granted to an ordinary filmmaker. Moreover British thinkers, psychiatrists and filmmakers have not been able to make up their minds one way or the other on the effects of violence depicted in the film. The question is whether the film's violence and rage were emulated by the British youth or whether it helped to reduce violence within them.

The way our censors function can be illustrated by an interesting example. A rule made on the advice of experts laid down that those films which had been screened at famous film festivals or those that had been written about in journals of international repute will henceforth be liberally censored. The objective was laudable but look at the results. Indian distributors started picking up those films that had met with artistic approval but showed nudity and sex in large doses. Here one example will suffice: Greek director Angeloupoulos' *The Beekeeper* is a serious and grim film. The problems in this film are existential. But the film's nubile heroine has been shown in the nude for long periods. Our distributors got this film imported and found it to be slow. And the film was subjected to arbitrary scissoring and reduced in length. Thus a good film came to be distributed in an improper shape. The result was that a serious viewer could hardly sit through it.

Should this policy be adopted under such conditions? Surprisingly in the west where sex films can be easily seen in cinema halls, the audience is usually very thin — the very old, the lonely, the sick and foreign labourers constitute the viewership. The result is that wrong type of audience does not flock to good films in some of which there are necessary depictions of sex and nudity.

After all, the coitus-depicting statues at Khajuraho and Konarak with all their intimate intricacies have not in any way led to the destruction of our nation. It is obvious that film is a more powerful and far-reaching medium but if our censors give a free rein to the depiction of sex and keep a strict curb on violence, this will go to better our film industry and film culture.

Once at a film festival in Bombay, producer-director Vijay Anand rightly said when no earthquake occurs in the morals of our nation during the screening of uncensored films in the two festival weeks, not much will change if such films were to be screened during the year.

Often doubts are expressed over Indian society's capacity to take in depictions of sex in film. But if once the censor gives a free hand to such depiction, then a large segment of our society will be found to be indifferent towards explicit sex. A free depiction of love on our screens is not as lethal as showing a villain taking out a knife and stabbing a pregnant woman in close-ups (this in fact is the theme of the film *Aaj Ka Arjun*).

Of course, the problems of film production are linked to this policy of our censors. A change in policy will preclude the hilarious possibility of such a serious film as *The Beekeeper* being advertised as a hot film. And the international film festivals will cease to be attractive only for their hot films.

Much more complex is the role played by the NFDC (National Film Development Corporation) in the production and distribution of films. FFC (Film Finance Corporation) was formed way back in 1960. The Corporation got accolades in 1969 on the release of Mrinal Sen's Hindi film *Bhuvan Shome*. It was later in 1980 that FFC got the new name of NFDC. Actually NFDC was born earlier, in 1975, but it was in 1980 on the merger of FFC and IMPEC (Indian Motion Picture Export Corporation) that NFDC got its final shape. And now NFDC has taken a new form through the medium of the Metro channel on television. Once again filmmakers are asking whether NFDC's role lies in regarding entertainment as an opiate or in setting new standards in healthy entertainment.

In fact, the debate on NFDC's role in the development of cinema has been going on since the last twenty-five years. 1960-61 saw the founding of the National Film and Television Institute (FTII) in Pune. The need for such an institution had been stressed earlier in 1951 by the Film Enquiry Committee.

Despite its limitations the Pune Film Institute has been Indian cinema's most significant and encouraging government body. The FTII together with the National Film Archive are the repository of the world's best films and almost anybody by seeing them and reading through a maze of books on film finds the path he is going to take. Its over 26,000 books and 1,600 films can help to change one's film perception. In this context the comment made by Shaji, the director of *Piravi* (1989), is interesting:

"The Pune Institute was a place where one got inducted rather than instructed into filmmaking. I'd mostly go to the National Film Archive, to its library. I'd never really venture out of the campus."

Even Adoor Gopalakrishnan, one of our most significant filmmakers today, on reaching Pune from his native Kerala, saw that the only way to educate himself in films was by seeing them. There he saw nearly five films every day as it was not easy to see them in Kerala.

Says Adoor: "I don't think film watching is divorced from theory. In fact, one learns more from watching films. Theories are important. But you must remember when the Institute had just started out in 1961, both students and teachers were probing their way through the medium. There was more freedom to choose from what we saw and read."

In its early days students came into contact with a great filmmaker like Ritwik Ghatak. The generation of Mani Kaul and Kumar Shahani belongs to this period. Admittedly, the list of the Pune Film Institute's alumni is attractive and long and includes such famous names as Adoor Gopalakrishnan, Mani Kaul, Kumar Shahani, Shaji S. Karun, Saeed Mirza, John Abraham, Ketan Mehta, Jahnu Barua, Subhash Ghai, Shabana Azmi, Om Puri, Naseeruddin Shah, Suresh Oberoi, Shatrugan Sinha, Virendra Saini, K. K. Mahajan, Venu, A.K. Bir, Renu Saluja, Santosh Sivan and Madhu Ambat.

From this rather imposing list, it is obvious that the FTII provides significant facilities in the field of direction, cinematography, editing and acting. But in order to reap the full advantages of such a progressive institution, it is necessary that complementary government facilities in the form of other institutions be available.

Film culture cried out for a new direction when the new crop of talent emerged from the FTII. A whole crop of directors, actors and technicians burst on the scene with newly acquired ideas and creativity.

After *Bhuvan Shome* the Indian film world changed its map as it were. It's true that good films used to be made earlier too but after 1969 there came about a radical change of the situation.

On a cursory look the achievements of NFDC in the field of film-making have been impressive. The Corporation produced over 200 films, 25 of which came out in flying colours on the international arena.

During this period a number of well-known filmmakers made their films, courtesy NFDC. Some of them are: Satyajit Ray, Shyam Benegal, Mrinal Sen, Tapan Sinha, Adoor Gopalakrishnan, G. Aravindan, Kumar Shahani, Mani Kaul, M.S. Sathyu, Ketan Mehta, Saeed Mirza, Girish Kasaravalli, Aparna Sen, Basu Chatterjee, Sudhir Mishra, Shaji N. Karun, Goutam Ghose, Prakash Jha, Pradip Krishen, Nirad Mahapatra and Govind Nihalani. The films were made in Hindi, Bengali, Kannada, Malayalam and Oriya. Famous Film Institute alumni got a chance to show their mettle in these films.

In the '70s, leaving aside a few exceptions, most of the new talked-about directors, actors and stars had been inspired by the Film Institute. During this period a healthy relationship came to be established between NFDC and the Film Institute.

From the release of *Bhuvan Shome* in 1969 to that of Shyam Benegal's *Suraj Ka Satvan Ghora* is a long period, and the situation has changed considerably. There was a wave of hope in the success of *Bhuvan Shome*. In 1993 this was not so. There may not be despondency, but today filmmakers think twice before deciding on a new project.

Years ago Mrinal Sen had said: "With a wider mobilisation of minority spectators which will eventually turn out to be quite a sizeable all-India crowd, I am sure low-budget films can be readily accepted as a sound commercial proposition. It is no surprise, to me therefore, that, low-budget films are being made in Hindi and not much in the regional languages. And from personal experience I can tell you that *Bhuvan Shome*, had it been made in Bengali, could not have made its money back. I am told that the FFC is planning to build a chain of art theatres throughout the country. This is fantastic." (Mrinal Sen: 'Views on Cinema'.)

Today Mrinal Sen's optimism cannot stir up enthusiasm among lovers of cinema. As compared to Hindi films, those in other languages like Bengali, Malayalam, Kannada and Oriya have proved to be more significant. NFDC's plan to open 'art' cinema houses in every corner of the country has been unsuccessful. Though it is true we have a fair population to support good cinema, yet art cinema has only been able to come up with government finance.

Few good films were made in Hindi because very few filmmakers emerged who were attached to the geography, history, and landscape of the Hindi-speaking states. In name some directors did make Hindi films. But these could just as well have been made in English.

Only good and serious cinema in Bengali and Malayalam got the support of viewers in some measure. In Bengal, Ray, Ghatak and Mrinal Sen had taken up the challenge of making good films even before the birth of the NFDC. The viewers of their films were limited but visible.

Both Adoor and Aravindan's Malayalam films were able to make their economic base in their own way. At one time Aravindan was making significant films with budgets that were so low that other filmmakers could not even dream of. Those days the cost of raw stock, processing etc. was not so high. And both these filmmakers had found regular viewers to watch their films.

Today it is not surprising that with the help of Doordarshan NFDC has made several significant films. It is not necessary that all of them will be premiered on Doordarshan. For example, Adoor's *Mathilukal* was made with Doordarshan's help but on condition that it would first be released in cinema halls.

It is not only in India that the good cinema is faced with difficulties. Even European cinema with films of directors like Fellini, Bergman, Tarkovsky and Wajda, which once provided a direction to world cinema, has now lost out to Hollywood's entertainment-oriented films like *Jurassic Park*. Art films continued to be made in Eastern Europe as long as they got government finance. Today these films are not being made.

In such a situation NFDC and Doordarshan can be expected to hold out some hope, but not much. Today the economics of cinema is not in favour of good, small-budget films. But the prospects for such filmmaking are not gloomy if the filmmaker is attuned to the soil and roots of his viewers.

The national film report of 1980 talked of setting up a cinema academy. Even today such an institution is badly needed. To quote

Ray's concurrence to this report:

"He supported the idea of setting up a Chalachitra Akademi exclusively devoted to the promotion of cinema as an art form and bringing the National Film Archive under the Akademi. He very strongly felt that cinema should be introduced as a subject of study at the university level."

We have had very little documentation on cinema. NFDC has ceased publication of its journal, *Cinema in India.* Even in a big city like Delhi, there is no library on cinema and there is no museum of cinema in India. Since 1964, the National Film Archive has done significant work but with a cinema academy all these could have been better organised. Even those institutions that have promoted cinema in the past are not in good shape. National Film awards have been given since 1954. However, an attempt to bag these awards through large viewer coteries is something recent.

Official and extra-professional pressures have been brought to bear on the Directorate of Film Festivals. Since 1978 at international film festivals the Indian Panorama section has been doing significant work. Since a few years even this section is being pressurised by the twin forces of economic viability and success. We have already referred to NFDC in this respect.

More important than opening up a cinema academy is the need to ensure the professional and artistic character of our present government institutions. The truth is — sweet or bitter — that without government understanding a cinema with artistic parameters cannot retain its individuality.

Today when, for reasons known and unknown, the entire filmmaking world is ready to accept Hollywood's dominion, the commitment towards good cinema assumes greater significance.

8

A Showcase for the New Indian Cinema: The Panorama

— *Sudhir Bose*

INTERNATIONAL FILM FESTIVALS of India (IFFIs) were held irregularly from 1952 to 1975 where the focus generally used to be on international cinema to give an opportunity to people working in the medium as well as film buffs to acquaint themselves with the latest developments. At the first IFFI held in Bombay in 1952 Indian cinema made an unslotted and, as it were, an anonymous appearance, with an important exception. Raj Kapoor's *Awara* (1951) had already been a box-office hit and captured the popular imagination with its tempting packaging of a sensitive theme — lineage versus upbringing — in songs, spectacle and romance verging on sensuality. Raj Kapoor and *Awara* have been popular across countries and continents since then.

It was at the fourth IFFI held in Delhi in 1969 that Mrinal Sen's *Bhuvan Shome*, a landmark film[1] for many reasons, was first shown. It was Sen's first Hindi film; it was a low-budget movie financed by the recently formed Film Finance Corporation; it is now credited with having heralded the Indian 'new cinema'; and it was a commercial success with discerning audiences. In the cliché-ridden, pan-Indian Hindi cinema *Bhuvan Shome* came as a breath of fresh air.

Even if one restricts oneself to the limited exposure of Indian films at these early IFFI's, *Bhuvan Shome*, Shyam Benegal's *Ankur* (1974) — which attracted even Satyajit Ray's attention for its camera work and newcomer Shabana Azmi's acting — and Awtar Krishna Kaul's *27 Down*, together with Ray's already established prestige in the international film festival circuit brought home the need for organized screenings of the latest films of "cinematic, thematic and aesthetic excellence" (Indian Panorama Regulations) in a section later called the Indian Panorama. Filmmakers who treated the cinematic medium in a creative manner (many of them graduates from the still new Film Institute of India) were thus given a slot to present their films before international gatherings at IFFIs and Filmotsavs (in alternate years from 1977 to 1988, and known as IFFIs since then).

The most notable absence at all these festivals was the erratic genius of Indian cinema, Ritwik Ghatak, so that when the Indian Panorama made its inaugural annual appearance at the Madras Filmotsav in 1978 he had been dead for two years. Thus the only way his contribution to Indian cinema could be recognized was by holding a retrospective of his films there.

Since then, inclusion in the Indian Panorama has been coveted as it ensures international showcasing and an avenue to foreign festivals. In addition, it almost always guarantees a television screening, very important for the makers of these films who may face the difficulty of theatrical release and thus even recovering the cost of the film.

Through the Indian Panorama, it is possible to trace the path that the new Indian cinema took, and where it stands today.

As one reviews the Panorama[2] lists down the years what strikes one is that the master, who had almost single-handedly forced the international film community to take notice of him — and Indian cinema — more than two decades before the inception of the Panorama, was now no longer at the peak of his creativity. Not many will include *Shatranj ke Khilari*[3] (1977)[4], *Joi Baba Felunath* (1978), *Hirak Rajar Deshe* (1980), *Pikoo* (1980), *Sadgati* (1981), *Ghare-Baire* (1984), *Ganashatru* (1989), *Shakha-Proshakha* (1990), and *Agantuk* (1991) among Ray's creative peaks. While there are flashes of genius all through these films, one has only to think of the lyricism of *Pather Panchali*, the perfection of *Charulata*, the relentlessness of *Jana Aranya* — the various attributes sustained through each work — to realize that the best of Ray predates the Panorama; he had been discovered long before. In fact, his death in April 1992 has made it necessary for film scholars to place his contribution in perspective, both in artistic and commercial terms. For most of Ray's films were commercial successes — and some of them box-office hits — in the limited Bengali circuit.

But that is not the case with Mrinal Sen, Ray's contemporary and still active. Although Sen had made sixteen films when the Panorama began, *Bhuvan Shome* (1969) was the first of his films, as described above, to place him on the festival circuit. *Chorus* and *Mrigaya* were considered well-crafted films, but it was with the inclusion of his films in the Panorama — notably *Oka Oorie Katha* (1977), the terseness and sense of urgency in almost every frame of *Ekdin Pratidin* (1979), the consummate artistry and subdued drama of *Akaler Sandhane* (1980), the economy and clinical quality of *Kharij* (1982) and the brooding nature of *Khandhar* (1983) — that Sen was recognized as next only to Ray. If there are as many troughs as peaks in his oeuvre, Sen has a body of films that presents a vision of life and times that have so deeply influenced him.

Among the next generation of filmmakers, who came into the limelight in the seventies and are still active, Adoor Gopalakrishnan probably stands the tallest, in spite of his meagre output of seven films. Five years after he made a promising debut with *Swayamvaram* (1972), every film by Adoor has been shown in the Panorama — *Kodiyettam* (1977), *Elippathayam* (1981), *Mukhamukham* (1984), *Anantaram* (1987), *Mathilukal* (1989), and *Vidheyan* (1993) — and

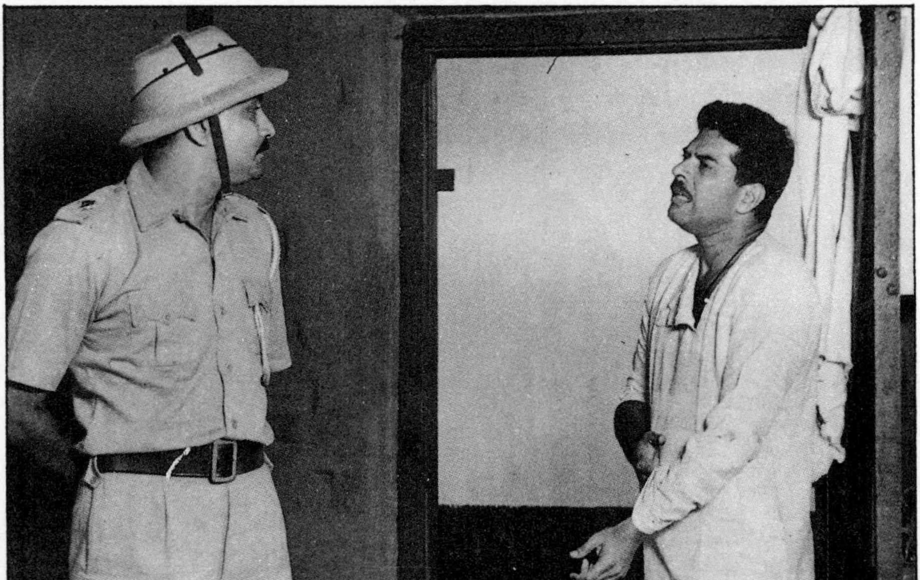

Mathilukal, 1989, Adoor Gopalakrishnan with Mammooty

added to his reputation as a visual artist. An Adoor film begins with his script, original or adapted, rich in literary and dramatic content, which gains in subtle nuances in the process of direction that shows his craftsmanship. Especially notable is his use of the soundtrack — silences to underline the dramatic moments in *Elippathayam*, natural sounds to enhance the changing moods in *Mukhamukham,* and music and silence to complement the visual design of *Anantaram*. Conscious of the need to reach the national and international film public at the earliest possible, Adoor has not waited for Panorama selection of his new film. *Elippathayam*, for instance, was not ready in time for selection for the Calcutta Filmotsav in January 1982. He was able to complete it only a few days before the Filmotsav began and screened it before the Filmotsav ended — to the applause of the international gathering. By the time *Elippathayam* was officially shown in the Panorama at the Delhi IFFI a year later, it had been screened at international festivals abroad and recognized as a major work (he was given the annual British Film Institute award of 1982 for 'the most original and imaginative film'). Adoor's lead in the way he has used the earliest opportunity to show his latest work has been followed by many other filmmakers in subsequent years.

G. Aravindan, Adoor's contemporary and like him from Kerala, also caught international attention through the Panorama. Like Adoor,

Neena Gupta in *Vasthuhara,* 1990, G. Aravindan

Aravindan had made only one film before the inception of the Panorama. Eight out of ten films by him since then have been featured in the Panorama, notably *Thampu* (1978), *Chidambaram* (1985), *Oridathu* (1986) and *Vasthuhara* (1990). He showed his last film privately at the Madras IFFI in January 1991 and within two months he was dead. But with eleven films he has established his place as the cartoonist (as in *Thampu* and *Oridathu*) and poet (notably *Chidambaram*, but the sensuous treatment of the landscape in many of his films has a lyrical quality) of Indian cinema. An unlikely combination in a creative artist until one takes a bird's-eye view of Aravindan's oeuvre; his background as a cartoonist can be only part of the explanation.

Shyam Benegal is a contemporary of Adoor and Aravindan, and had also made his mark before the inception of the Panorama with his debut, *Ankur*. But there the similarity ends. Benegal's importance lies in the fact that he was the first filmmaker of the seventies in the pan-Indian Hindi cinema to break the mould of its formula-ridden filmmaking and make a place for himself as a conscious artist whose films held their own in the commercial circuit. *Ankur, Nishant* and *Manthan* — sometimes described as a trilogy of tyranny and exploitation in rural India — did a number of things: a view of life rooted in reality; humanism underlying the treatment of social issues; flesh-and-blood characters (Benegal's women characters are vastly different from the dolls of popular Hindi cinema of the time); and discovery of a talented group of performers (Shabana Azmi, Smita Patil, Om Puri and Naseeruddin Shah, among others) and technical crew (notably Govind Nihalani as cameraman). His record in the Panorama has, however, been somewhat patchy, with *Bhumika* (1977) standing out. *Junoon* (1978), *Kalyug* (1981), *Mandi* (1983), *Trikal* (1985), and *Suraj ka Satvan Ghoda* (1992) are, of course, notable films; but they somehow lack the sustained intensity of his earlier work. *Mammo* (1994), however, shows Benegal's earlier narrative power and ability to extract an inspired performance — by Farida Jalal, in this case.

Mani Kaul and Kumar Shahani are the two unusual filmmakers to have been featured in the Panorama but predate it. Kaul's debut in the Panorama was with *Satah se Uthata Admi* (1980). His earlier *Uski Roti* (1970) had shown an entirely new approach to filmmaking: a personal style and avoidance of the conventional narrative mode. His next film in the Panorama, *Mati Manas* (1985), was also in the same vein. But with *Nazar* (1990) Kaul took another new direction: use of a European literary work — Dostoevsky's "The Meek One" — as the basis of his artistic concerns.

Shahani had to wait longer to be featured in the Panorama, with *Tarang* (1984) — twelve years after his first, *Maya Darpan*, which had an originality of treatment. His next film came five years later, *Khayal Gatha* (1989), followed by *Kasba* (based on Chekhov's "In the Gully", 1990).

Although Kaul has made more films than shown in the Panorama since its beginning, Shahani's output has been relatively meagre. Their reputation as intellectual filmmakers rests on their theoretical explorations in their films. It is as if film is for them a vehicle for delving into the self more than for reaching out to the other — the spectator — on the one hand, and for experimentation with form on the other.

Govind Nihalani, who had achieved fame as the cameraman of Benegal's films in the seventies, made an impressive beginning as a director with *Aakrosh* (1980) with a courageous theme — the indictment of a system that allows injustice — in the unfolding of which he showed his cinematic flair. *Ardh Satya* (1983) is an exploration of the inner conflict of a principled police officer caught in the present-day's socio-political maze. *Party* (1984) takes a look at people whose sense of unfulfilment is set off against their image of well-being — socially as well as artistically. These films are centred on individuals. *Tamas* (1987) is, however, made on an epic scale around communal bloodletting and conflagration at a cataclysmic time in recent Indian history; it is a fictionalized recreation of the events leading to the partition of the Indian subcontinent in 1947 — a major work on the subject. In *Drishti* (1990) Nihalani cast, for the first time, the then star of the popular Hindi cinema, Dimple Kapadia, in the role of a career woman in a big city whose married life is convulsed by extra-marital affairs.

Among the young filmmakers who made their presence felt in the Hindi cinema in the early years of the Panorama is Saeed Akhtar Mirza with *Arvind Desai ki Ajeeb Dastan* (1978) and *Albert Pinto ko Gussa Kyon Aata Hai* (1980). With *Mohan Joshi Haazir Ho!* (1984) he showed great skill in exposing the inequities in the social and judicial systems that virtually bludgeon a common man in his struggle for his rights. *Salim Langde Pe Mat Ro* (1989) showed Mirza's ability to use camera work (Virendra Saini has been the cameraman of all his

Naseeruddin Shah and Shabana Azmi in
Albert Pinto ko Gussa Kyon Aata Hai, 1980,
Saeed Akhtar Mirza

films) to evoke the ambience of the penumbral world of crime and marginalization of a section of Indian society — poor Muslims this time — a thematic flashback to the predicament of underprivileged Christians in *Albert Pinto*.... Since then Mirza has been lost to television serials although he is now ready to start shooting a new film.

Ketan Mehta's *Bhavni Bhavai* (1980) marked the emergence of both its then young director and Gujarati cinema in the Panorama. Mehta fuses the various folk performing arts — mime, dance, earthy humour and songs as narrative links — to tell the story of a continuing social evil, untouchability. In its attention to detail it is almost a period film with contemporary relevance. With *Holi* (1984) Mehta switched to Hindi; its camerawork (by Jehangir Chaudhary) captures the mood of the subject: rebellious youth in a moribund system. *Mirch Masala* (1986) charts a new direction: a woman as the central figure symbolizing struggle against male sexual feudalism, while *Maya Memsaab* (1992) is a cinematic transplant of a European literary masterpiece: Gustave Flaubert's *Madame Bovary,* in the context of the emergent middle-class young woman in present-day India with the kind of camerawork that tends to assume a life of its own. *Sardar* (1993), around the gigantic personality of Sardar Patel, is an epic film that uses editing (by Renu Saluja) to weld diverse historical events in the turbulent times before and after India's independence into a coherent saga of Indian nationalism.

Girish Kasaravalli led the entry of the Kannada cinema in the Panorama with his debut *Ghatashraddha* (1977). A cruel story told by the then young filmmaker with compassion, it shows his ability to extract outstanding performances — even from child actor Ajit Kumar, an ability he put to good use in his next important film *Tabarana Kathe* (1986). Tabara (a touching and restrained performance by Charu Hasan, elder brother of Kamal Hasan) waits for his pension — and justice — in a manner that reminds one of Samuel Beckett's *Waiting for Godot*, with the difference that the pension does come but too late for use. *Mane* (1989) is a peek at another aspect of social malaise as a young couple search for a home — not a house — to live in privacy and with dignity.

The Marathi cinema's best representative in the Panorama is probably Jabbar Patel. He appeared at the Madras Filmotsav with *Jait Re Jait* (1977). But it was *Simhasan* (1979), perhaps the first objective look at the world of Indian politicians, that made viewers, both in the popular and festival circuits, take notice of him. *Umbartha* (1981) is almost a feminist film in its focus on a woman seeking an identity through a career; and *Ek Hota Vidushak* (1992) fuses a traditional folk theatre form (*tamasha*) in Maharashtra with the theme of a talented but simple-minded performer used by a boyhood friend turned politician.

Among the generation of filmmakers in Bengal who began their careers after the Panorama came into existence, Goutam Ghose and Buddhadeb Dasgupta have probably achieved the maximum recognition in the international festival circuit. Ghose began with *Ma Bhoomi* (1979), followed by *Dakhal* (1981). But it was with *Paar* (1984) that Ghose — director and cinematographer — achieved international recognition, although it was Naseeruddin Shah who won the Best Actor prize for it at the Venice film festival that year. *Antarjali Yatra* (1987) and *Padma Nadir Majhi* (1992) had their international premieres at Cannes, and the former won the top award at the Tashkent film festival in 1988. Considering the vastness of the locale which is *the* theme, *Padma Nadir Majhi* is a magnificent effort, a continuation of Ghose's preoccupation with the mighty elements of untameable water and inhospitable landscape; in his latest film *Patang* (1993), the locale changes, less successfully, to the railway tracks.

Dasgupta also entered the Panorama circuit with his debut *Dooratwa* (1978) and has been there with most of his films. A former teacher who turned to poetry and filmmaking, he tends to look at his themes in prismatic hues: the alienation of an individual in an environment of materialism and acquisitiveness, for instance, in *Dooratwa, Grihajuddha* (1982), *Andhi Gali* (1984), and *Tahader Katha* (1992). The dilemma of an artist is a facet of the dilemma of an individual, as in *Phera* (1986), probably Dasgupta's cinematic peak till now, and *Bagh Bahadur* (1989). His most recent film is *Charachar* (1993), the story of a bird catcher-and-seller as the metaphor for a creative artist. Looking at his oeuvre one feels that Dasgupta has yet to realize his full potential.

The Film Institute at Pune had attracted hopeful filmmakers from all corners of the country. Until the '60s the cinema of the northeastern part of the country — in Assam, Orissa or Manipur — was virtually unknown. As the Film Institute graduates returned home to try and start work, a new consciousness of cinema arose, leading others into the field as well. With the awards they won, and with nationwide exposure through the Panorama as well as television, a socially and geographically distant part of the country became drawn into the mainstream of Indian life.

Jahnu Barua from Assam, after graduating from the Film Institute, made a beginning in the Panorama with his debut *Aparoopa* (1982) and achieved international recognition with *Halodhia Choraye Baodhan Khai* (1987), an authentic depiction of the Indian rural problem and of human dignity in the face of the most trying social circumstances. It is the literal translation of the original title, "The yellow bird (looking beautiful in a long shot) eating the grain in the fields (in a close-up)", that gives one an insight into Barua's handling of the cinematic medium. Although he has had two more films in the Panorama, *Banani* (1989) and *Firingoti* (1991), they lack the visual intensity of *Halodhia Choraye Baodhan Khai.*

Biju Phukan and Suhasini Mulay in
Aparoopa, 1982, Jahnu Barua

Bhabendra Nath Saikia, also from Assam, entered the scene with his debut *Sandhyarag* (1977), but had to wait quite a few years until his next film was selected for the Panorama. *Agnisnaan* (1985) was followed by *Kolahal* (1988), *Sarothi* (1991) and *Abartan* (1993). A writer who uses his own stories for his films, Saikia has shown a sensibility that seeks to explore the feminine psyche emerging from the shadow of the male to create a place for itself in the sun, as it were. He, too, is a filmmaker who has yet to realize his full potential.

Aribam Syam Sharma came from Manipur to the Calcutta Filmotsav with *Imagi Ningthem* (1981), which attracted attention for its charm, simplicity and freshness of approach in handling the theme of a child yearning for a mother's love. Many years later, *Ishanou* (1990) took the viewer on a journey into the world of the supernatural in the context of a society that associates supernaturalism with divinity, a divinity in a woman that makes her an object of awe. An international award for *Imagi Ningthem* (at Nantes) and inclusion in the 'Certain Regard' section at Cannes for *Ishanou* are impressive achievements by this soft-spoken director.

Ishanou, **1990, Aribam Syam Sharma**

With the importance accorded to the Panorama, filmmakers operating within the parameters of popular cinema have also aspired to respectability through inclusion in it. The most successful among them has been Mani Ratnam with *Mouna Ragam* (1986). It was with *Nayakan* (1987), *Anjali* (1990) and *Roja* (1992) that he showed how the ingredients of Indian popular cinema — melodrama, songs, dances — could, with high production values, enjoy a double life as a box-office hit and a Panorama selection. In fact, *Roja* was a commercial success in Tamilnadu before its Panorama screening at the Delhi IFFI in January 1993; it was then dubbed from Tamil into Hindi and became an all-India hit (no other dubbed Indian film has matched its success).

The short history of the Panorama has thrown up a number of filmmakers who have not always been able to build on their beginnings. There is a long list of such filmmakers, but a few examples should suffice. Utpalendu Chakraborty made a promising entry into the Panorama with *Chokh* (1982), an impassioned exposé of various aspects of social injustice that shows the then young filmmaker's admirable command of the cinematic medium. But *Debshishu* (1985) and *Chhandaneer* (1989) were not of the same class or level. Nirad Mahapatra also made a promising beginning with *Maya Miriga* (1983), a restrained and insightful observation of changing middle-class realities in a town in Orissa, done with sensitivity and compassion. But he has done nothing since then.

Shaji N. Karun was well known as the cameraman of most of Aravindan's films before he shot to international fame with *Piravi* (1988), which had its international premiere at Cannes in May 1989. Shaji had held private screenings of his debut film at the Delhi IFFI in January 1989, and by the time it had its Panorama screening at the Calcutta IFFI the following January it had already been shown in the major international film festivals and won many awards. Described by some as the most outstanding Indian debut film since *Pather Panchali* (1955), *Piravi*, a story of human pathos based on an actual incident, has been noted for cinematic sensitivity, achieving new heights of cinematic aesthetics with its fusion of various elements, especially restrained performances and a creative use of the soundtrack that records seasonal moods to reflect emotional states. The notable quality of Shaji's second film, *Swaham* (1994), which also had its premiere at Cannes, is its use of black-and-white and colour to contrast the stark realities of the present with the memories of a happy past.

A chart can be as cruel as the camera; the former by its nature and the latter by choice present their subjects without make-up. The charts (given at the end of the book) of filmmakers and their films as they appeared in the Panorama from 1978 to 1995 is revealing: it shows how new names appeared each year; only a few reappeared in the following years while others dropped by the wayside. The chart also reveals how the cinema scene is heavily dominated by male filmmakers. Thus, although some women filmmakers have appeared in the Panorama from time to time hardly anyone has really made an outstanding contribution to the cinematic idiom. Among them Aparna Sen stands out with her *36 Chowringhee Lane* (1981): a sensitive debut that recreates cinematically the motif of anachronism, as it were, in a multifaceted manner — Anglo-Indians in independent India, old age and loneliness, English literature or language. Prema Karanth has so far made just one film — *Phaniyamma* (1982) — but established an international reputation with it. Sai Paranjpye and, more recently, Kalpana Lajmi, are two capable directors whose films show a successful combination of commercial viability and an underlying thread of seriousness.

The Panorama as "a showcase for the latest and 'best' in Indian cinema" (*Indian Cinema '82/'83)*, then, has had its ups and downs. A regular watcher of the Indian film scene cannot but come to the conclusion that, in spite of its continuing prolific output, Indian cinema is at present passing through a lean phase in terms of "cinematic, thematic and aesthetic excellence." The last Indian film to make a strong impression at international festivals was *Piravi.* And that was in 1989.

Notes

1. In this article 'film' is restricted to what is commonly known as a feature film.
2. From here onwards, 'Panorama' will stand for Indian Panorama sections of IFFIs and Filmotsavs put together, unless otherwise specified.
3. Henceforth, only the films shown in the Panorama are discussed, except when there is a reference to a pre-Panorama film.
4. The Panorama films' years are those of production/completion. The films usually appeared in the Panorama at an IFFI/Filmotsav the next year, and sometimes the year after that.

9

Form and Content

— *Chidananda Das Gupta*

THE POSITION OF D.G. Phalke at the fountainhead of Indian cinema has been inscribed in text-books and in the psyche of the film buff for decades. Despite occasional claims pressed on behalf of Hiralal Sen or others as the real "first", Phalke's position has come to be firmly accepted and his iconic frontality and modernisation of imagery in conjunction with Raja Ravi Verma glorified, but his influence on the later course of Indian cinema has hardly been analysed. What did he bequeath in terms of form and content?

Of the one hundred or so films that Phalke made, the overwhelming majority from *Harishchandra* (1913) to *Gangavataran* (1937) were mythologicals[1]. By 1920, when Phalke was making *Jalandhara Vrinda*, *Kansa Vadha*, *Ram Janma*, *Shri Krishna Leela*, Dhiren Ganguly had embarked on *Bilet-Pherat* (England Returned), possibly India's first film on a contemporary social issue. In 1937 Phalke was making his second talkie, *Gangavataran*, still celebrating Hindu myths and reinforcing them in the new medium that equated seeing with believing. In that year, V. Shantaram made *Duniya na Mane*, a trenchant critique of the traditional Hindu treatment of woman as a sex object for buying and selling. In the same year Master Vinayak poked powerful fun at traditionalism, and, like Shantaram, made a spirited defence of the modern woman in *Brahmachari*. New Theatres and Bombay Talkies had both made films committed to social reform arising from the dominant progressive trends of the day — the movement towards independence. To think that Phalke stayed away completely from this social ferment is to realise that his close association with *Kesari* was, like his films, an indicator of his Hindu fundamentalism which, if anything, exceeded that of his mentor and the editor of *Kesari*, Bal

Gangadhar Tilak. Tilak was partially redeemed by his anti-British politics, his historical pursuits and insights into ancient Indian astronomy; his protege was locked into a much narrower focus of vision. Somnath Zutshi notes how Phalke, in being inspired by the film *Life of Christ* to turn it into Swadeshi, never paused to think of some eighteen hundred years of the Christian presence in India and similarly erased the Muslims (presence of about one thousand years) from the 'Indian Scene[2]. For him, as for the fundamentalist today 'Indian' equalled upper caste Hindu.

The form Phalke established in his films was the objective correlative of his fundamentalism. His other mentor, Raja Ravi Verma, used the worst of contemporary standards in art, the British academic, to give a new credibility to the Hindu pantheon and, like him, gave no indication of the slightest interest in the dominant social movements or new trends in the arts of the time. Verma and Phalke combined to produce a plentitude of oleographs depicting the Hindu gods that had little or nothing to do with Indian art traditions or scriptural prescriptions on the making of images of divinity[3]. They launched a travesty of Indian art very akin to what the Hindu fundamentalist today is making of the heights of Hindu religious thought.

No such thing happened to traditions in Indian classical music; no one raises questions about its Indianness in the way they do in painting and sculpture. In virtually all encounters with western music, Indian music has derived nothing; it has only given, and often enriched, western music. Indian painting and sculpture appear mostly derivative to the world; Indian music does not. This is because there has been no break in Indian musical tradition, whereas in Indian art, there has been a complete break with tradition caused mainly by Ravi Verma and his followers, after which modern Indian painting found it impossible to pick up the pieces. Its major streams either lost their way in revivalism as in the orthodox Bengal school or in derivation from the west as in much that goes by the name of modern Indian art. Between these Scylla and Charybdis, a slender channel is navigated by certain individuals and minority cults.

In folk art, the impact of the west and of industrialisation has been reflected and subsumed into traditional forms whether in Madhubani or Orissa paintings on detachable surfaces or a variety of wall painting genres. Even in Bengal's *Baluchar* sarees, a social commentary on western lifestyles proceeded from within the tradition; in the Kalighat *pat* and in Tanjore and "company" paintings, the modifications in traditional forms took place without any surrender of stylistic identity. The Kalighat *pat,* as W.G. Archer points out, adopted the British medium of water colour in place of tempera and shading in order to emphasize volume[4] but these did not constitute a stylistic break with tradition; the new was subsumed into the old without conflict.

In terms of cinema, the Phalke-Verma mode was by no means inevitable. Low reliefs exist in Sanchi or Amaravati or Pallava while in the paintings of Ajanta, there is a marvellous method and ability to handle narrative, to relate human figures to each other in meaningful interaction of facial and gestural expressions, angles and lines of vision (the "lookline matching" of narrative cinema). Ravi Verma's and Phalke's iconic frontality is also not of Indian origin. In the European tradition, the saint or the subject of the portrait looks directly at the beholder. Indian gods face the devotee, ready to receive his prayer, but do not look directly at him. When Prahlad faces Vishnu and Lakshmi in profile in Phalke's *Bhakta Prahlada*, there is an instant sense of eye contact and the whole scene with the divine pair reclining luxuriously before a lowly devotee, is oddly reminiscent of a feudal lord receiving a bonded supplicant. In other words a typical Indian hierarchical social content is put into a western framework. In dealing with the moving image, Phalke struggles with the movement from the frontal to the horizontal position to avoid having the character turn away from the audience.[5]

The Phalke-Verma frontality imparted a stiffness to the limbs of India's moving imagery which it never quite shook off. It held Indian cinema back from exploring the essence of a medium created in response to the need to reflect new perceptions of spatial relationships arising from highly accelerated relative speed of objects encountered in daily experience after the industrial revolution. There was also a quantum jump in both the variety and the shift of viewpoints such as with skyscrapers and the extreme high, low and wide angles that new geometrical scales brought into play. The cinema became a new way of seeing. The big close-up and the extreme long shot dramatically illustrated the uniqueness of the cinematic medium alongside its movement in time. However much one might play with their juxtaposition, the unit of the cinematic shot remained a naturalistic image of the object in front of the camera. Naturalism was also inherent in the movement of an object within the area reproduced by a static camera or by the shifting viewpoint of a panning, tilting or lateral tracking shot to which Indian reliefs and murals bear such a unique resemblance. Phalke-Verma iconics destroyed this rich, flowing spatial relationship between human figures, faces and objects, and carried away by the "modernity" of the British academic portrait, reduced this traditional richness to a narrow, static, literalism of form as well as content. By rejecting the classical scriptural models[6] for the depiction of the gods, they took away the noble, supra human radiations from the images of the Hindu pantheon, and reduced them to ordinary humans in fancy dress. This is what we see in Ramanand Sagar's TV Rama or B.R. Chopra's TV Krishna. Even today, the Durga image worshipped in Bengal, for instance, has a quality that is both human and divine by virtue of the concept and the fashioning of the image itself; in the Verma oleograph or the Phalke screen, she is saturated with a dreary ordinariness.

The non-mythological cinema inherited many of these characteristics. Iconic frontality was reinforced by the influence of the Parsi theatre and the elementary treatment of the proscenium stage made fashionable by western examples displayed by the English rulers and internalised by the west-influenced educated Indian. Allied to this was the alignment of figures along a horizontal axis across the stage with entry and exit on left and right, instead of the asymmetrical balance of grouping so noticeable in traditional reliefs and murals. The mark of early theatre is also visible in the lighting tradition in popular cinema which demands a uniformly bright light on everything, making every part of the stage totally visible and inhibiting the cinematic use of movement through light and shade which emphasizes the three dimensionality and dynamics of moving objects. Stage-like also is the convention which still demands the absence of foreground obstruction to the total horizontal view; the side of the oblong stage-box open to the audience must remain open and clear. Characters must not disappear behind obstructions and reappear in view. In action scenes this convention has yielded a lot of ground but in dialogue sequences it is observed fairly strictly to this day. Action and dialogue are generally kept separate for that reason. The link with Ravi Verma lived through all this, for he himself "draped the figures in the costumes of the stage, posed them in stances and attitudes that too recalled the theatre".[7]

An additional element — the most important, successful, original and yet traditional aspect of popular Indian cinema — was added by the *lavani* tradition in *Sangeetbari Tamasha*, the vigorous folk theatre of Maharashtra. The song represents the philosophical, transcendental core of the popular cinema, especially in Hindi-Urdu in which the lyrics have often been written by famous literary men and set to music by highly talented composers. A unique aspect of the rendition of songs is derived directly from *Tamasha* — high pitch of the female singer typified by Lata Mangeshkar. There are occasional exceptions to this which only prove the rule. Thus the aesthetics of the Hindi popular film came from a mix of indigenous and foreign models, the visual dimensions of which are derived from the Phalke-Verma approach itself, formed by a somewhat uneducated and ill-informed apprehension of the west. Ravi Verma did not know what impressionism was any more than Phalke knew what Eisenstein was doing. Admittedly, it was not easy to be informed at the time they began their work. But later, when new horizons were explored in Indian painting, Phalke took no more cognizance of it than he had of traditional styles of visual narrative. By contrast, in 1921, two years after the *Bauhaus* movement was founded, the Tagores had an exhibition on it in Calcutta.[8]

The New Cinema

India's new cinema since Independence represents in many ways a protest against the dead form and content bequeathed to it by the Phalke-Verma domination of the mainstream cinema which continues to this day. Instead of making a mock-Indian imitation of the worst of available models in cinema, it honestly acknowledged the source of the cinema in the industrial revolution and the new world of perception brought about by it. It borrowed the narrative mode developed by the poineers of western cinema much as the novel in Indian literature(s) did from European fiction from the 18th century onwards. As is well known, in most Indian literatures the major medium was verse; prose either did not exist or was acutely undernourished until Christian missionary translations of the Bible provided a fresh impetus, first by the use of prose itself and thereafter its dissemination through printing. Once these first awkward steps had been taken, the novel followed in no time, and over a period of some two hundred and fifty years, grew into a mammoth production including a significant measure of fiction of enduring quality.

Despite this derivation of a fairly naturalistic form in a branch of literature that had hardly existed within our tradition, Indian literatures were able to absorb it into their examination of society and the projection of its needs and aspirations. Its content was intensely Indian and reflected the urges for social reform and projections of overlapping images of India of the future. After independence, the novel did not lose its momentum; today it retains its influence and much of its role in social engineering.

The new cinema carved out its path in a similar manner. The first impetus which Satyajit Ray gave it was a kind of transfusion of Indian renaissance energies stored up in Bengali literature. At the beginning of the Ray period, Bengali cinema was bound up in obsolete conventions and had used the cinema for literary theatrical story-telling without a discovery of the essence of the cinematic medium. Partly, this was due to lack of acquaintance with models outside of Hollywood. British cinema had hardly any tradition worth relying upon until World War II when the British documentary realism gave it a sort of magic touch. Partly, the lack of innovation in Bengali cinema of the time was also due to the absence of a vital link with the renaissance strand. Its lack of formal development had made it too inadequate as an instrument for energising social change. It lagged far behind Bengali literature in innovations in either form or content. Ray's cinema emerged as a kind of culmination of the renaissance in Bengali literature, often surpassing it in its subtle orchestration of elements from the other arts. The initiative seized by Ray had an immediate impact on other filmmakers whose talents had been unable to find adequate expression. Foremost among these and the most brilliant was Ritwik Ghatak whose conformity to Bengali cinema tradition in *Nagarik* (1952) bore no relation to its freedom of expression in *Ajantrik* (1958), three years after *Pather Panchali* (1955) broke through all conventions of Bengali and indeed Indian cinema. Ray's trilogy not only transferred the values of Bibhuti Bhushan Banerjee's epic work to the cinema but declared its own formal self-sufficiency with a more complete reach of expressiveness. Ray had, as he once said, learnt from Hollywood narrative both what to do and what not to do. The slow rhythm and the contemplative humanist realism of his early work, in particular, drew upon the resources of Indian tradition and defied western categories and conventions. For instance, his humanism bore no relation to the anthrocentrism of the European variety: it reached back into the Buddhist concepts of *karuna* and *ahimsa* on the one hand and, on the other, an Upanishadic awareness of the vastness of time and space and the insignificance of man, the evanescence of his life and its doings. This enabled him constantly to see "the mythic in the ordinary" and radiate suggestions well beyond the limits of the film frame.

Another force that entered into the arena to generate a wider range of new cinema was the government. By setting up an infra-structure designed to enable imaginative new cinema to appear, it paved the way for the emergence of a body of pro-governmental, pro-constitutional, pro-social-reform cinema. This new cinema, stretching from Manipur to Kerala on a mainly north-east to south-west axis, was critical of government not for its professed aims but for its non-performance. Unlike the commercial cinema, it has never gone against the values expressed in the Constitution. The bulk of commercial cinema encourages people to take the law in their own hands, to perpetuate superstitions and to replace one set of repressions by another, promoting violence almost as a drug habit. The denigration of the position of woman has also been a major part of its agenda — sometimes even in films purporting to defend her.

By and large, the new cinema bears the stamp of the Ray model. Its financial approach has been disciplined and in tune with the economic conditions of the country. The director's authorship of the film and his control over all aspects of its making have been fully accepted. In terms of rhythm, the frenetic tempo of both western films and the Indian commercial cinema has been eschewed in favour of a more traditional pace suited to the rhythm of Indian life. The new cinema moves more slowly; it is more of a cinema that makes the audience think. The bulk of this cinema is in the realistic narrative form. Its approach to film technique issues out of its commitment to art and to society. Its approach to action, make-up, lighting and direction, mise-en-scéne, editing and music bear a basic resemblance to the Ray model and to the realities of the Indian situation. It has so far failed to forge a popular all-India medium; but this is in great measure due to the nature of its commitments and to the system of ownership of the instruments of dissemination of popular cinema.

An all-India cinema perforce relies on the abandonment of regional characteristics and their role in the development of the integrity of a film. It also pressurizes the producers of the all-India film to define their central focus on the Hindi-Hindu-North Indian model since it reflects the largest audience segment. What it does in that process is to marginalise all other linguistic religious-regional combinations. Thus Manipur, for instance, needs a cinema of its own to reflect its regional character and aspirations and the assertion of its pre-Hindu identity, which today is a significant element in its self-image. Thus the projection of regional realities becomes the driving force in generating a new, serious "art" cinema. The commercial or "money-first" regional cinema tends to imitate the all-India model (this is partly true even in the South), making the new cinema the sole representative of the trends, characteristics and aspirations of the region. This regional truth tends to universalize the best films of these areas and makes itself accessible to national and international observers. The language barrier, apart from other things, denies these subtitled films a wide audience outside their natural areas. Even Satyajit Ray is more heard about than seen on the all-India level. Yet by capturing the attention of the national and international intelligentsia, his films have acted as messengers not only of Bengal but of India generally. International attention made it impossible to marginalise him somewhat in the way that makes it impossible for the Myanmar government to kill Aung San Suu Kyi. The reality of this equation must be seen in the content of the outlook of the average bureaucrat or politician's standard of personal judgement: "If I can't understand it, how can it be good?"

This problem is intimately linked to the fact that Ray's films and many of the others who came in his wake are of an equal standard to the highest reaches of literature in various Indian languages irrespective of their accessibility; the "money-first" film corresponds to pulp fiction. The need for reflecting these higher levels of thought in the cinema is sometimes denied even by wide sections of the educated middle class in power which in its ignorance clings to the traditional view of cinema as ephemeral entertainment close to a form of sin that one has come to tolerate indulgently. Only the mythological, with its load of religious convention, escaped this sense of guilt, which is why it retained its popularity for a long time and became a conduit for the induction of new audiences into the cinema. The decline of the mythological was very marked in the post-Independence period until it reappeared with redoubled vigour before the TV audience in the shape of the money-spinning, Phalke-Verma inspired *Ramayana* and *Mahabharata* serials.

One must also remark on the fact that the mythological element has run as an undercurrent in the commercial cinema ever since. Mythologicals mythologised the past; their spin-off into the rest of Indian commercial cinema appeared as an instrument of mythologising the present, much as the popular American cinema today mythologises the future. The mytholigising of past and present perpetuates the pre-industrial inability to distinguish fact from myth and makes it difficult to treat them as two distinct planes interacting with each other in social and individual decision-making. It reinforces the traditional Hindu indifference to historicity to which oral transmission contributed so significantly and to this day helps to retain the puranic-epic right to rewrite history according to present convenience, making it impossible to sift fact from a confusing network of often contradictory myths. The sanctity of myth overwhelms the sanctity of fact.

Social Codes

The episodes in Shyam Benegal's serial *Discovery of India* taken from the epics treat myths in a totally different manner, sharing an awareness of the thought articulated by Roland Barthes, that "in myth, things lose the memory that they were once made". His treatment of episodes from the *Ramayana* and the *Mahabharata* attempt (not with uniform success) to project them in historical terms, showing real human beings as they were likely to have been at a certain range of time. Thus kings here are not superhuman beings possessed of enormous wealth and power and magnificence, but tribal chiefs trying to come to terms with events and conditions on a scale appropriate to that stage of economic and technological development. Ritwik Ghatak used myths in a film like *Meghe Dhaka Tara* to underline the inner strength of woman in the midst of her suffering. Ketan Mehta's *Bhavni Bhavai* used a folk form to highlight, with mordant irony, the extreme inhumanity of the traditional Hindu attitude towards the untouchable. Govind Nihalani's *Aakrosh* drew pointed attention to the traditional exploitation of the tribal by the caste Hindu. Buddhadeb Das Gupta's *Grihayuddha* portrayed the sense of guilt suffered by the revolutionary who betrayed the socialist cause to seek wealth for himself. Saeed Mirza examined a car mechanic's illusions of personal equality with the bourgeoisie in *Albert Pinto Ko Gussa Kyon Ata Hai* to confirm the Marxist view of class struggle in the Brechtian mode of distanciation, also used by Ketan Mehta and other directors. Pattabhi Rama Reddy, Girish Kasaravalli and other directors in Karnataka stressed the suffering and injustice caused by a Hinduism clinging to superstitious and exploitative traditions. Mrinal Sen constantly explored the mores of the middle class and confirmed and reconfirmed his Marxist conviction. Ray himself, perhaps goaded by the criticism he faced, attacked the exploitative caste-class hierarchy of Hinduism in *Sadgati* and the dilemma of the educated, both employed and unemployed, in a series of four urban contemporary films — *Aranyer din Ratri, Pratidwandi Seemabaddha* and *Jana Aranya.*

But the new cinema's preoccupation with social justice soon became, in the hands of lesser artists than Ray, as formula-ridden as the commercial cinema they professed to counter. Adoor Gopalakrishnan

36 Chowringhee Lane, 1981, Aparna Sen
with Debashree Roy

powerfully questioned this in *Mukhamukham*, much to the wrath of the conventional leftist. G. Aravindan stayed completely outside it and made films that bespoke a very gentle respect for the individual, seeing man almost as a part of nature. His *Pokkuveyil* portrayed an insane youth with a fine delicacy of touch and a depth of insight. In the eighties, well before the collapse of the Soviet Union, the turn-away from "the system" towards the individual became marked also in Aparna Sen's *36 Chowringhee Lane* and in Buddhadeb Das Gupta's work from *Phera* onwards. Soon after *Ankur,* Shyam Benegal had already veered away from the Marxist formula. When the Soviet Union, the living symbol of the worth of Communism, simply vanished into the thin air, it only became the culmination of a trend already set away from it. Ray, who had always stood above these formulae, reemphasized the value of individual ethics in *Ghare Baire* and later in *Shakha-Proshakha*, and sought answers to larger questions of the future of society in his last film, *Agantuk.*

The formal aspect of this change was to disengage from the remnants of neorealism and to come out of the long shadow of socialist realism, in particular, of the Indian People's Theatre Association's attitudes and techniques so obvious in some of Mirnal Sen's middle period films. Sen later turned to a series of examinations of middle class social mores seen in a more individualised form, and worked himself free of the shackles of Marxism. The most important achievement of this period of his work was *Khandar*, a delicate and poetic evocation of the gulf of silence that divides the urban middle class from the rural. Formal experimentation had often been a passion with Sen but in his Marxist period it had often been a decorative element at variance with the conformism of his political credo. His later films achieved greater integration directly as a result of his freedom from both formal and ideological obsessions. The form became less and less of a strident appendage and matured in the way it turned itself into the content.

Mani Kaul and Kumar Shahani have made a clearing for themselves in the welter of theory and practice of filmmaking in India. With their markedly non-narrative 'non-pornographic' approach, they reject causality and naturalism as well as the need to communicate with a wide audience. Kaul has given proof of his visual imagination in a series of films from *Uski Roti* (1970) to *The Idiot* (1992) as well as his 'documentaries' like *Dhrupad* or *Before My Eyes* which are not

Uski Roti, 1970, Mani Kaul

essentially different from his feature films. Kumar Shahani followed in his wake but not without individuality. This school of filmmakers and critics is limited in size but articulate and compelling in its dissent, although defined perhaps more by what it is not than by what it is. Its theoretical contribution to the alignment of form and content in future developments in India's art cinema cannot be gainsaid.

By the nineties, the government appeared to have given up its commitment to serious cinema. It politicised and bureaucratised the infrastructure once built as a support system for a more creative cinema and used its growth centres to exploit the political advantages of alliance with the commercial cinema. It tended more and more to equate film as industry with film as art and began to marginalise the higher creative use of cinema. Sadly, this shrinkage of the new cinema's space coincided with its ideological and technical freedom and maturity, and inhibited its growth. Ketan Mehtas *Maya Memsahib* is totally free from the

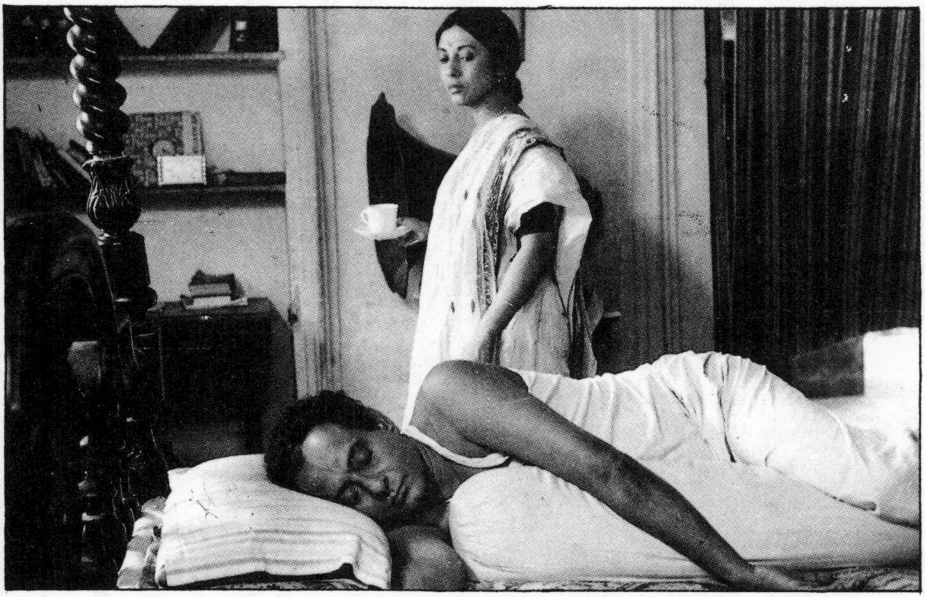

Phera, 1986 by Buddhadeb Das Gupta

shadows of neo-realism, of socialist realism and the IPTA; it is made with a real sense of power over the medium and almost seems to celebrate its freedom from ideology. But the number of films is shrinking with funds drying up and exhibition outlets even more limited than before. Already, budget constraints are imposing a minimalism on most of the filmmakers, forcing them into one-set, one-location films with very few characters. It will become more and more difficult for them to repeat the relative expensiveness of *Maya Memsaab* or the elegance of Shyam Benegal's *Trikal*. Thinness of texture has already begun to hit the international acceptability of the Indian art film. Its presence at international film festivals has visibly dropped.

On the other hand, the commercial cinema's resource mobilisation for individual films keeps climbing in terms no longer of lakhs but of crores of rupees. This divergence of resource base only pushes the two cinemas further apart and makes the coming together of art and commerce more difficult than ever before. The higher the investment, the more conformist the commercial cinema tends to become in order to recover its investment; the lower its investment sinks, the less the art cinema is able to innovate because the point is being reached where innovation no longer makes its possible to overcome budget constraints. Thus the gains made in the highest reaches of innovative cinema in India in terms of both form and content — one issuing out of the other — are in grave danger of being lost.

Notes

1. *70 Years of Indian Cinema*, Ed. by T.M. Ramachandran, Filmography at the end of *Dadasaheb Phalke*: *Father of Indian Cinema* by B.V. Dharap, pub. by Cinema-India International, Bombay, 1985.
2. Somnath Zutshi, *Woman, Nation and the Outsider in Contemporary Hindi Cinema*, eassy in *Interrogating Modernity*, Seagull Books, Calcutta, 1993.
3. Vishnudharmottara Purana.
4. Archer, W.G., quoted by Ashis Rajadhyaksha in *Interrogating Modernity*, *op. cit.*
5. Das Gupta, Chidananda, *The Painted Face* : *Studies in India's Popular Cinema*, Roli Books, New Delhi, 1991.
6. *Op. cit.*
7. Krishna Chaitanya, *Ravi Verma*, Lalit Kala Akademi, New Delhi, 1960.
8. Parimoo, Ratan, *The Three Tagores*, Baroda.

10

The Technicians

— Amrit Gangar

THE TIME IS OF 1942. And of a love story. It might seem *Romeo & Juilet,* but it sounds Dolby. Vidhu Vinod Chopra's much-awaited production *1942 — A Love Story* is released in Bombay's Metro theatre. And now the city has an accoustically equipped theatre which can screen a film recorded on state-of-the-art Dolby sound system. Greeting the good news, the film weekly *Screen* said editorially, "...one of the few efficiently-run theatres in the metropolis is going to treat its patrons to the wonderful aural pleasures of the Dolby with *1942 — A Love Story* as the opening attraction. Assuming that it provides the incentive for other cinemas in the city to convert to Dolby, the onus is now on the Hindi film industry to visualise its future products accordingly." These products are considered to "break the monotony of plain viewing".

The breaking of the monotony of plain viewing is generally part of technical innovation and not of aesthetic delineation. In the realm of the arts, especially of the cinema, the term technic/technique would signify certain underlying polarities in filmmaking practices. "Technic" is essentially a part of the commercial filmmaking strategy. In order to achieve certain "effects", the commercial film producer/director needs technics. The effects may be achieved through camera, editing, sound or sets generally determined by the market-view. But a filmmaker, who does not have any desire for "effects", would not need "technic" and therefore no technic-ian in a strict sense. While taking note of the polemics of filmmaking and the world-views that underlie it, I would use the term technician as a person who is skilled in the technique of an art, especially a mechanical or industrial art. His skill is at the disposal of a producer or director. The expanded fraternity of new technicians today includes software/computer graphic designers. And virtual realists, too.

The cinema requires a number of production/post-production optimalities. From shoot to screen, there is always one thing that is present between the director and the end-product — the apparatus. It is the 'apparatus' that actually distinguishes the cinema from other arts and crafts. It is the 'apparatus' that makes the cinema a collective art or enterprise. The technician can command the apparatus to realise the director's vision.

The Indian filmmaker and the technician have always worked in the sub-optimal circumstance. He has never had the wherewithal available to his western counterpart; through his urge and will he has always found ways to overcome the technical limitations.

Leading filmmaker Shyam Benegal has all praise for our technicians. He rates our cameramen among the best in the world, our editors highly competent, our sound recordists improving. What is, however, dismal is the condition of our processing labs which need to be qualitatively compatible with other departments of filmmaking.

Four decades ago, one of our popular filmmakers, Mehboob Khan (*Mother India*), had echoed Benegal's sentiments. He said, "Whatever the limited technical facilities and resources we have with us, we have expert technical crews who can deliver the goods." Mehboob Khan produced India's first technicolor film *Aan* (1952) with the co-operation of technicians in London.

Around 1949, reacting against television, Hollywood was busy inventing new methods to break what *Screen* said in mid-1994, 'the monotony of plain viewing.' Patrons were now treated to novelties such as widescreen, cinemascope, cinemascope 55, cinerama, technirama, vista vision, Todd-AO, panavision and ultra panavision, 3-D films, *et al.* All these involved substantial alterations in theatres. Big budget, long films were now favoured (eg. Cecil B. de Mille's *The Ten Commandments*, William Wyler's *Ben Hur*, Stanley Kubrick's *Spartacus*). Such films were made in order to make the cinema a different viewing experience from that of television. There was another stream too, which leaned towards the creation of highly personal and individual films, very austere and *avant-garde*.

Today, computer and video technologies have changed the audio-visual ecology, sometime creating a techno-phobia among the artists who fear the imminent death of motion pictures. However, the new technician sounds more hopeful.

The changing technical conditions always require the technician to modify and update his skills and perceptions. They do not, however, subjugate the aesthetics of cinematography, the term "cinematography" in the Bressonian sense of creative filmmaking and not as cameraman's work.

Who is the new technician? In a sense, I would find the good old Dadasaheb Phalke brand even today. Look at Phalke, how he elevated the technical craft of Indian cinema eight decades ago. He did all kinds of experiments with his apparatus. He was like a multi-purpose machine himself — producer, director, writer, cameraman, set designer, editor, make-up man, you name it. He was a mega-technician. The renaissance of Indian cinema found yet another remarkable "technician" in Satyajit Ray, who could master almost all aspects of filmmaking himself.

The new technician of old times perhaps had the privilege of a stronger sense of wonder than the new technician of new times, in terms of fundamental research. The former's apparatus had a stronger element of speculation.

The present generation of camerapersons, editors, sound recordists, stage designers, art directors is in a totally new situation because of the presence of television, video and computer technology. The world has already moved from the analog orbit into the digital one. And even for the newest technician it is difficult to prognosticate about further technological moves. The new technician dealing with motion pictures may be happy to learn about Europe's leading lab Eclair (France) investing huge money in a state-of-the-art release print facility. This at a time of diminishing world-wide theatre attendance! "Everyone is amazed but we believe in the future of cinema," said the Lab's Director, Alain Comudet. "But cinema has to differentiate itself from television in order to get people back to theatres. This means quality in the movie theatre, from comfort of the seat on up. And this means the best quality prints."[6]

This is extremely crucial for the survival of the cinema, even in India where the general condition of theatres is more than dismal. The new technician has always worried about the projection and accoustical conditions of our theatres, which can completely mar whatever technical finesse there is in a film. It is said the legendary cameraman Subrota

Mitra (*Pather Panchali*) was so anguished about the wretched projection conditions of our theatres that he decided to give up his work. In an international film festival, red chillies in Ketan Mehta's film *Mirch Masala* looked greenish in a Delhi theatre! The condition of Calcutta's theatres is much worse. Only in the South are there some redeeming features as far as the overall infrastructure is concerned. But this is a city-based situation; what about theatres in smaller places all over India? The new Indian film technician finds himself/herself in changed cinematographic geo-politics today, but he/she has to face the anachronism nevertheless, which is due more to attitudinal reasons on the part of financiers, producers, distributors of films rather than the so-called third-world poverty of means.

In the near 1,000 films being manufactured every year, we could perhaps detect some distinct styles and flashes of technical brilliance here and there. *Screen* said, "A good augury for the Hindi film industry is that it has at least ten brilliant directors at present who are capable of innovation."[7] This also augurs well for the new technician. Most of the technicians today do admit that their role is being increasingly recognised by the producers/directors which was not the case earlier.

In India, the establishment of the Film and Television Institute and the National Film Archive made a vital contribution to expanding aesthetic/technical horizons of the cinema. An FTII-alumnus and the cameraman-director Balu Mahendra recalled, "The technical aspects of films and filmmaking which I know now were learnt mostly at the institute. Learning these things in a systematic and scientific way was important."[8] Younger technicians such as today's leading cameraman Piyush Shah and sound-recordist Joglekar, would also recognise the FTII's contribution to their technical creativity, especially in terms of exposure to cinema and interaction with outside practitioners who would visit the institute as guest lecturers.

In India, it has taken decades for technicians to be taken seriously by producers of films, who now know how they can enhance the quality and market value of their products. But there has always been an implicit tension between technical sophistication and aesthetic depth. Many of our films (as it is anywhere else) have a tendency to overwhelm the audience by their technical gimmickry. Such a mindset is evident in the plethora of mythologicals and stunts that we have produced over the years. Special effects always played a lead role in mainstream filmmaking. Today, every film producer must be dreaming of producing something like *Jurassic Park.*

The journey of the Indian film technician from the earliest days till now has been arduous, though innovatively satisfying at times. Let us see how individual technical journeys have evolved.

Camerawork

The Indian cameraman's heyday was during the silent era, but the moment films began to talk and sing, the sound recordist took over. An early cameraman Bibhuti Laha said, "The man behind the camera was more of a photographer than a cinematographer. His prime duty was to photograph the artiste's delivery of dialogues as clearly as possible. Practically, he used to have no say in the whole matter of the filmmaking process and the sound engineer was the all-important person on the set. Sometimes the poor cameraman had to photograph even wrong and bad compositions completely against his will, just because the sound engineer wanted to place 'the mike' that particular way."[9] A cameraman was appreciated if he could produce the sharpest possible images. He was always baffled by artificial lights. As Laha remarked, for lack of proper knowledge and technique of artificial lighting, our cameramen used to flood their sets and the characters with lights from all possible angles, which resulted in absolutely flat photography. "Modelling, mood and effect were terms they were not at all conversant with."

But nevertheless there was indomitable perseverance and energy to fight against difficulties. Many sensitive technicians revolted against the primitive ways of filmmaking then, which resulted in stage plays becoming at least photoplays. It was V.B. Joshi who first introduced the reflector to control the direction of sunlight. And Gordhanbhai Patel who first took the crane shot long before any Indian studio had a crane. With an Eyemo camera, he sat on a trolley and cranked away. The trolley was pulled by ropes and pulleys up an inclined plank.

A special effects innovator, Patel was the first cameraman to shoot a scene in which horses approached the camera and jumped right over it. For this he used the spring-driven Debrie camera, which could be locked in the running position. The camera inside a strong protective box was placed in a bench and allowed to run by itself as the horses leapt over it. The late Patel was very agile and active when, over a decade ago, I met him in his Dadar Studio in Central Bombay. Among his other innovations, he demonstrated a cinescope lens devised by him. This lens when attached to a projector could enlarge the image four times. And by appropriate cropping of the screen image, it was possible to exhibit normal 35 mm film in cinemascope format. Today state-of-the-art lensing technology has reached great heights but the Indian technician still needs to be as innovative as Patel was then since we still continue to work in sub-optimal conditions.

"We still use chicken coop light, a kind of simplistic light that was used in the '40s and '50s," says Shah commenting on the poor quality lighting fixtures and equipment here. But how about the mindless use of the zoom lens in our films even now? "The zoom lens in our cinema has completely destroyed the fundamentals of mise-en-scène." There is a joke about a filmmaker profusely preferring "dandi ooper, dandi neeche" (turning the lens knob up and down, for zooming in and out). Leading cameraman and an FTII-alumnus K.K. Mahajan (who has a high reputation both in mainstream and parallel cinema) is said to have recommended taking the "dandi" off the zoom lens permanently to stop its misuse. But who dictates zooming? Is it the producer, director or cameraman himself? Shah would blame the high level of ignorance because it's not that the zoom can't be used for specific aesthetics as one would find it in the Latin American films, in their extremely potent, image-building violence.

The lensing aesthetics of the mainstream cinema is greatly deformed. Lighting has to have 80-100 per cent visibility. Rembrandt lighting[10] will hardly ever be found. One day looking at Subrata Mitra shooting Satyajit Ray's first colour film *Kanchenjungha* (1962) in Darjeeling, technicians of a Hindi commercial film, *Professor*, being shot there, laughed at Mitra shooting in low lights. At that time, every one thought that the colour film had to be shot in bright sunlight to obtain proper colour contrasts. Obviously, innovative Mitra was breaking the conventional rule, and he found his director in Satyajit Ray.[11]

Of late the use of lighting is rather interesting in the main stream Tamil films, which have an ambience of the science fiction films in the use of back lighting. It has no fixed source, within the 360 degrees circle. In the films of Mani Ratnam who usually likes to use different cameramen, different artistes and different art directors with every new film, we find an interesting use of travelling matte.

In the non-availability of proper gelatines or light filters, our cameramen today are not able to achieve the proper balance between harsh and soft shades. The colour emulsion in film stock varies between 3200 Kelvins to 5600 Kelvins. By using proper gelatines, it is possible to control colour temperatures.

However, in the evolving technological environment, the new camera-technician is not pessimistic about the future of motion picture. It is very interesting to see the kind of work Bernado Bertolucci's cameraman, Vittorio Storaro, does now. In *Little Buddha*, Storaro has mixed 65 mm and 35 mm formats. The first scene is shot in 35 mm anamorphic format (2.4:1 aspect ratio) while the second scene, set in India some 2,500 years ago, is shot in 65 mm (2.2:1 aspect ratio). According to Storaro, the 65 mm format will take filmmaking to a higher plane in the HDTV era. Surprisingly he has announced that henceforth all his feature projects will be only in 65 mm, as he believes many of the old concerns about shooting in 65 mm format are no longer relevant. Such moves augur well for motion pictures, and should help artists/technicians rid of the techno-phobia.

Video and computer technologies offer immense post-production possibilities. The new technician may find ways of reciprocal exchange between video and motion picture. But essentially video and celluloid are completely different media. Video cannot have a frozen frame like the motion picture. At a given light, lens size, focal length and aperture, you cannot have the depth of field and focus in video the way you can have it in motion picture. But the digital "mystery" is yet to be revealed fully.

Talking about *Tamas*, the controversial televised serial, its cameraman-director Govind Nihalani commented, "television photography is different from cinematography, but not to the extent it is made out to be. Visually, image-wise, one does make the necessary adjustments for the small screen image. Also, because of the technical development in television it was possible to achieve dramatic high contrast and low key cinematography successfully."[12]

In Bollywood, Baba Azmi (*Tezaab, Roop ki Rani, Choron ka Raja, Mr. India*) is a busy young cameraman today. He prefers working with younger and newer directors. "They are not rigid in their thinking. The film cameraman has a specific job — hum sirf dabbe bharne ke liye nahin hain (we are not here just to fill up cans.)"[13] The new technician is also more assertive today about his creative contribution in a film.

A couple of years ago in Calcutta, I happened to meet an old-timer, retired cameraman Devjibhai Padhiar (79) who had done the preliminary outdoor coverage for Jean Renoir's film *The River*, in 1949. Padhiar worked with Renoir's cameraman, Clyde De Vinna, an expert in outdoor shooting. The *American Cinematograph* had published Padhiar's photograph along with De Vinna. Padhiar, who had a short stint at Ambalal Patel's Film Centre in Bombay, remembers some technicians of those days — cameramen such as Gordhanbhai Patel, Dwarkadas Divecha and Faredoon Irani; sound recordist Minoo Desai; lab technician R.B. Mehta, and L.V. Prasad.

In Calcutta he found the technicians more educated and enlightened, some of whom had worked in UFA studios in Germany. Among his contemporary cameramen were Vidyapati Ghosh, Ajay Kar, Bibhuti Laha, Jyotin Das, Nitin Bose, Bimal Roy, etc. In those days of non-availability of fast film, Padhiar did some remarkable low-light shooting. "We never took it as a handicap. In 1937, I had taken a real moon shot on a 50 ASA film. It was absolutely a correct shot in which one could see the sky with all details." Padhiar also remembers the leading cameraman Krishna Gopal, who had set up a two-colour process lab. Krishna Gopal also lamented the state of film processing labs in India, which were like "dhobi ghats where instead of cloth, film was washed, with the same potentiality of the dhobi to ruin the product."

Quoting Kodak's Rajesh Singh, Shah reveals that the bad quality prints are due to the quality of our water! And our labs simply cannot afford to set up water filtration plants for distilled water to obtain the right quality prints. Rhetoric apart, even today most of our people don't have even potable water to consume! Sub-optimal circumstances are part of our political-economy; it's the technician's ingenuity that is challenged all the time.

However, the level of technical awareness among the new generation of cameramen is quite high. They have given a new look to the Indian cinema. One can easily find an array of young camerapersons whose work would demand recognition: Ashok Mehta is remarkable for his lighting, so is Navroze Contractor, Nadim Khan who has trained cameramen such as Deepak Duggal, Kiran Rajhans, Bashir Ali and Ashok Behl — once at the top in the mainstream cinema, where he created unusual trolley movements and "disco" lighting. Manmohan Singh

(*Darr*) and Binode Pradhan (*1942 — A Love Story*) are other names to reckon with. In the south there are wonderful young cameramen including Madhu Ambat, Sunny Joseph and Venugopal. Nambiar — who teaches at the FTII — is yet another sensitive cameraman. Video/ television camerawork is getting more and more fluid and slick (eg. Sunil Sharma's work in the teleserial *Karamchand*), thanks to better cameras and imaginative technical abilities.

Sound Recording

The advent of sound changed the entire style of production and projection of motion pictures. It also led to the growth and adaptation of new equipment, and the creation of the new profession of sound engineering.

In the early days, producers were happy if the dialogue was audible, and as veteran sound recordist Bani Dutt commented, sound engineer was congratulated if only 80 per cent of the dialogues were clear and distinct.[14] India's first talkie, *Alam Ara*, was made on the single system, i.e. the sound track was printed on one edge of the frame. There were no separate sound negative and picture negative for printing the final positive. There was no play-back, no dubbing facilities.

Obviously, the Indian film sound recordist has travelled from working on a studio floor which looked like a "jute or rice godown" to accoustically more sophisticated times. The cameras were noisy and had to be controlled by using cotton blimps or cover. Even today, in the whole of India, I am told, there are only two silent cameras available. There are constraints that independent filmmakers face since for them location recording is very important. Even today, in a city like Bombay, dubbing theatres are not treated and airconditioners keep emitting whirring noises, despite the fact that over last few years post-production technology has made tremendous strides.

On the other hand, the modern digital audio workstation concept is revolutionising the idea of sound recording. Mani Kaul's short film, *The Cloud Door*, using Dolby SR was transferred from negative stage to Beta video format to Avid (digitised computer system, storing pictures and sounds on hard disc) which is a non-linear editing system. You can edit both picture and sound together on it. With Avid, we now have non-destructive editing, where original sound is not destroyed while cutting. *The Cloud Door* was edited on Avid by Lalitha Krishna, at Media Artists studio in Madras, considered to be the best in India. At Prasad Lab (Madras) we have good processing facilities available in the country. The attitude towards sound in films is changing. Sound technicians also hope to get better sound negatives. Sound processing in labs is also getting standardised, which was not the case earlier. More and more labs are becoming conscious about sound quality. As Joglekar says, "Labs are now prepared to carry tests on sound." Theatres, too, are becoming better. In India today (mostly in big cities) there must be at least a dozen theatres with Dolby sound system.

Young sound recordists, however, feel that filmmakers should involve them from the film's planning stage itself. With new technology, the sound recordist/engineer has the role of sound editor or designer.

As a sound designer, Rajat Dholakia, for example, has produced some wonderful sound figuration for films such as *Before My Eyes*, *Siddheshwari* (both directed by Mani Kaul), *Parinda* (Vidhu Vinod Chopra), *Hun Hunshi Hunshilal* (Sanjiv Shah), *Om Dar-B-Dar* (Kamal Swarup), *Mirch Masala* (Ketan Mehta), *Figures of Thought* (Arun Khopkar) etc. Working with Mani Kaul opened the doors of his mind, believes Dholakia. In Kaul's *Siddheshwari*, Dholakia synched the sound, besides recording it on location. In Benaras where *Siddheshwari* was shot, he would hire a boat and sail with his Nagra recorder to record the whole gamut of environmental sounds. "It was a real experience, going beyond music to know how can one create musicality, a symphony of sounds. The great thumri singer Siddheshwari Devi had environmental influences; I tried to evoke them through sounds," says Dholakia. Each film of Dholakia is quite distinct for its sound figuration. But all this seems to be possible only in a non-commercial set-up.

In the commercial film world, the role of the sound recordist begins mainly at the dubbing level. And that is the reason Vijay Bhope, a very busy young FTII-trained sound recordist, got bored there. Bhope, who works from early morning to past midnight every day, enjoys himself doing television serials because here his involvement is total — from beginning to end. "Around the time I came out from the Institute, the technology had already moved from optical to magnetic. Now optical is used only in the final stage of filmmaking. Magnetic technology has more sound range than the mono-optical system. The earlier loop system of recording also changed to rock-n-roll system. In loop system, sound mixing was done in one go. (Legendary Mangesh

Desai used to do that. Satyajit Ray appreciated his work very much). Initially Bhope assisted the senior sound recordist, Hitendra Ghosh[15] on India's earliest classic television serial *Khandan*. He considers Dayal Nihalani's film *Andha Yudhdh* his favourite since it had used sounds in a very natural way. Bhope has worked with Shyam Benegal, Aparna Sen, Pravin Bhatt, Amol Palekar, and a number of TV series producers.

The positive fallout of the technological change will be a greater sensitivity among Indian audiences to sound in films; perhaps we may develop Indian-ness in sound in the way we use sound in Indian films, like our relationship with music. The new technology has made the hierarchy of sounds more complex, more exciting.

So far sound in Indian films has largely been used for reinstating realism. It has not been used to substantiate the visual. Innovative sound designers Joglekar and D. Wood are doing very interesting experiments : processing sound effects, bringing them close to music (not necessarily musicalising it), sampling sound effects, taking real-life sounds and arranging them in a certain way. Like Dholakia, it was while working on Mani Kaul's films that Joglekar found newer ways of using sound. "He changed the concept of the use of sound in films that I had learnt at the FTII, where I was taught about the continuity of tone between scenes," says Joglekar.

Mani Kaul has dynamised the use of sound in Indian cinema. He has tried to explore it at multiple levels of intelligibility. He would play around the middle-spectrum and change tones while laying or re-laying tracks. He would not go in for the conventional tendency to synch effect foleys. He would also change the concept of sound-matching. In Indian cinema, Mani Kaul's films are the most significant for the use of non-linear sound narratives. In his *Nazar*, there are no live sounds in the film, but it has long ambiences of sounds that evoke the idea of simultaneity of melody. This aspect, as Joglekar says, comes to fruition in his last film *Cloud Door*.

Ritwik Ghatak was another filmmaker who used sound in films in the most imaginative, yet simple, manner, which was both dynamic and free. In his essay, "Sound in Film"[16] he gives interesting instances of the use of sound. One instantly remembers the sound of the whiplash in his *Meghe Dhaka Tara*, or the sound of old marriage songs in *Komal Gandhar*. There is also a contrapuntal use of sound in his films. In the bar scene in *Subarnarekha,* for instance, we hear the

Patricia tune "quoted" from the final orgy in Fellini's *La Dolce Vita*. Fellini used it to crack his whip at the hollowness of western civilization. In Ghatak's *Subarnarekha* it is a commentative sound that we hear with reference to a context.

Satyajit Ray's sound/musical patterns are more lyrical. Ray took over the composition of his background music from *Teen Kanya* onwards, after working with Ravi Shankar on the *Apu Trilogy* and *Paras Pathar*, Vilayat Khan on *Jalsaghar*, Ali Akbar Khan on *Devi* and Jyotindra Mitra on *Rabindranath Tagore*. Since then he evolved his own style and method of composition. The use of background music in his films always remained austere, at times very finely blending Indian and western musical traditions. Needless to say, all those exciting sound-tracks in Indian cinema were created through almost primitive machines.

The new technician today has better equipment and facilities for recording, mixing and dubbing. Video is better in sound reproduction as it is on tape (Beta or U-Matic) unlike films whose output format is optical, with its very limited dynamic range. But now with Dolby this shortcoming will be controlled. There is no restriction on sound on video as it can have all kinds of tonal ranges. With computer technology the sound ambience will further expand amazingly. In the Indian cinema today, digital sound quality is much cleaner.

However, the aesthetics of sound in Indian cinema does not have the maturity it should have. The commercial cinema does not accept "silence" as part of sound.[17] A technician said that it is a deliberate decision to fill the films with loud music and sounds because of the wretched theatre conditions, especially in smaller towns and villages. Loudness makes itself at least audible to people. Sound aesthetics thus acquires yet another dimension in our cinema!

In his essay "Notes for an Aesthetic of Cinema Sound," Kumar Shahani says that incidental and atmospheric sounds in the cinema lie between the organised sounds (music) drifting into entropy and contextual sounds (speech), while the rest is silence. However, silence does not exist in an absolute sense. Shahani elaborates on what Bresson said: "On the most obvious level, silence in music relates to space indirectly. In the cinema, on the other hand, it relates to space in movement."[18] For the cinema, sound is the most crucial element.

Among our young technicians today we find extremely good sound recordists/technicians. Some of the names that come to my mind besides Hitendra Ghosh, Vikram Joglekar, D. Wood and Bhope already referred to, include Padamanabha (Paddy, who has his own recording studio in Bombay), Indrajit Niyogi, Bhagatsingh Rathod, Kuldeep Sood, B.V. Chaturvedi, Rakesh Ranjan, Namita Nayak (the only practising woman sound recordist, an FTII-alumnus). Bhope says there was also Lochana Subramaniam, his batchmate at the FTII; she is now settled in Bangalore, perhaps a non-practitioner. The earlier generation also include such names as Ishan Ghosh, R. Kaushik, Dinshaw Billimoria, Manohar Amberkar, etc.

Editing

"Editing is the stage when a film really begins to come to life," wrote Satyajit Ray in 1966, "and one is never more aware of the uniqueness of the film medium than in watching a well-cut scene pulsate with a life of its own."

In the art of cinema, it was David Wark Griffith who first revolutionised the concept of editing. In his very first year, Griffith broke all the rules. Until then, that had been established. Scenes usually began with an entrance and ended with an exit. Directors never used more than one angle in a scene, they stuck to medium shots, following the dictum of Charles Pathe, who said, "Will you gentleman never learn that in the cinema an actor must be photographed so that his feet touch the bottom of the screen and his head the top?"[19]

Griffith made his camera give him a set of images that he could shape into a complex scene or sequences. The best effects he achieved came from the relation of one shot to another. Griffith didn't invent the close-up, but he knew how to use it in a new way. Griffith introduced two truly revolutionary types of editing in a film called *After Many Years*, adapted from Tennyson's *Enoch Arden*. They were more important than the intercutting of parallel action that he was to develop in *The Birth of a Nation*. Griffith and Russian filmmakers such as Pudovkin and Eisenstein, revealed the potential of film editing. Filmmakers the world over follow their editing designs even now. In India the editing patterns have generally revolved around the freak-out (but matching most of the time) cuts in song-and-dance popular films and the linear ones in the so-called realistic films.

In an interview, filmmaker K. Hariharan questioned Aparna Sen about her obsession with match-cuts, which was the most basic principle of realism. The director's answer was: "That's more out of a commitment to rhythm, to a continuity of action. It is a commitment of my actors, to the cameraman, the music director and to myself. The way songs and scenes are picturised, it looks as if jump-cuts are an excuse for incompetence rather than design. It reflects a kind of indiscipline."[20] Sen considers ad films as the essence of this kind of indiscipline, a total destruction of a beautiful art-form.

Editing is not always a post-production exercise. There are many filmmakers who already edit their films in their mind and then in the camera. Sen herself says, "I frame the shot as if it was on the editing table. My poor editor has very little room to improvise. Even my inserts are planned beforehand." It is a matter of an individual director's working style and attitude to his fimmaking.

While talking to the editor Yashwant Chavhan who edited Guru Dutt's films including *Pyaasa*, *Sahib, Bibi aur Ghulam* and *Kagaz ke Phool*, I came to understand the deep interest Dutt used to take in editing. Now 70-plus, Chavhan recalls how Guru Dutt would sit with him at the editing table for long hours and discuss every cut. Emphasising the importance of editing he cites some examples of films and how he saved them from going completely haywire in the post-production stage.

Guru Dutt used to insist on achieving emotional effects of his choice. It was easy to get proper cuts because there was a complicity between the director, cameraman and editor. Chavhan laments the state of editing in today's popular films. "It's all cut to cut," he says and thinks that such a trend was started by Raj Khosla.

This is what Bollywood's top young editors Waman Bhonsle and Gurudutt Shirali (Waman-Guru) say about editing, "Editing is an extremely important department by itself. After all, it was the invention of editing that led to the development of cinema as we see it today.[21] Waman-Guru who have worked with directors such as Subhash Ghai, Raj N. Sippy, Shekhar Kapur, Gulzar, Anil Ganguly, K. Bappaiah, K. Vishwanath, etc. have re-edited big-budget films such as *Yaarana, Mr. India, Agneepath* and *Angar* "because the producers were unhappy with the previous quality of editing."

For Waman-Guru the technical job of editing is also an art form. Unlike Guru Dutt sitting with his editor Chavhan, today's editors, especially in the mainstream cinema, don't allow the directors to meddle until they are through with their first edited version. Many a time, some editors' styles are known to the directors and they don't even bother to see the cut version.

The mainstream editor, Afaque Hussain, who has also edited films of Pankuj Parashar and Prakash Jha, has developed his own distinct style of editing. His "repeat cuts" (used in *Jalwa*) is not a conventional mainstream cinema style, he says. *Jalwa* was one of the finest edited film in the mainstream cinema, according to Hussain. In Parashar's film *Ab Ayega Maza* and *Aatish*, his cutting style was absolutely 'freaked-out', in fact he had mastered the wild cut style of editing with its own patterning. He also uses flash cuts, as he did in the "Becho, Becho" 30-second, 21 cut song in *Aatish*. Hussain taught editing for a brief while at the FTII.

Having his own editing set-up in Bombay with Steenbeck ST-701C, Hussain still feels the good old editing Moviola machine (which is a terror to many) was better in a way as it had its own precision. When you stop the Steenbeck while editing, you miss 2 or 3 frames. The Moviola could be stopped precisely at the frame you wanted. As today's technician, he feels the producers of films have to change their attitude to the work of editors. Hussain would not allow the director to enter his room until he was ready with his edited version. He is apprehensive about video technology, about the depth it can achieve vis-a-vis motion picture. Renu Saluja (*1942 — A Love Story* and Ketan Mehta's later films) is the most busiest editor today in Bombay.

Lalitha Krishna, who has edited most of Mani Kaul's films, edited *The Cloud Door* on the Avid editing digital machine at Media Artists. She is so fascinated by the facility the Avid offers in editing, with which one can not only avoid a rush print, but have as many as five versions of a film at a time. "It suits filmmakers like Mani Kaul, for whom editing is a continuing process at any time — even after the final cut of the film," says Lalitha. What is existing is that Avid has been made especially for motion picture. You can develop dissolves from 15 frames to 18 frames to 21 frames without depending on intuition or speculation.

Stage Designing/Art Direction

It is generally believed that the art director's job is only to make a setting for a film-shooting for purposes of describing the locale of a particular scene. But this is not all about it, as the art director has to tackle other more important aspects of the job in its emotional and aesthetic context. The Indian technicians dealing with stage designing have developed their individual styles and approaches.

Veteran art director Souren Sen specified three matrices of art direction in films, viz. physical matrix (dealing with the physical aspect of the setting), emotional matrix (the quality of a particular setting, which contributes to the emotional context of the scene to be enacted), and aesthetic matrix (particular property of the setting which harmonises with the efforts of the other departments that stand up to create a feature film, to a complete whole).[22] It is the last matrix that is "only the product of careful attention and extreme self-control, the craftman in him creates and the critic in him controls him to shape the humble technician —the art director."

In the realm of stage designing one of the top new names is Nitin Desai (his latest are *1942 — A Love Story* and Walt Disney Production's *Jungle Book*). 1965-born Desai is a commercial art diploma holder from Bombay's JJ School of Arts. He started as assistant to the veteran Nitish Roy. Now independent, he has worked with directors such as Kumar Shahani, Gulzar, Ketan Mehta, Shyam Benegal, Govind Nihalani, Raj Kumar Santoshi, etc. and cameramen V.K. Murthy, K.K. Mahajan, Ashok Mehta, Jehangir Chowdhary, W.B. Rao, Binode Pradhan.

Working mainly in the realistic mode, Desai's forte is his meticulous pre-planning. He has his own set-up at Bombay's film city. He uses all kinds of materials for the sets from plaster of Paris to modern plastics. For Ketan Mehta's film *Oh Darling Yeh Hai India*, Desai has incorporated a futuristic ambience (as imagined by the director) in his sets. He does substantial research before he ventures into designing the sets. But he still envies the time of Bansi Chandragupta and laments the working environments today — "everyone is in a hurry". In the teleserial *Chanakya*, for example, he has one single set of a town with 26 structures, four main lanes and six bylanes. He always imagined the possible movements of the trolley while designing the sets. As a set designer he familiarises himself with the language of an architect, a builder and a master carpenter. Most of the set designers/art directors believe that the sets should be as realistic and as flexible as possible.

Earlier the senior art director, Sudhendu Roy, developed a technique (after his visit to Hollywood few years earlier) of panels made of cloth and wooden frames, which he would paste with brown paper and coat with colours. This was very lightweight, cheap and easy to operate. At present in the Bollywood of South India there are several young set designers/art directors capable of building sets of any size and type. As a set designer, Desai claims he can produce better effects than actual locations. But today, we have films with either high or low budget. In the high-budget projects, stars get the major chunk and in the process film producers cut down on other aspects of filmmaking. Locations are preferred to sets.

The realistic craft or technique of set designing was mastered by Satyajit Ray and Bansi Chandragupta. Chandragupta believed that the sets existed only in relation to the script. He said, "It is not a replica of what already exists, otherwise there would be no need for designers. A film set is built for the camera and for the camera-angles only. Anything that is not effective through the lens is a waste of good money and effort, however pleasing it might look to the naked eye... Ray has a keen camera eye and each carefully picked details helps to build the atmosphere."[23]

Chandragupta changed the conventional idea of set designing in films as it had existed before in the time of early mythologicals and the *Mughal-e-Azam*, not to talk about the sets of Gemini's *Chandralekha* and other films.

The new set-designer technician though follows the photographic-reproduction approach; he has to find alternative ways reducing wastage, material cost and as much flexibility. He has to keep the requirement of the cameraman in mind and the ultimate look of the film. Desai and other young stage designers/art directors (some of whom include Samir Chanda, R. Varman, Saboo Syril, Madhukar Shinde, L.S. Sawant, Suresh Sawant, etc.) are equally cautious about the condition of our theatres where projectors can radically damage the "look" of the film they had imagined! Earlier in black and white as well as colour films there were Rusi Banker, Kanu Desai, M.R. Achrekar, Sant Singh, Ajit Banerjee, etc.

The New Audio-Visual Ecology

With all technical anachronism around, what is evolving is the new audio-visual ecology. The marriage of motion picture, video and computer technologies should facilitate certain modes of filmmaking finally. As with Avid, the whole elaborate labour of handling celluloid can be avoided while editing. Digital technology has still many more mysteries in its bag.

Computer technology is an increasingly crucial ingredient in visual art today and virtual reality, which is still evolving. The latter gives the technician/artist creative possibilities that haven't been available through other digital media such as video or computer graphics. Its immersive nature differentiates it from looking at a monitor screen: viewers are totally surrounded by the computer-generated environments. In nutshell, dimensions of both audio and visual are expanding immensely, which should make the cinema richer.

And we still have Storaro and 65 mm film! We still have hopeful young technicians, if you like to call so.

(Names of technicians given here do not necessarily make an exhaustive list, any omission is not intended — AG)

Notes:

1. Dolby SR is a noise reduction-cum-sound compression and expansion device. Two encoded audio tracks are decoded as left-centre-right-surround. In other words, it has a multi-dimensional sound ambience.
2. *Screen,* July 15, 1994.
3. *Indian Talkie, 1931-56*, Silver Jubilee Souvenir, Film Federation of India, 1956.
4. The size of the image on the screen was enlarged and stereophonic sound was introduced, the features which television would lack. In Todd-AO (combination of the name of the inventor, Michael Todd and the initials of the American Optical Corp.), the negative film is 70 mm wide.
5. In his Notes on Cinematography, one of the world's great living filmmakers in France, Robert Bresson, says, "Two types of films, those that employ the resources of theatre (actors, directors, etc.) and use the camera in order to produce; those that employ the resources of cinematography and use the camera to create. For Bresson, cinematography has the special meaning of creative filmmaking, which thoroughly exploits the nature of film as such.
6. *American Cinematographer,* March 1993.
7. *Screen,* July 15, 1994.
8. *Deep Focus,* Vol. III, No.3, 1990.
9. *Indian Talkie* 1931-56, Silver Jubilee Souvenir, Film Federation of India.
10. Producer Goldwyn wrote to Cecil De Mille about the shadowed lighting the

latter had used in a film directed by him that he would have trouble selling a picture in which "you couldn't even see the characters' faces half the time." Dismissing Goldwyn's reaction Cecil asked the messenger, "Tell him it's Rembdrandt lighting."

11. Author's interview with Soumendu Roy, then Mitra's assistant.
12. *Cinema in India,* October-November, 1992.
13. *Cinema in India*, February, 1993.
14. *Indian Talkie* 1931-56. Silver Jubilee Souvenir.
15. Ghosh now works at the re-recording studio of Rajkamal in Bombay, in place of the late Mangesh Desai. Though Ghosh belongs to the realist school, he appreciates the work of filmmakers such as Ritwik Ghatak.
16. *Cinema and I*, Ritwik Ghatak Ritwik Memorial Trust, 1987.
17. Bresson said, "The sound-track invented silence".
18. Framework No. 30/31.
19. *Behind the Screen : The History and Techniques of the Motion Picture,* Kenneth MacGowan, Delacorte Press, New York, 1965.
20. *Cinema in India*, December 1991.
21. *Indian Talkie 1931-56,* Silver Jubilee Souvenir. Sen's thoughts in response to Mr. Acharekar's paper on art direction, presented at a film seminar in 1955, New Delhi.
22. *Cinema in India,* June 1992, *Satyajit Ray : The Inner Eye,* Andrew Robinson, Rupa & Co. Also refer to an interesting interview with Bansi Chandragupta, *Inside-Outside* Magazine, March-April, 1978.

11

Ideologies of Underdevelopment

— *Aruna Vasudev*

FOR SOME YEARS the opposition between the mainstream cinema and a new movement variously labelled parallel, alternate, serious or art çinema was intense, angry, deeply partisan. The polarisation was absolute: either commerce or art. Since the fifties there had been few directors able to arrive at a form of entertainment where there was any evidence of understanding of the cinema as a form of artistic expression. Technically proficient under extremely difficult working conditions, with inadequate equipment and ill-equipped studios, with fierce competition for stars, for screening time in the limited number of theatres, heavy taxation and the difficulty of finding legitimate funding, the mainstream directors arrived at a formula which, it seemed, satisfied the audience for which it was meant, and continued to produce a blend of song and dance, melodrama and farce and later, sex and violence. The style of acting showed little variation; stereotypes in familiar situations carried the day.

When Satyajit Ray said he did not think that 'popularity is incompatible with seriousness or with art,' it was not a surprising statement in itself. It applies to the best of Hollywood; to Renoir, Chabrol, Truffaut; to Chaplin, Ford or Hitchcock, and many others. It even applied to the situation in Bengal at the time Ray made it, but it did not apply to the entirety of Indian cinema. Within an Indian context, Shantaram or Raj Kapoor, Mehboob or Bimal Roy achieved some distinction without adding anything new to the language of cinema. To an extent, Guru Dutt arrived at a more personal idiom within the commercial framework. It was only Ritwik Ghatak and Satyajit Ray in Bengal in the late '50s and '60s who broke the pattern and, in very different ways, showed the possibilities of other kinds of cinema.

When the new movement arose at the start of the '70s, the rupture with the mainstream cinema was total.

In the mid-'80s the bitter polarisation between art and commerce was aggravated into a further, clear-cut division; a three-way split between entertainment, seriousness which was equated with social realism, and art which was regarded as a form of self-indulgence and, therefore, irrelevant.

In all this, the role of the government has been a key factor. Initially, in the '60s, by creating a Film School (the Film and Television Institute of India) patterned on France's famous IDHEC (Institut des Hautes Etudes Cinematographiques), a National Film Archive with its huge collection of the great classics and contemporary films from all over the world and last, perhaps most importantly, the Film Finance Corporation to provide institutional funding for 'non-commercial' films, it actively promoted the emergence of a new cinema in the early '70s, in direct opposition to the mainstream. It was the government that recognised the work that was then produced through national awards and international promotion; it established the Indian Panorama as a significant part of India's annual international film festival and later, through the revamped Film Finance Corporation into the National Film Development Corporation, it looked for international outlets through theatrical release and television for these films. It was a radical opening up of the means of production and it led to a fundamental shift in perceptions of cinema.

On the face of it, it was an ideal situation — full structural support from the government without any government interference in the creative process. An ironic twist was added when films funded by one government organisation (the NFDC) would sometimes be refused a certificate, initially, by the Censor Board for their extreme critical positions, only to go on and win a national award given by a government-instituted jury, or selected for inclusion in the Indian Panorama by another government-appointed committee. In the halcyon early days, art and imagination were as greatly respected as 'seriousness' of purpose. There was a sense of pride in the genesis of another language of film, pride in the many shapes it was taking. Everything was new, from a coherently structured narrative to an exploration of the medium that quickened the imagination, from the arrival of an entirely new breed of actors trained principally at the National School of Drama to technicians with a thorough grounding in film technique acquired as much through a sustained exposure to great cinema at the National Film Archive as to practical training at the Film Institute.

With an impressive line-up of talent, a considerable body of work revealing a variety of approaches, the alternate movement, despite the several pulls in different directions, shared an attitude towards cinema that set it definitively apart from the mainstream.

In the '70s, as the initial enthusiasm settled into a sustained movement, positions became clearer, both among filmmakers and their votaries as well as among the authorities. It became increasingly apparent that the odds would be more in favour of 'realism' than 'art', that ideology would prevail over imaginative innovation. In a sense it was inevitable. This cinema is the creation of a sophisticated, cosmopolitan, articulate, urban filmmakers, carrying a burden of guilt for inherited privilege, conscious of a sense of responsibility for atoning for centuries of exploitation and injustice, for working towards a more equitable society by attacking not just economic disparities but also social ills made acceptable through traditional practice.

A limitless number of issues were waiting to be raised, introduced by the rapidly changing social and political environment. Not all of them were taken up for the first time: the denunciation of casteism, feudalism, the oppression practised by a class, by wealth and power or by men on women, the suppression and exploitation of the weak, recalled the '30s but the approach had hardened — from helpless emotionalism into anger and a call for action. A change in the Indian reality brought forth new subjects: the rural-urban conflict, direct criticism of the political system, the joyous and traumatic birth of identity for the woman, corruption, the growing lumpenisation in the cities, the rage of the young in the face of a hostile future, the disruption of the cohesive family structure causing psychological and social dislocations, the hesitant emergence of the individual.

All these, and more, are areas in which both the audience for these films and the authorities that supported and rewarded them are implicated in and affected by. The films themselves are couched in a language that is easy to grasp, evoking immediate identification and an emotionally-charged response. It is also a kind of expiation of guilt. And by recognising and rewarding it, the government against which the criticism is frequently directed, appropriates it, aligns itself with it, assimilates the film and its message claiming that this, in fact, is the ideal for which all are striving. To an extent, of course, it is true. These ideals are enshrined in the Constitution of India and by pointing to the failures, such films do uphold their goals. Therefore, to suppress them or even ignore them becomes tantamount to denying the legitimacy of this ideology.

The result, however, does not approximate to the Third Cinema as defined by Solanas and Gettino in their celebrated essay, or upheld by Teshome Gabriel. It is not, as the former write: 'a revolutionary cinema...that attempts to intervene in the situation as an element providing thrust or rectification...'

This kind of realism is neither critical nor subversive. Protest, an active confrontation with the world — the only worthwhile motive for realism — results, as has been said, from 'a realism that is recreated through artifice.' This cinema by its superficial reproduction of reality confirms the existence of what it shows; it is the stuff of conventional documentary, affirming what we already know. And the style in which it captures images of misery makes it possible to consume them with impunity. The *status quo* is not disturbed, the general public is not estranged. Instead, there is a sense of righteousness, of guilt dissolved in the very fact of having witnessed such representations. This is not to infer that the filmmakers themselves are not men and women of conscience, concerned and committed to their beliefs, but when issues are dealt with without an analytical, intellectual understanding of the manner in which cinema operates, the result can be a subversion of the text.

The press and media played an ambivalent role. By responding with enthusiasm to the subject of a film, confusing content with form and labelling it 'art', they conferred upon it a legitimacy that springs from an emotional, not critical, reaction.

In the determination to appear liberal, the support offered to these films led to a marginalisation of the filmmaker as artist. Haile Gerima, passionate advocate of the cinema as a weapon, has also upheld 'the crucial and historic right to have the freedom to stumble and explore and experiment.... While it is very important for food and shelter to be the primary objectives of any government the development of the human intellect culturally is of equal importance.

In sidelining the artist-filmmaker, in deflecting the art/non-art debate into one between ideology and art, we seem to be subscribing to a notion of ourselves as underdeveloped, upholding the paternalistic view of ourselves and our cinema held by the West. It is an attitude that has done incalculable harm to the cinema in 'developing countries'. It is a benevolent attitude which Turkish critic Mehment Basutçu sums up ironically as: "You filmmakers from poor countries lacking in the financial and technical wherewithal, pray do not try to compare yourselves with western masters by experimenting with style when treating existential or metaphysical themes. Not too much philosophy, please ! Confine yourselves to descriptions of harsh, economic realities in your countries; denounce the injustices of which you people are victims; we will support you. And you will not only be espousing a noble cause, but will also find a western audience for your films. Moreover, we will defend you without any pangs of conscience since you are doing useful work. As for technical shortcomings or the mediocre aesthetic quality of your films, we will excuse them and any other awkwardness we may find, all the more easily since you speak of the essential..." *

Basutçu concedes that this approach "is somewhat caricaturised and is now thankfully on the decline". But for some time it did severe damage. For it was an encouragement to filmmakers to continue along such lines, achieve a certain reputation internationally with it and because of that, at home as well. Often, international critics unfamiliar with the cultural codes necessary for deciphering meaning fully, praise a work for its 'uncompromising realism', little realising that in its context it is a repetition of well-worn clichés. The international praise showered on a film or filmmaker makes it impossible for national critics to point to its weaknesses in either/both text and technique without appearing either churlish or disgruntled. So a consensualist paradigm prevails where the standards set are dictated from outside. A situation thus approved leads to a further marginalisation of the artist-filmmaker who is castigated for his lack of a social conscience and accused of self-indulgent individualism. This gets extended to the minority audience for such films and to critics looking not for ideologies of underdevelopment but for an aesthetics of cinema.

---

* This essay is based on a paper first presented at the Asian Cinema Studies conference at La Trobe University, Melbourne, Australia, in 1992. Mehment Basutçu in *Cinemaya,* 7, Spring 1990, p.16

In the late '80s, the citations for national award-winning films almost always lauded films that "portray the steady destruction of rural folk traditions...", or "the political and social hypocrisy...of the middle class", "the bleak narration of an unemployed youth becoming unemployable due to callous social attitudes...."

As one filmmaker whose imaginative use of cinema does not fall within these parameters commented: "If a film is about poverty or politics, it is sure to win awards and accolades."

Not to be outdone, the mainstream cinema also acquired the appurtenances of a social conscience. But the falseness behind the appearance was easily detectable. There was no real commitment to the ideas being advanced; instead, an exploitation of patterns of domination and dependence to wrench the heartstrings of a susceptible audience; along the way, fakery and play acting.

The Nineties

The past few years have seen a complete overthrow of all accepted conventions: in the 'serious' cinema — of neo-realism or of artistic expression — as much as in the mainstream. For a variety of reasons, the former did not succeed in acquiring a large enough audience to make itself commercially viable. The dependence continued on government support, whether the National Film Development Corporation or later on television. An alternate distribution network did not come into being; the bleakness in most of these films could not compete in the marketplace for screening time in the cinemas against the increasingly extravagant spectacles being profferred by the mainstream producers — multi-starrers, huge budgets, wild and vulgar song and dance sequences alternating with explosive violence....

Family audiences, long the mainstay of the popular cinema, abandoned the run-down theatres (the international trend of multiplexes in attractive surroundings not having been followed), leaving the once-splendid picture palaces to riff raff audiences of unemployed young men for whose delectation these films seem to be designed. The once-clear lines dividing villain from hero, vamp from heroine, are gone. Anything that sells is the apparent motivating factor, raising a despairing cry for stricter censorship.

In the parallel cinema the picture is dark. The hope for financing and distribution comes principally from television, the NFDC grudgingly releases small amounts for 'serious' films, vetting scripts and cutting down budgets until there is just enough to make the film, but never enough to make it well. The look remains 'low-budget'. The idea that 'art' equals 'small' in concept and execution persists.

As films from China and Iran, Taiwan and Korea begin to compete for audiences internationally through films that are large in concept, lavish in production, with no money spared to achieve technical quality or, later, on promotion, Indian cinema seems determined to uphold values of austerity, almost of self-effacement. In content and form, the canvas has been reduced, not enlarged, an ideology of underdevelopment perpetuated.

12

The Space of Encounter: A Re-reading of *Sant Tukaram*

— Madan Gopal Singh

IN HIS OPENING COMMENTS at a symposium on the Theory and Politics of Location, John Akomfrah, a third cinema practitioner, spoke about 'the desire to build a living room out of the layers of politics, cinema and theory'. The spatial metaphor, in view of a film practice that deflects its arguments and stories across a series of mythical/historical diasporas, assumes a special significance. For, the desire to build does not refer merely to an assured spatial presence — the living room, that is — but, much more symptomatically, to an original absence — home! However, this yearning seems to have been very carefully camouflaged in a paradox that does not cease to compound itself. Thus, on the one hand, one hears of third cinema as a 'counter cultural movement that has on its side the possibility of national liberation', on the other, one finds it dispensing with the 'certainty of place, location and subjectivity'. The professed rhetoric of third cinema being uncertainty, it aspires to 'devise a way of speaking in broken tongues'. Within the space of cultural autonomy, it refuses to debate the 'rhetorics of the original scene'. The question about the irretrievably lost home is, thus, successfully held in abeyance.

These metaphors of space and speech are important in our context for a very different reason. The Indian Sufis of the 16-17th century Punjab and Sind proposed, not without a degree of intransigence, the concepts of *laamakaani* or homelessness and *saraayki* or the articulation born of the inn. If, in our context, we were to look beyond the colonial-post-colonial inscriptions of modernity, we may find that these wandering mendicants were the first ones to envision the moving face of the 'new'. Whereas the concept of *laamakaani* was borrowed from the Arabic/Persian Sufi traditions, that of the new speech, *saraayki*, was developed almost indigenously. The creative joy consisted in arriving at a familiar-non-familiar speech through a grand identity-dissolve that the journeys of these Sufi mendicant-poets inevitably entailed. There was no living room for there was no sense of home any more. What remained was a topographic passion that grappled with the idea of unity through an ethic of separation.

Arguing on behalf of third cinema, in a somewhat similar circumstance, art historian Geeta Kapur emphasized 'the articulation of the colonised individual, the absent subject, into history'. This argument formed part of her presentation on Ritwik Ghatak's *Jukti Takko ar Gappo* (Arguments, Stories, 1975). Thinking through the 'relationship of the spatial with the narrative situation', she invoked the image of the wandering saint-poets to show how Ghatak's own staging of the self within the overall problematic of (contemporary) history was sanctioned by their vanguard reformist-revolutionary positions and how, by consequence, he attained 'access to a collective and communitarian identity'. However, the question of creating a time outside the implicated destiny of 'reflection' is not answered by a dynamic, of movement through space, which merely reaffirms a narrative that has been played out, always already! In other words, the question is: which is that history that stands outside the reflection of history or, for that matter, an ethic that stands outside of the categorical imperative? In cinema, for instance, the space exists both inside the narrative universe as well as outside it. As a (descriptive-affective-mental) category of thought and perception, it needs to constantly renew itself through the creation of time outside time (or, better still, a history outside history) within the diegesis of cinema. Here, as in a certain classicity of music, one enters home only to leave it. The living room may, thus, be a mere reflectionist sleight created by an innocent stalker in the third zone. It has very little to do with the wandering of poets and, by consequence, with the reflexivity of the third space in cinema.

How does this cinema of 'self-reflexivity' grapple with a near narcissistic enigma of its own birth in a third context such as ours? For, even though the romance of national liberation has not fully receded and the institutional structures of modernity have not been even partially exhausted, we have already strayed into a rhetoric of visual anthropology where militancy and nationalism come together to foreclose the space of encounter between cinema and its 'real'. Instead, what we have here are socio-psychological reflections of the narrative anxiety interceding on behalf of modernity and nationality. Cinema has become more of a minuscule totem worn as an amulet around the filmic discourse. This would, then, mean that we have to, above all, address ourselves to that un-negotiated split that has occurred within the subject whereby the 'epistemic self' aspires towards the ideal of creating beyond the nation and the 'practical self' locates its creativity firmly within the national mythos. We have, here, quite a range of contradictory mappings to contend with: the ideological construct of persona, the pragmatic construct of institutions, weighty cultural formations around a fixed controlling centre, the floating centres of fluid materialities and choreographic excess...There are so many aporias within the space of this third!

If one were to push the paradox of 'time outside of time' a little further, one could actually see, here, the beginning of a 'cinema outside cinema'. What is space independent of the narrative in which it is imaged? What is the ontological energy of movement in cinema? What is the life of cinema outside of realism? What is the implication of image under the power of gaze? For a long time, a number of our filmmakers continued to critically engage themselves with not only the filmic narrative space — its diegesis, i.e., with all its strategies of spectavizing — but, equally rigorously, with the very narrative of cinema itself — its implicated history and, therefore, its ontology. They tried to understand cinema beyond its capacity as a medium and a mode — beyond the original site, i.e. — and, in trying to do that they tried to move beyond their own implicated positions. They tried to shift the space of encounter beyond the shadow of destiny.

There were those seminal film texts from the history of Indian cinema which tried to examine how this new engagement with historicontologies, which is, in fact, an engagement with the sensuous core of narratives, negotiated the undercurrents of these inside-outside conjunctions. One could think of *Sant Tukaram* (1936) by Fatehlal and Damle, *Pather Panchali* (Song of the Road, 1955) by Satyajit Ray and *Meghe Dhaka Tara* (The Cloud-Capped Star, 1959) by Ritwik Ghatak. The central motif of these texts is constituted, both literally and figuratively, around the space of home; their central impulse is geared towards a dissolution of this space. The narrative structure unfolds a simple schema of repetition in which the circular return movement towards home is seen to become more and more difficult even as the idea of 'home' loses its original sense of benign and nurturing containment. In the process, we discover a series of new responses to the idea of cinematic time, materiality and the staging of the persona being worked out either as spiritual affect (as in *Tukaram*), realist balance (as in *Pather Panchali*) or through the subterfuge of memory and melodrama (as in *Meghe Dhaka Tara*). In varying degrees and from different positions of cultural creativity, the three texts try to negotiate the problematic of homelessness in relation to cinema, filmic universe and history. However, only Ritwik Ghatak amongst the three addresses himself to the problematic of articulation through the grand identity-dissolve with a sense of critical urgency.

The spiritual affect in *Sant Tukaram* does not merely relate to the 'face' as it would in a more pronounced hagiographic tradition of representation in Christianity. The construction of iconicity, which Geeta Kapur has so exhaustively dealt with in her seminal essay, 'Mythic Material in Indian Cinema', is, as such, not answered without reference to Fatehlal-Damle's construction of the durative. Following Gilles Deleuze, durative may be described as the image of time recovered during the dissolution of sugar granules in water marking 'a qualitative change from water which contains a sugar lump to the state of sugared water'. In a definitive sense, *Sant Tukaram* is the first Indian filmmaker

Sant Tukaram, 1936, S. Damle and Fatehlal

to explore the concepts of persona, space and movement within, at first, the overall edifice of film-narrative, and, then, the ontology of cinema itself.

At the level of plot — in this case, plot quite literally laid out as the English 'plotting' or the French 'intrigue' — the schema of narration is split along two sections — the dividing line being the consecration of Tuka and his poetry. The story unfolds through a series of intrigues against the low-caste village poet who stays absolutely at the outermost margin of the social life by the high-caste temple performer Salomalo who builds his precarious reputation as a *bhakti* poet by stealing Tuka's verses. Tuka has no idea of the causality that such intrigues inevitably harbour. He stays and creates in just about any-space-whatever unlike Salomalo who literally owns the temple as the arena of his performance. He passes through the narrative space as if in an a-causal trance; as if it (the narrative) is not happening to him at all. He does nothing to either consciously invite intrigue or to get out of its consequences. Unbeknown to him, there is always a miracle — optical, as in the folklore of cinema — which brings about the resolution and, thereby, invites the structure of intrigue to be upgraded in the next plotting.

This semiotic of silence continues to steer the film till Tuka himself begins to demand a miracle and, thereby, brings the benign and a-causal folklore of optical effects to an end and converts it into a tool of causality and social power. In this way, from an initial celebration of homelessness, the film moves inexorably towards a recovery of home and, therefore, a possible standardization of the folk articulations. There comes a time when almost the entire village community, with the exception of the lone resistant figure of Tuka's wife Jijai, completely immerses itself within Tuka's verses wiping out its earlier musical expressions of productivity in the lap of nature. Home, within this newly received narrative sense, being a communitarian space and, therefore, enlarged much beyond the family, becomes an area of influence and power and creates an entrenched rhetoric of identity. However, homelessness in the earlier narrative section consists of the recovery of spiritual affect in any-space-whatever and is interlinked to the identity-dissolve one associates with the self-reflexivity of the third space. This shift is, therefore, not just an interfacial transition from one thematic strand to another but a real split concerning an entire attitude on narrative and cinema and, possibly, about an understanding of history itself. Against the received history of the magico-realist thrust of cinema, the opposing metaphysic of myth and folklore holds out for a considerable length and then, as if, gives up (without a warning) and allows itself to be inundated by the realism and magicality of the cause. It needs to be emphasised that, given its semiotic of silence vis-a-vis its understanding of the narrative mode founded solely on the principle of causality, it has a double register of 'magicality': magic as pure optical effect and magic as power. There is no 'Melies-like magicality (via Phalke)' here as long as the pure optical nature of magic is sustained and as long as it functions as the carrier of an a-causal narrativity.

In her analysis of *Sant Tukaram,* Geeta Kapur speaks about "the childlike, indeed childish, set of miracles" in terms of a dual function they perform: there is, in her opinion, "a never fading thrill in technical transformation..." of hitherto static iconography" and, secondly, "the magic induced into the everyday life of the little community" becomes "a motivating impulse towards a materially plentiful, therefore generous, existence". This seems to be a somewhat literal mapping of the optical effects onto the elements of miracle in the narrative. The point about these miracles and opticals is that they emerge alongside the semiotic of silence as a key strategy of the non-narrative which is linked, through ontology, to a critique of the 'resemblance complex' of cinematic aspiration on the one hand and a silent exegesis on the auteur's own location within a colonial context with absolutely no lineage of the realist conscience on the other.

The hegemony of the realist narrative and magico-realist cinema is countered with not only the magic of mythology and folklore but also, and far more importantly, with the 'optical effects'. As against the grounding of 'magic' within realist aspirations, *Sant Tukaram* seems to celebrate the pure possibilities of the optical effects. In both Dadasaheb Phalke and Fatehlal-Damle, miracles and optical effects explore the space of pure possibilities that cinema opened up vis-a-vis the narrative in a colonial context. The iconic dynamism in the miraculous transformations of the narrative and cinema could be understood only in reference to the possibilities inherent in the affection-image even if the sensuous in *Sant Tukaram's* use of the miracle/ optical effects is severely restricted in that it is allowed only a skeletal presence across the film.

Because of the obvious differences of historicity, the two magicalities are indeed as incomparable — Melies' being oriented towards a future sensuousness and Fatehlal-Damle's being located in the presence of the pure optical — as is Falconetti's performance in Carl Dreyer's *Passion of Joan of Arc* to that of Vishnupant Pagnis in *Sant Tukaram.* Geeta Kapur adduces 'ideal alienation' in the very style of representation and performance of Vishnupant Pagnis as Tukaram. "How does this man 'play' the saint; what subject-image-sign does he transmit," she asks. She invokes what she believes to be comparable films — Dreyer's *Passion of Joan of Arc* and Bresson's *Diary of a Country Priest* — to attempt an answer. She quotes from Andre Bazin to emphasise how the 'countenance as flesh, when not involved in playing a role, bears a man's true imprint, the most visible mark of his soul'. However, in this shift from the 'psychology to the physiology of existence', the dynamic of movement and causality, with which the performance of Falconetti in *Passion of Joan of Arc* is suffused, is almost strategically denied to Pagnis within the overall semiotics of *Sant Tukaram.* Pagnis's performance is, in fact, definitively inscribed within a denial of narrative action through a spiritual stillness which permeates Tuka's being as possibly the beginning of a new persona. Falconettii, on the other hand, lives through the weight of narrative induced under obsessive framings and tight close-ups. Likewise, Bresson's *Country Priest*, the other comparative reference in Kapur, achieves 'a man's true imprint' only through obsessive movements going invariably out-of-frame and eventually out-of-field. Instead of the continuous mobility and obsession of these performances, we have, here, a stillness, silence and, if at all, a narrativity without motive. There are no close-ups and even less of movements going out of frame. It is not as if the film lacks in the use of the dramatic. There is, indeed, a profusion of the action-image but it is placed, within the agency of plot, as a self-enclosed narrative strategy. Within the overall schema of intrigue, one hardly comes across a causal experience of the realist narrative or, for that matter, the magico-realist cinema. What one finds instead is the construction of durative as spiritual affect.

From the very beginning, the attempt is to explore the possibility of durative in space by holding the image-object in real time and, thereby, recovering the real time itself within the filmic time as such. This truly remarkable spiritual affect is brought about, for instance, through a construction of time in music — through the non-durative singing of the arch-pretender Salomalo and the prostitute Sundara as against the durative singing of the people of Dehu and, especially, Jijai at work, and Tuka, for whom singing as work merely extends his being.

In the opening sequence, for instance, Tuka is seen squatting in a centralized mid-close shot, singing in an indistinct space. The upper part of his body sways gently and rhythmically to his own singing. His face is awash with soft light and the glint in his eyes is not directed at a real object in space. In this durative shot the actual singing and the shot become indistinct. The more the durative grows in real time, the more the camera loses its gaze. The time moves out of the diegesis of cinema and becomes organic. Only in this sense, the iconicity brings about the shift in focus from performance to physiognomy. But more importantly, the persistence with the durative transgresses the notion of balance in a realist image. It is important to note that within the genre of the mythological, the use of durative is most uncommon. In a sense, such a take may be likened to the notion of time as it obtained at the beginning of cinema where the focus fell upon the mechanistic rather than psychological time.

In recent critical writings on *Sant Tukaram* (cf. Kumar Shahani, Ashish Rajadhyaksha, Geeta Kapur, *et al.*), one comes across recurrent reference to Vishnupant Pagnis's style of singing. Almost always, the intent is to underline 'narrative effect of the performance'. Tuka's durative mode — though never ever recognised as such — is compared with the near parodic, excessively embellished mode of singing with emphatic pauses on the name of the plagiarist-author, Salomalo, going equally dramatically with literal representations of some of the key-words through exaggerated *bhavs.* Translated literally, *abhang* means an uninterrupted singing in praise of God. Translated further into cinematic terms in *Sant Tukaram,* it harbours the very essence of time as durative. Throughout the first section, the singing of *abhangs* is presented as the uninterrupted time constituting the image as durative. In a sense, the point is crucial to the debate of history as signification. For, in pitching the durative image — as both movement and time — within the constituted space and time of diegesis, it seems to question the received notions of cinema and begins afresh a thinking on the ontology of the cinematic image. Music becomes a defining principle of the film: the conception of space, the construction of time, personae, the physical and narrative movements all become rhythmically interlinked to create the 'new' image as durative. In the first section, almost all major characters are found existentially steeped in some form of music or the other. Tuka's very being is defined by the *abhangs* he writes, composes and sings in absolutely any-space-whatever and to no one in particular. This is the only 'activity' he engages in. Regardless of what he may have to say to Ramshastri in the Inquest sequence, his singing is beyond the pale of both *bhakti* and *yoga marg* (or, by extension, the imaginary and the symbolic).

Salomalo's singing, on the other hand, is projective precisely because it is an integral part of his profession. Hence, the performance! It is not just a question of his *tamasha* style singing as against Tuka's mode of reposeful interiority. His singing creates, on the other hand, a fictional space, assembled time and, in short, a narrative of realist causality. The mimicry, the side-glances, the fragmentation of space, the stories — all these are explainable in reference to a diegesis of realist causality. Tuka's simplicity through durative against Salomalo's complexity through the realist causality reverses the image-equation within the context of the cinematic ontology. There is a near-professional affinity between Salomalo and Sundara, the prostitute, even though the latter is in a more continuous flow of time.

However, the real counterpoint to Tuka's mode of singing and, therefore, his being is constituted not so much by Salomalo's elliptical mode of being as by Jijai's singing which mingles perfectly with her work. She sings even as she bathes her milk-dry buffalo, she sings while pasting the floor in anticipation of surprising Tuka, she sings while grinding the grain that has fortuitously come her way. Her singing, like Tuka's, is not directed towards a listener. It evolves in close tandem with work which happens to be her gesture of affection. Her idiom and mode of singing is predominantly folk and more than holds its own against Tuka's *abhangs*. This singing in conjunction with work is symptomatic of life in Dehu. Women work in the fields during harvest time, men measure heaps of grain, cartwheel drivers move in a procession — the entire carnival of life is in a state of natural musicality until it is usurped by the neo-morality of Tuka's *abhangs*. However, against the time durative created by Tuka in the first section, there is always the movement/energy durative created by Jijai on the margin, which seems to critique Tuka's understanding of social action. Jijai's movement through space reveals the dynamic side of realism which rejects both the conventional plot-narrative as well as the cinema that seems to develop in conjunction with pure spiritual affect. This the opening of another third — the gender as both the folk and the feminine — dislocating the centre from the margin. The argument is even extendable to Sundara the prostitute.

The question of ontology of the image and movement in cinema as it was subsequently debated in the west pertained basically to the realist lineage of cinema itself. The invention of cinema itself was part of a larger mimetic drive in which the 'self' was sought to be produced as the 'other'. However, as the example of *Sant Tukaram* shows so decisively, there was a life for cinema beyond realism, especially by way of a semiotic of silence within the context of resistance to colonialism. It refused to construct a living room within the lap of a realist cinema or, what Bazin calls, "a kind of decal or transfer" of realism. It aspired, on the other hand, to construct a sense of homelessness through a denial of the realist causality and, hence, of an entire narrative tradition. For, it saw the image of the thing also as the image of its duration. Object had become not just time but its outside as well.

This denial was not brought about by sharp discontinuities or by a radical change of perception on the construction of subjectivity itself. Despite the biographical folklore used by the filmmakers, the conjunction between the persona and history continued to be dictated by the reflections of these filmmakers on both the narratives of cinema as well as the narratives of their own existential condition. These reflections began invariably with self-critical engagements with the ontology of the image, movement, space and duration itself. These were, then, the first marks of the grand identity-dissolve which were to subsequently so infuse the poetic conscience of a filmmaker like Ritwik Ghatak. If the split between the epistemic and the practical subject did not show up, it was because the epistemic self had strategically hidden its ethic from the realist gaze.

Part III

13

Documentary Cinema: A Visual Metaphor for Cultural Pluralism

— Shoma A. Chatterjee

All methods of recording on celluloid, any aspect of reality interpreted either by actual shooting or sincere and justifiable reconstruction, so as to appeal either to reason or to emotion, for the purpose of stimulating the desire for, and widening of, human knowledge and undetrstanding, and of truthfully posing problems and their solutions in the spheres of economics, culture and human relations.

The World Union of Documentary Filmmakers, 1948

It is difficult, in a period of ideological wariness where scepticism prevails, to make works that persist in claiming objectivity of observation, transparency of description or immediacy of experience, without even questioning the place from which interpreters (whether they are writers or filmmakers) construct their cultural accounts.

Trin T. Minh-ha, in
Re-thinking the Subject of Ethno-documentary, 1992

The documentary idea demands no more than that the affairs of our time shall be brought to the screen in a fashion which strikes the imagination and makes observation a little richer than it was. At one level, the vision may be journalistic, at another, it may rise to poetry and drama. At another level again, its aesthetic quality may be in the mere lucidity of its expression.

— John Grierson

In keeping with the cultural pluralism India represents, our cinema, too, reveals tremendous cultural diversity. If cinema is to be viewed in spatial perspective, its prismic dimensions are as multi-coloured and multi-hued as life itself: the mainstream cinema, the parallel or art cinema, the cinema made for the specific purpose of advertising a product or a service, (either for commercial purposes, or for public service), and the documentary cinema. But the very fact that we use the term 'mainstream' to qualify cinema as a commercial product, automatically positions the world of the documentary on the margin. Is it, therefore, a part of marginalised cinema? In terms of exhibition in public outlets that would evolve a culture of mass viewership, it is. In terms of its traditionally self-defined stereotype of the Films Division newsreel, yes, it is a victim of its own making. But in terms of international recognition, in terms of trying to make a strong statement about a little-known ethnic group, in terms of narrating the life-story of an artiste or a writer or a theatre person, in terms of investigating a fact, in terms of using the camera politically, the Indian documentary has surely come into its own. It has created islands of recognition in world cinema. It has shaped and honed itself technically as a mode of audiovisual expression which offers infinite room for improvement, experimentation and expression. Above all, it has defined itself as a powerful force of representation, realisation, argument, debate and question.

The documentary in India is not just 'cinema' *per se,* which begins and ends with the making, exhibiting and viewing of a film. It is a movement. The word 'movement' suggests a sense of fluidity, of moving forward, of an ongoing journey that never quite ends, which is ambivalent unto itself, which amoeba-like can stretch itself to any shape it wishes. Documentary cinema in India does not restrict itself within the periphery of a retrospective of films made by Mani Kaul or Kumar Shahani. It is all of this, of course, but it is much, much more. It offers a panoramic view of life: in the past, in the present, and in the distant future.

All this has emerged and taken concrete shape in recent years, mainly due to three forces that gave the Indian documentary a place of its own, and a place of respect and dignity in the marginalised environment of economic bankruptcy and poverty of viewership. These three forces are:

(a) International documentary film festivals like the ones held at

Mannheim and Leipzig where Indian documentaries have bagged awards, thus bringing these films and their makers into the Indian limelight at least temporarily;

(b) The Bombay International Festival for Documentary, Short and Animation Films (BIFF), begun in 1990, offered a world platform to Indian makers of documentary films who could now have a formidable Indian and foreign audience viewing their films at least once, something definitely better than the films never being offered for viewing at all!

(c) The banning of some strong political statements from being screened both on the large and on the small screen by the administration simply because they questioned the administration in different ways for different reasons and thus would place the Government in a rather embarrassing light!

Wide coverage given to all these three forces in the print media has brought the Indian documentary sharply into focus in recent years.

What are the kinds of documentaries that are being made? Who are the people making them? Why are they making them? And, above everything else, how are they making them? Are they being seen at all by Indian audiences, except through the film festivals here? Or do they remain in the cans for some exhibition in some remote school or college where the maker pitifully passes a hat around to try and break even so that he can use the money for his next film? Seeking answers to these questions might hint at the evolution of documentary cinema as a mode of cultural expression, reflection, representation, interpretation and analysis in India.

Coming to the first question — what are the kinds of documentaries that are being made — the answer might sound incredible by the very definitions of quality and quantity. That apart, artificial categorisations of the documentary format into classes like the biographical documentary, the ethnographic documentary, the historical documentary, the geographical documentary, the documentary of culture and arts, the environmental documentary, the political documentary, the documentary of social relevance, would be a misnomer since all these classes, if one might call them so, are subject to considerable overlapping, thus blurring the dividing line between the one and the other. For example, Gulzar's film on Pandit Bhimsen Joshi is as much a biographical documentary as it is a historical one because it traces the history of one school of Hindustani classical music, the Kirana gharana, without which the history of Hindustani classical music can never be complete. Arun Khopkar's *Colours of Absence* on cubist-abstract painter Jehangir Sabavala unfolds the painter's evolution as one of the better-known painters of modern India. But in terms of form, it can also fall under the slot of the experimental documentary since Khopkar interweaves his narrative with the painter's views on Nature through variable chromatic light, through sounds that sometimes directly relate to the visuals and sometimes create a contrapuntal tension, aiming at capturing the spirit of the paintings. In this sense, it becomes an art-centric, aesthetic documentary. And, of course, it makes its way into the Archives as a film that would form part of India's art history.

Take Sudhanshu Mishra's documentary, *Mithak Bhang* (The Disappearing Poem). On the surface, it is clearly an ethnographic documentary because it traces the lifestyle of the Agarias, a group of tribal iron smelters living in the forests which form the margins of the Kanha National Park in Madhya Pradesh. But on deeper probing, one discovers it is also a film of social concern, since Mishra seems concerned about the increasing economic desperation these people are being driven into, consequently leading to their social disintegration because of the growing economic irrelevance of their age-old craft. Yet, looked at from a totally different viewpoint, it emerges as a film that determinedly digs into a remote, unknown part of the country's indigenous culture, through these tribal groups' rituals performed through song and dance. How would you slot this kind of film?

The merit of these filmmakers lies in that they do not allow the power-relationships that might emerge between the filmmaker and his subject to surface as the film unfolds itself. They do not interpret the subject as the inheritor of a specific mentality, which places qualitative limitations on the subject. Nor do they perpetuate definite modes of objectification.

Zafar Hai's *Hyderabad: A Place in the Past* sounds like a blend of history and geography. It is indeed, both, but extends its horizons to be much more. As its maker himself says: "It is a cinematic tribute to the Nawabi culture of Hyderabad, evoking the grand lifestyle of more than a century ago." The magic of the camera evokes, through photographs, the flavour of things past. And nostalgia carries within itself the tragic reality of decay and alienation. Centuries of Mughal traditions that have filtered down from the north to the south has been subtly hinted at. What kind of film would you like to call this?

Jill Misquitta's *The Clap Trap* is a telling documentary, captured from two major first-persona accounts, a story of the 'extras' in Bombay's film industry consoled through the tautological trick of being labelled 'junior artistes'. It is, at once, a human-interest story, an investigative story, and an enthnographic film. It is also a political film since, through celebrating these marginal people's struggle for survival, the director takes open potshots at the dehumanisation of human beings in an industry where the stars earn in six and seven figures but where their 'juniors' are victims of exploitation : economic, emotional, even sexual.

What one is trying to stress is that, over the past decade, beginning around the mid-eighties, so far as documentary cinema in India is concerned, there has been a visible shift from the making of a genre of film to the making of a wide range of genres of film in which the making itself is political.[1]

And looked at from this standpoint every documentary made in India, away from the august body of the Films Division, is a political documentary. These films are made independently by filmmakers without government funding, or assistance either in terms of manpower or of infrastructure. Doordarshan and sources of state-patronage are also circumspect in the kind of films they choose to fund. The Films Division, as the 'public sector' of filmmaking, has kept on manufacturing newsreels and illustrative films in the nature of an assembly-line production.[2] Whatever funding the FD has made available to private directors has remained largely confined to films that are 'politically correct' by their very definition. Such films are : *Lamp in the Niche* (Girish Karnad), *Amjad Ali Khan* (Gulzar), *Nargis* (Priya Dutt). The only notable documentary to be funded by Doordarshan in recent years has been Nilita Vachani's *Eyes of Stone*. Interestingly, Krishnendu Bose, who now makes ecological films for INTACH (Indian National Trust for Art and Cultural Heritage) under the banner of his company, Fluid Head Films, was assigned a current affairs programme ('Focus') by Doordarshan in 1988. A 30-minute documentary entitled *The Godfathers of Dhanbad*, the film dealt with the coal mafia. But Doordarshan has still not got around to telecasting it. The ban comes as a surprise, because, having seen the film, one does not find any logic in Doordarshan's negative attitude towards a film which it has itself commissioned.

In the circumstances, therefore, it would be better to club these independent documentaries as 'alternative cinema', or 'counter-cinema', because their makers are indeed attempting to counter the *masala* that is dished out in the mainstream, while they are also countering all attempts to abort their mission in making socially relevant documentary films by the establishment.

What are the characteristics of a 'socially useful' film that forms part of this counter-cinema? Gaston Roberge[3] describes the socially useful film as follows:

a. A film that raises the spectator's awareness of certain issues even if the issues are not dealt with exhaustively.
b. A film that educates the sensibilities of the spectator about these issues and suggests the possibility of different worlds.
c. A film that gives some information about the actual mechanisms of alienation and of oppression. (However, too much information might make the film 'objectionable' and cause it to be banned)[4].
d. A film that features a hero who is imitable and rational in his approach to problems — not just violent.
e. A film that promotes human virtues that make life worth living, such as hope and compassion.

From the above, this writer agrees to the first three points but is sceptic about the fourth and fifth points since they are so ambiguous and ambivalent that they might easily permit entry to mainstream films and make the entire subject of social relevance a futile and a meaningless argument.

Who defines counter-cinema? Pankaj Butalia,[5] himself an economics lecturer-turned documentary filmmaker, places the credit for pioneering a kind of vibrant, angry questioning movement in cinema on the able shoulders of Anand Patwardhan "for creating conditions in which such a cinema could become respectable".

For nearly two decades now, Patwardhan has been making documentaries on many themes that an earlier documentary filmmaker would never have dreamt of. He has paved the way for similar activists who followed him. Patwardhan says: "In every film I make, I strive to make the elements of filmmaking subservient to what is happening in the film. I measure the success of my films by their ability to make people think about the issues generated. Personally, I don't like using the word 'art' because it is used badly and wrongly all the time. I don't think art can be divorced from society. Not that everything has to be political in the sense of everyday politics. But I think everything is political in the deep sense."[6]

Patwardhan's career in documentary films began with *Prisoners of Conscience* (1978) followed by *A Time to Rise* (1981). He hit the headlines in 1985 with his film on the victimisation of slum-dwellers in Bombay. *Bombay, Our City* brought him the national award for the best documentary of the year. But it was promptly banned from public exhibition by the same government that bestowed the award on the film! A powerful and lucid essay on the politics of space and structure that have dictated the blueprint of our country's irrational development,[7] the film marks a turning point towards a more specific definition of the political documentary which doubles as sociological comment. The film unwittingly led to the evolution of a movement towards the formation of a counter-cinema.

His later films, *In Memory of My Friends* and *Ram ke Naam,* deal with communalism placed in its own perspective. The first, rooted in Punjab, the second, in Ayodhya. In both these films, Patwardhan takes the position of a left-wing rationalist interviewing scores of common people living in the areas of conflict. He uses their pragmatic good sense to make his point.

Ram ke Naam, 1992, Anand Patwardhan

His point is that holocausts occur when passions are deliberately whipped up by manipulators for their own selfish reasons. After *Ram ke Naam*, he said : "It's not so much that I've made the film from a Left perspective as that I made it as a contribution to the fight against communalism and the Left has been at the forefront of that struggle. During the Ayodhya Rath Yatra, no one else was opposing the BJP. But Marxism is not the only way of fighting communalism. We have a secular tradition in India which Mahatma Gandhi emphasised, that is also opposed to religious fundamentalism. My support is for both."

The success of Patwardhan's films in India and abroad has inspired many filmmakers to record on celluloid their perceptions of Indian socio-political reality. Some of the investigative films that form the crux of this counter-cinema are Utpalendu Chakraborty's documentary on political prisoners, *Mukti Chai* (We Demand Freedom), shot mainly with a hand-held camera. Chakraborty insisted that from the time of the Rowlatt Act till the proclamation of the emergency, individual freedom continued to be held in grip by repressive forces; Goutam Ghose's *Hungry Autumn* which took off from actual famine conditions in West Bengal in 1974 and went on to analyse the basic situation of agriculture, widespread destitution and their repercussions on society at large. *An Indian Story* was jointly directed by Tapan Bose and Suhasini Mulay. The film probed into the forced blinding of 34 prisoners of Bhagalpur by the police. The news made front-page headlines in the national press. The film tried to examine the whole pattern of police brutality in India. The duo then went on to make *Bhopal : The Genocide* on the Bhopal gas tragedy. The film won a national award but was kept away from public screening by the Government. The censors banned the film and it had to be saved by a court order. The film was a straightforward, brilliantly-researched and painstakingly-shot documentary about a great human tragedy that turned technology and industrial development with foreign funding into one of the sickest jokes of the modern world. Actual footage of sick and pregnant women, blind men, dying babies, helped the film to evolve its own strong statement. This film, too, was banned and was saved once again by a court order.

Had Ranjan Palit and Vasudha Joshi not made *Voices from Baliapal*, few Indians would have ever known about the collective, peaceful, yet active, resistance of an ethnic mass against a wrong government policy: the setting up of a nuclear base in Baliapal which would uproot these groups from their natural habitat where they are economically self-sufficient through the local crops and through fishing.

Does feminine sensibility differ from male sensibility? Is the feminine aesthetic sense in terms of cinematic image, while reconstructing reality, distanced from such counter-cinema in the form of documentaries made by men? Not really, if one were to go by the telling works of women who have shattered the myth of cinema being a male creative field through their strong efforts at creating counter-cinema.

This question assumes topicality in view of the *Filmfare* award for the best documentary film of 1993 having gone to *I Live in Behrampada*, the debut-film of activist-theatre person Madhushree Dutta. The film came out of her close interaction with the largely Muslim residents of a densely populated slum, sandwiched between a growing, largely middle-class Hindu colony and a suburban railway station in Bombay. Dutta brings a transparently caring camera to the lives and the terrifying experiences of these ghettoised people and also allows the hostile and middle-class neighbours to voice their fears and their mistrust.[8]

Deepa Dhanraj of Bangalore is a spirited young woman who has traversed the rough terrain of counter-cinema. In the '80s, she made four films for an organisation called "Yugantar". These were *Molkarin,* on the unionisation of women domestic servants in Pune, *Tabaku ki Aag,* on the struggle of tobacco workers in Nippani, *Yeh Sirf Kahani Nahin Hai* on marital violence, and *Sudesha*, the portrait of a woman activist in the Chipko movement against deforestation. She later broke away from Yugantar to become part of the Stree Shakti Sanghatana, and made a film on the communal riots in Hyderabad and their bloody aftermath in *Kya Hua is Shaher ko*. At the 2nd BIFF in 1992, one got to see Dhanraj's *Something Like a War,* a daring exposé on the lopsided and inhuman aspects of family planning tilted against women in the country.

Nilita Vachani, who studied communications at the University of Pennsylvania, made *Sabzi Mandi ke Heere*, an hour-long Cinema-verité kind of a documentary funded by a German television company. It offers an interesting, behind-the-scenes look at inter-state travel in North India focusing on the vendors who travel on these buses. She then made an award-winning film, *Eyes of Stone*, a close, camera-involved study of a young Rajasthani woman who is prone to fits of demonic possession. The study of this individual case actually reflects on an entire social system where an individual becomes a helpless victim of social and superstitious forces she herself comes to believe in.

Manjira Dutta, who formed Media Workshop in Delhi, made her first independent documentary on the lop-sided nature of development programmes which ignores remote parts of northern India called *All Roads Are Closed.* In *The Sacrifice of Bablulal Bhuiyan*, she dealt with the death of a colliery worker who was shot by security personnel. She tried to recreate the sequence of events that led to his death. *Portraits of a Dream Show* is about circus people while *Seeds of Plenty, Seeds of Sorrow* is an indictment of the American capitalist design behind the Green Revolution. However, since the film was commissioned by the BBC for the Rio Summit and was screened in 77 countries, questions have been raised about the 'independence' of its stance.

Mediastorm, a Delhi-based activist group, made a series of video films wide-ranging in their coverage of socially significant women's issues like the Shah Bano judgement, *sati*, female foeticide and dowry.

Meera Dewan, in *Gift of Love*, branded the gory, pre-meditated murder of a dowry victim. She also made another film on women as victims of violence which was telecast on the national television network. And after this, she made a subtly understated film on child-labourers who are victims of exploitation and are exposed to occupational hazards within the work-environment of U.P.'s unsafe bangle factories.

Sumitra Bhave, a trained sociologist based in Pune, turned filmmaker when she became an active member of Streevani, a women's organisation in Pune. Together with Sunil Sukhtankar she made *Bai,* based on the oral life history of a Dalit woman and on her coming to terms with her alcoholic husband; *Pani,* a fictionalised account based on the true incident of women's collective effort to bring drinking water to their village; *Mukti*, on drug addicts; *Samvad*, on two Gandhian women working for the tribals in Gujarat, and *Sahyog*, on a dairy cooperative formed by Rajasthani women in a Delhi slum. She broke away from Streevani to work independently. And then came *Chakori,* which carried off an award at the 3rd BIFF in 1994. This is a strong, simply-stated story of a young, abandoned wife whose entire life undergoes a radical change through the apparently simple device of her learning to ride a bicycle, which itself is a revolutionary step in her village.

Suma Josson's *Bombay's Blood Yatra*, Teesta Setalvad's *Bombay: A Myth Shattered*, the late Uma Segal's *Shelter*, Rinki Bhattacharya's and Gulan Kripalani's *Char Diwari*, Shibani Ghosh's *Sadak Chaap*, Sai Paranjpye's *Choodiya*, Sehjo Singh's *The Women Betrayed*, are other films that define the evolution of women who have come to form an integral part of the movement in counter-cinema.

***The Women Betrayed*, 1993, Sehjo Singh**

If these films lead one to believe that the feminine aesthetic sensibility is concentric towards social concern and women's issues only, then this would be taking a rather myopic view of things. A look at Rina Mohan's *Kamlabai*, Sheila Dutta's *Portrait of an Actress*, Shyamasree Tagore's *A Sculptor Speaks*, Balaka Ghosh's *Anukampan*, Soudhamini's *It Rested* and *Pitru Chhaya*, Victoria M. Mukherjee's *Billy Arjan Singh*, Neena Gupta's *Bazar Sitaram,* offer examples of the versatility of the woman documentarist, though all women filmmakers strongly protest against any kind of ghettoisation on grounds of sex.

Kamlabai, 1991, Rina Mohan

However, Gaston Roberge sounds a note of caution in saying: "The necessity of breaking through often leads a filmmaker to be more aggressive towards society than he actually will be once he has broken through. Success in this effort to break through often results in the metamorphosis of the filmmaker from a rebel to a complacent artist." Has this happened? Unfortunately, it has, in the case of talented and creative filmmakers who began with brilliant documentaries but perhaps used these as the stepping stone to the more lucrative and popular arena of feature films. Goutam Ghose, Utpalendu Chakraborty, even people like Mani Kaul, Kumar Shahani, Shyam Benegal and Vidhu Vinod Chopra seem no longer interested in making documentary films. Dilip Ghosh, whose debut documentary, *Children of the Silver Screen,* marked a unique step in the direction of probing the world of child-stars in Hindi cinema, still sticks largely to making ad films.

There is yet another danger. By treating film as a mere data-collecting and recording instrument, therefore turning it into a pawn in the game of power, the cultural, political and sociological interpreter gives up, in a way, any attempt at understanding the very elements that structure his or her experience. When analysis becomes an end in itself, instead of remaining a creative tool for social change, it becomes a deadly circle.[9] As a Cuban writer has remarked on the role of cinema: "To show a process is not exactly equivalent to analysing it. To analyse the problem is to show the problem permeated with judgements which the analysis itself generates *a priori*. To analyse is to block off from the outset any possibility of analysis on the part of the interlocutor."[10]

The above, however, seems more true of documentaries made by the Films Division and by other Governmental departments at the Central and State levels and not really, barring a few exceptions, of films made by those committed to the cause of furthering the counter-cinema movement. One bright light in terms of funding for such cinema has recently opened up. Foreign companies like the BBC and the German ZDF have given an impetus to filmmakers who might never have been able to make their films for lack of funding. This is mainly due to the almost non-existent structure for screening documentary films.[11]

But where are the audiences? The documentary, or counter-cinema, as one chooses to call it, like any medium of art, can survive only if there is a perceptive and demanding audience. The commercial cinema-goer cannot be considered an audience for the documentary. Under these circumstances, it is extremely doubtful whether the documentary can take root in our country independent of the television.[12]

But Sanjit Narwekar, ex-News Editor, *Screen*, does not agree. "Markets for Indian documentary films would automatically open up if audiences began to see these films as a matter of choice rather than as a matter of compulsion. In fact, when a documentary film, however well made, is tagged on compulsorily with a feature, it arouses resentment and rejection in an audience which is not attuned to the subject matter at that moment."

Some filmmakers suggest that the film society movement could prove to be an excellent vehicle for the promotion of documentary and short films. Unfortunately, such a movement for the exhibition and public screening of these films remains confined within a few regional pockets and there seems to be no sign of the late John Abraham's *Odessa* catching on.

Despite the growth of the tribe of filmmakers like Shashi Anand, Chalam Benurakar, Anwar Jamal, Sudipto Bose, Ruchir Joshi, Yash Choudhary, M.A. Rahman, Aribam Syam Sharma, P. Ashok Kumar, etc. (an exhaustive list is impossible) one critic opines that few films are formally satisfying.[13] This is because the style of documentary filmmaking has remained limited to the depiction of crisis, spectacle or oppression. A cinema attempting to go beyond needs to re-examine modes of representation. Filmmakers need to extricate themselves from the dominance of the empirical and explore the domain of interior, subjective worlds.

Under critical analysis, the 'scientific' use of film and its strategies of neutrality is no more exempt from the workings of dominant ideology than is the commercial cinema.[14] All one must do, in these circumstances then, is to work at setting into relief the more invisible strategies of subjection and at shaking values that dominate society down to the smallest detail, starting with the system of cinematic values on which its politics is entirely dependent, that a politically made film assumes its informative role.

Notes:

1. Trinh T. Minh-ha : "Rethinking the Subject of Ethno-documentary"; *Visual Anthrology and India*, Ed. K.S.Singh, 1992.
2. Monica Narula : "To Direct A Gaze"; *Indian Cinema, 1992*, Directorate of Film Festivals, Delhi.
3. Gaston Roberge : "Problems and Prospects of Short Filmmaking in Third World Countries"; *Deep Focus*.
4. The parenthesis is Roberge's.
5. Pankaj Butalia : *The Indian Documentary in the '80s*; Paper on "Tendencies of Development in the Three Continents", 1988.
6. Meher Pestonji : "Getting Rid of Slumdwellers is not the Solution"; *Express* Magazine, July 21,1985.
7. Vishwa Priya : "Patwardhan's *Bombay, Our City* : A Blueprint for Irrational Development"; *Deep Focus.*
8. Maithili Rao : "Women to the Forefront": *Spectrum India*, BIFF, 1994.
9. *Ibid.*
10. Bourdieu, Pierre : "Outline of a Theory of Practice", Trans. R. Nice (New York, 1977).
11. *Ibid* 2.
12. C.J. Paulose : "What Ails the Indian Documentary?" *Deep Focus.*
13. Ibid 2 & 11
14. Trinh T. Minh-ha: "Mechanical Eye, Electronic Ear and The Lure of Authenticity", *Wide Angle,* 6:2 (Summer 1984).

14

Hindi Commercial Cinema: Changing Narrative Strategies

— Rashmi Doraiswamy

THE ERA OF THE persona as a sign expressive of the anxieties of the time, extending over several narratives and providing the motor impulse for the development of these narratives, is over. The persona is, as such, both in and out of the narrative, a part of the narrative and yet bigger than it. Over the last decade, however, the hero, heroine and villain have displayed the ability to contain within themselves more than one — if not many — stereotypic selves. Shah Rukh Khan in *Baazigar* (1993) and *Darr* (1993) is the villainous hero. The villain in many films today also carries the onus of providing comic relief in the narrative; Anupam Kher and Kader Khan, followed by Shakti Kapoor, are the new villian-comedians. And the heroine has taken on several functions of the vamp of yesteryears. Karishma Kapoor, for instance, in her dance sequences in *Raja Babu* (1994) and *Khuddaar*

Karishma Kapoor and Govinda in *Khuddaar*, 1994, Iqbal Durrani

(1994) outdoes any cavorting that the Helens and Bindus indulged in earlier in the explicitness of the sexually suggestive poses that are simulated. One of the main functions of the vamp in the past, apart from being aide and consort to the male villain, was to execute titillating song-and-dance numbers that the heroine in all her modesty could not do. Bindu's "Mera Naam Hai Shabnam" from *Kati Patang* (1971) and Helen's dance to the song "Mehbooba, Mehbooba" in *Sholay* (1975) are two such memorable vamp sequences in the history of Indian film music.

Deewar, 1975, Yash Chopra

Of course, as signs, these new multi-functional characters do stretch their significations across several films; but they do not achieve the status of personae because they just *are*; the narratives they are inscribed in do not offer any logic, *in the form of a debate on social being,* for the acts being performed. It is here that the major difference between the 'anti-hero' image of Shah Rukh Khan and the 'angry young man' persona of Amitabh Bachchan, who held sway in commercial Hindi cinema from the early seventies to the mid-eighties, lies. *Zanjeer* (1973) charted out for the first time Bachchan's smouldering presence, haunted by the childhood memory of his parents being killed and his desire for revenge. However, it was *Deewar* (1975) in which Bachchan plays a smuggler, that finally pinned the persona down and gave voice to a debate on the path to be chosen of living within or without the boundaries of law. It was this transcendant logic that defined his being in all the films he acted, even in those in which, as in Manmohan Desai's films, for example, the spirit of carnival and excess of coincidences was the dominant, rather than a single-minded desire for revenge. Such a logic or debate is completely absent from films like *Baazigar* or *Darr*. What is offered is an apology for villainy, that even in terms of causal relationships is a weak justification. In the narrative logic of commercial cinema in the seventies and early eighties, film time is first devoted to the extenuating circumstances that cause the hero to embark on his path of revenge, and only evil is dispensed with evil, thus retaining a sense of justice in the moral universe created. In *Baazigar* the reasons for the hero's killing of three innocent people are not given dominant exposition and occur later in the film; it is also the first film in which an innocent girl is brutally thrown off a terrace to her death by the (anti) hero, who wishes to avenge the wrongs committed by the girl's father against his family. No sense of moral justice finally prevails in the world created by this film.

One of the reasons for the collapse of the persona is the dispersal of narrative categories. The displacement of the initial segment, normally involving childhood experience of villainy, to a later part in the film's narrative has already been referred to. By imparting to this experience of villainy the status of a beginning, a chain of causal relationships was established in the moral universe simulated by the film. This was true of films with accents on different generic elements: revenge-centred productions in which Bachchan starred — like *Zanjeer* and *Deewar* — as well as musicals like Nazir Hussain's *Yaadon ki Baarat* (1972) and Desai's *Amar, Akbar, Anthony* (1978). In films today, the segment providing the logic for the behaviour of the protagonist rarely occurs in the beginning: it is provided much later in the film. As such the actions of the protagonist have to be taken at their face value, the spectator having no clue to the origins of this pathological behaviour. Crucial to this narrative displacement is the role the flashback — a well-worn technique in commercial melodramas — is now accorded.

Narrative Dispersals

The flashback has traditionally served to recall, to highlight, to fit in pieces of a puzzle, to justify an action currently being carried out. This access to memory was the prerogative only of the lead protagonists, and the memory usually concerned only him/herself. The box-office hit *Tezaab* (1989) is a landmark film in the dispersal of narrative categories and the new deployment of the flashback. The film consists of three major narrative segments, with two large flashback chunks: one recounts from the point of view of a police officer the youthful idealism of the protagonist Mahesh Deshmukh, and the other is Deshmukh's own recounting of why he now lives off the limits of the city, forbidden by law to enter it. This recalling of the decisive moments of the hero's life by another character gives it a new status of objectivity and is a break from the conception of flashbacks in the preceding decades. Subhash Ghai's *Khalnayak* (1993) develops this notion of 'objectivity' even further: mother and son recount separately, to two different listeners, the advent of the villainous Roshi-baba into their lives, leading to the break-up of the family and the son becoming the villain's chief aide. The flashbacks are intercut so smoothly that we witness not just events from the mother's or the son's memories, but a coincident but independent *objective time that is past* takes shape.

Many other narrative elements have lost their position of centrality. There are now, very often, several subplots that do not directly relate to the main story. In *Gardish* (1993), for instance, a semi-lumpen character played by Annu Kapoor moves to Bombay from a small town at the same time as Jackie Shroff (the hero) and his family. Annu Kapoor begins by begging with the aid of electronic gadgets and goes on to become the rich don of the beggar industry. This 'history' is in stark contrast to Jackie Shroff who not only does not make it big in the city but almost gets criminalised. Annu Kapoor's rise is given a certain autonomy in the narrative without it serving as an obvious contrast to the hero's life. Even the love story, the mainstay of all narratives irrespective of genre, is no longer necessarily an important narrative ingredient (except, of course, in films specifically about teenage romances). In films like *Gardish, Tiranga* (1992), *Dhartiputra* (1993) the love-interest is of secondary importance. In *Gardish,* for example, the hero loses out with the heroine because of his constant skirmishes with the police. Another woman in his locality whose husband and child have been incinerated by the villain, and who is now a prostitute, falls in love with him. But love now in Hindi films has many nuances and shades. She clarifies that her feeling for him is a form of *shraddha*: a respect, devotion and affection of the kind that is accorded to God. The hero's relationship with her, to the very end, is ambiguous. Wrongs, too, are avenged not just by the hero with single-minded energy, but by a community of avengers. In *Dhartiputra,* for instance, the women prisoners of the jail take it upon themselves to defend the heroine and her son from the onslaughts of the villains.

Doubles also have not been exempt from this dispersal of significance. Doubles have traditionally been twins, separated at birth and moulded differently by contrasting environments. One would turn out to be gentle and subdued and the other volatile. In recent films, doubles do not have the mandatory common origin of birth. The look-alikes merely serve thematic functions, without any transcendent narrative significance as in the blockbuster *Aankhen* (1992), or the hit *Bol Radha Bol* (1990)

Signs of Villainy

With changing narrative strategies, the network of signs constituting the villain has also changed. Certain actors like Amrish Puri still bank on a frightening physical appearance as the hallmark of a villainous presence. There is a new tendency, however, to use speech as part of the physiognomy of the villain; Paresh Rawal's distinctive Hindi, or Amrish Puri's Haryanvi-oriented Hindi not only points to certain biases and prejudices against certain regions, but also to a new sensitivity to the details that contribute to 'realism'. It is also interesting that the distinctive Bombay-ized Hindi is used by characters who carry neutral or positive values in the narrative system. The only linguistic differentiation that was prevalent in Hindi commercial cinema earlier was that of a South Indian brand of Hindi that used to be passed off as humour by comedians like Mehmood. Even in a relatively non-violent film like *Hum Hain Rahi Pyar Ke* (1993) the humour — apart from that which arises out of the antics of the children — is anchored in the speech of three different linguistic groups — Tamil (spoken by the heroine and her father), Bihari-Hindi (spoken by the factory manager) and Sindhi-influenced Hindi spoken by a rival industrialist whose daughter wants to marry the hero. The treatment, however, in this film is benign.

This recent charting of linguistic differences in the way Hindi is spoken is also expressive of the silent struggles for political hegemony within the North Indian belt among various regional groups. That this is not too far-fetched a reading is borne out also by the thematic inscribing of these struggles in commercial films. *Tezaab,* for instance, has this sequence in the first segment of the film: Mahesh Deshmukh, who is now known as Munna, lives off the limits of the city and collects *hafta* (a weekly contribution from the residents of the locality for protection — against himself!) and gets into a fight with a Mukut Bihari, vanquishes him and shoves into a train compartment in which there are buffaloes. This is one of those segments that signify the narrative dispersal referred to earlier: Mukut Bihari does not feature again in the film and if a point had to be made about the power Munna wielded in the locality it could have been done just as well with any other villain. But pushing away Mukut Bihari with the buffaloes — an image of rural backwardness associated, in the minds of people, with a region like Bihar — from the limits of a metropolitan city has its own connotations. In fact, it fits in with the film's peculiar logic of targeting specific communities.

The spaces villains inhabit, too, have undergone drastic changes. The villain's world today is in the here and now. Earlier, the space he inhabited was an-other. Some amount of film time had to be spent in order to get to the villain's joint, at least the more spectacular of them. Reaching Gabbar Singh's hideout in the ravines in *Sholay* (1975) was itself a daunting task and several dangerous paths had to be traversed. Today's villain inhabits the same spaces that the other characters do. A few cuts are all that is needed to reach him.

It is only recently that the space of the family has emerged as the space of villainy. It is not as if members of the family — a father, or a brother, were earlier not villains. Their villainy, even when it was directed at family members, did not occur within the familial space, or was at least seen to be a violation of that space and the villainous family members — mostly vying for family money and property — were considered 'outsiders'. *Tezaab* changed this notion of the sanctity of the familial space. For the first time possibly in commercial cinema, a father forces his wife and daughter to dance, for the love of money, while he himself is idle. In *Angaar* (1993) a family of dons is shown to be sitting and eating food together and talking of their plans. Villains in preceding decades have never been shown in the intimate space of the family, particularly consuming food, which is an activity surrounded by an aura of sanctity. Even the ultimate sacred space — the space for prayer — is no longer exempt from the misdeeds of the villain. In *Divyashakti* (1993), Amrish Puri indulges in daily dialogues with God where he asks for forgiveness for his misdeeds. In one sequence he is so disgusted with himself that he actually shoots himself in the prayer-room. Since the bullet does not kill him, he tells God that he interprets this as a sign that He did not want him to die. It is only later we learn that the pistol had been so fixed by Amrish Puri himself that he could not have committed suicide with it! This villain has an unusual self-consciousness of himself as villain and Life, Death and God are reduced to a play, which goes far beyond the boundaries of merely lying to God or making false promises of repentance.

It is not just physical characteristics and the spaces villains are inscribed in that have changed. The very factors that contributed to villainy have changed. Villainy used to be associated with vice — a moral category. The villains were bosses of dens of vice — 'bad' characters and vamps hung around drinking, gambling, smoking. In fact, these dens included a vision of modernity: they were equipped or surrounded by technological gadgets, lifts, hotel lobbies, buttons to be pushed at crucial moments that would open and close doors, false floors, false walls, false ceilings. Today's villains inhabit indigenous body-building gyms (*akhadas*), homes realistically set up, or just walk in and out of spaces that the protagonists move in. If villainy was earlier tied up with the ethics of money, today it is tied up with the nexus of power, that extends to the police, law and governance of the State. Its tentacles reach out to these arms of justice. The villain or his boss attempting to escape in a helicopter in the penultimate sequence of the film was a pointer to the international connections of the criminal appropriate to an era when the 'Foreign Hand' was seen as a real threat to the stability of the country. But as we as a nation advance technologically, the paradox is that our villains seem to be able to dispense with technical gizmos. In fact, the new villain is totally an indigenous product. The less modern he is, the more involved he is in the corruption as it exists in the law-enforcing agencies of the state, the more convincing he is. One of the main reasons for the failure of the most expensive Hindi film ever made — *Roop ki Rani, Choron ka Raja* (1993) — can be traced to the outdated notion of villainy that the film tries to resurrect, replete with doors that open and close to facilitate the change of identity of the villain.

The Rise of the Community

The fight between good and evil is now fought out not only in the arena of the family but also in the arena of the community. This is a very subtle yet significant change in the topography of violence and is a contributing factor to the break-up of the persona. Earlier, the reference point was mainly the family; it was against this social unit that all values were tested. In *Deewar,* for instance, the argument for and against traversing a path that lay beyond the pale of law was to extend hegemony over the mother, to win her over to one's side. Several films today, notable among which are *Tezaab, Angaar* and *Gardish,* chart out the community spatially and as a force that serves as a testing ground for the protagonist to gauge his social self. There are many factors that go into the constituting of the community: a territory is marked out with a consequent understanding of insider/outsider and inclusion/intrusion. This territory is usually a set created in the spirit of a *chawl*; it normally consists of the fronts of houses, with streets, narrow lanes and squares playing a very important role in the lay of this territory. A few houses may be particularised, not as 'interiors' — that is, as spaces that can be entered and traversed from room to room, but as frontalities. Refer, for example, to Amrish Puri's house in the *chawl* in *Gardish.* The villain and hero fight for mastery over this space. The villain normally 'owns' this space, he collects *hafta* and enters and leaves it at will. Members of this community are engaged in non-intellectual activity: selling vegetables, betel, carrying loads on their heads, and washing, dyeing, drying clothes. Their main function, apart from going about their activity, is to be spectators to violence. This is an absolutely new and frightening aspect of 'mass' culture that cinema has internalised. The spectators are mute and will not interfere or intervene, or even give evidence later. They watch within the frame and magnify the terror of the violence that is being experienced. Their very passivity is a background against which physical violence stands out in stark contrast. One of the most devastating of such mass scenes in recent times has been in *Jigar* (1993) where the protagonist's sister is raped publicly in a square to teach the brother a lesson. The mother runs from pillar to post and even tries to enlist the help of a policeman nearby, but to no avail. The girl then publicly commits suicide. Rape has always been a staple ingredient of the villain's villainy, but it has always been committed as an act away from public gaze: in the privacy of a room, in the jungle but always in a *lonely, isolated* spot. The voyeuristic gaze in this particular instance also includes an incestuous one, since the brother is tied up at a height and has perforce to witness the rape and death of his sister.

The community gives a sense of belonging, but also imparts a sense of siege. It expresses all the anxieties of a middle class on the brink. The protagonist is, more often than not, the only educated member of this community. Even in the group of 'friends' he moves about, the others are semi-lumpen. That the protagonist today moves around in a group (Anil Kapoor is the quintessential mob-hero — refer, for example, to his role in *Ram Lakhan*, 1990) is yet another pointer to the collapse of the persona. A persona does not require male-bonding, particularly of the kind where the underprivileged instinctively move in a clannish group. It is not as if Amitabh Bachchan as the persona par excellence of the seventies and eighties did not have bonds with other male characters — as, for example, in *Sholay* where he and Dharamendra are partners in petty crimes. However, an aspect of the personality that he always cultivated was that of a loner, and a nonchalant one at that.

Dances, too, are choreographed differently, projecting the group as a force with aggressive intent. The dances now have less of folk/ classical pretensions and the emphasis is more on aerobics when the movements are not specifically sexual. The group is not conceived as 'extras' providing a background to the hero/heroine who is set off against it. The group now represents a *volume*, a *mass* of force that has to be reckoned with and the hero/heroine forms part of this aggressive mass. An aggressive sexuality is also in vogue. There have been several songs in recent times where the hero with a group of young men dances and sings to a woman who may be the heroine (as in *Dil*) or may not — as in the song 'Yeh ladki hai kya' in *Laadla*. The male members are almost teasing the girl in a derogatory manner. This is a disturbing phenomenon — even more so than songs whose lyrics capitalise on sexual innuendo. In recent times one of the most

Dharmendra and Amitabh Bachchan in *Sholay*, 1975, Ramesh Sippy

violent-in-intent vis-a-vis women is a song from a film called *Parwane* in which the hero with his band tells the girl that she takes too much pride in her youthfulness and that they would break her spirit: the last line of the refrain is 'Isko na kahin ka chodenge'. There are very few exceptions to these numbers: one of the notable ones being *Chaalbaaz* (1989) in which the heroine emerges onto a square after having had a few drinks at the bar. Here she accidently meets a band and a song bursts forth energising the space of the square. The group of band players have been benignly picturised and one or two of them are even etched out as characters, during the short temporal duration of the song — an achievement in itself.

The Politics of Songs

Melodies have made a comeback in commercial films, but with a difference. It was *Maine Pyar Kiya* that initiated the return to melodies in films. A record number of audio cassettes of this film were sold and the popularity of the songs outdid hits of the preceding decade. The film was produced by Rajshri Productions who were known for their small-budget, modest-return films based on rural, non-violent themes and featured new stars and a new director. The film became a super-hit, surpassing *Sholay*, mainly because of the popularity of the songs (of course, the theme of teen romance with a conflict between the rich and the poor, which was a welcome break from the long spate of violence-oriented films of that period, also contributed to this). This, more than any other recent film, can be called a 'musical' (though not in the Hollywood sense of the term). Set for most part in a large urban house of a well-to-do businessman, the songs are used to gently nudge along the narrative of love between a not-so-well-to-do girl from the countryside who is staying for a short while at the house and the America-returned son of the household. In a situation of spatial closure in the house, of hiding feelings from each other as well as from other members of the household, the songs serve as 'openings' from situations of spatial closure onto different emotional spaces as in the song 'Tu chal main ayee'.

Songs are now on priority in terms of picturisation and are released first. If they make it to the popularity charts on radio and television they ensure a better run for the film. Their becoming hits are now all the more important because of the redeployment of the value of the star system. Star names can no longer ensure the running of films as they did a decade ago. One, very often, has a feeling of *deja vu* when listening to new songs: there is a definite trend towards plagiarisation. Earlier popular western numbers were lifted; now even hits from the Hindi cinema of yesteryears are not safe from plunder. A change of note here, a chord there and a bit of re-orchestration, and a 'new' song is born. This is a tendency that began with Gulshan Kumar who, in the early eighties, worked his way through loopholes in the copyright law to re-orchestrate old hits and have them sung by young singers. The cassettes were low-priced and they sold well making him a mega millionaire in a short time. He, as Bhappi Lahiri had done on a smaller scale with regard to lifting western tunes, inaugurated a new era of 'freedom of conscience' in music: song-makers could now feel at liberty to pick their choice from hits of the past. There are several such instances: The recent chart buster 'Yeh kali kali ankhen' from *Baazigar* is a variation of 'Lehron pe lehar' from *Chhabili;* or a song that has become popular from *Gopi Kishen* 'Bati na bujha mujhe lagta hai darr' that is a mix of popular R.D. Burman numbers of the '70s 'Dum maro dum' and 'Sapna mera tut gaya'. Directors are cashing in on this nostalgia for songs of past. Film titles, too, evoke lines from well-known songs of yesteryears: *Eena, Meena, Deeka* ; *Pehla, Pehla Pyar*; *Hum Hain Rahi Pyar ke* and *Bol, Radha, Bol* are some examples.

Since songs are uncensored — only completed films are subject to censorship — and aired prior to the release of the film they can be as sexy as they like. Controversy, in fact, sometimes helps the film run. 'Choli ke peeche' from *Khalnayak* was a trendsetter in this respect, getting involved in a court case against alleged obscenity. The irony is that Subhash Ghai's own ouvre has songs with far greater sexual innuendo: refer to 'Saat saheliyaan khadi khadi' from *Vidhaata* or to 'Imli ka boota' in *Saudagar* picturised with the aging thespians Dilip Kumar and Raaj Kumar. This number opens up new avenues in notions of male bonding in Hindi commercial cinema: Dilip Kumar's actions and 'mudras' are more feminine of the two and at the end of the song the two actors are on the bed. The 'Sexy sexy' song from *Khuddaar* is another example of the ineffectivity of censorship. After the film was censored the wording was changed to 'Baby, baby' but in the minds of the audiences the song, that topped the charts on television for several weeks, will forever be associated with the word 'sexy'. The paradox is that the very mode of picturisation — the close-ups of Karishma Kapoor's bottom and her explicitly sexual gyrations — was not found worthy of censorship, all the more so in a film where much is made of the fact, thematically, of the villain and his cahoots who make a living by photographing girls (like the heroine) in compromising positions and blackmailing them!

What the songs have gained in terms of sexually explicit poses and movements and in vigour they have lost in emotional and rhythmic impact and thematic dovetailing. It is difficult nowadays to find a song that has the significance in narrative of, say, 'Pyar kiya to darna kya'; today the song is a packaged product that has been *inserted* into the film. Writers of songs too are explicit about sexual references: 'Gutar, gutar' from *Dalal* is just one recent exmple. 'Choli ke peeche' has ushered in another trend: that is of an arousal of an expectation of a sexual reference in the first two or three lines of the song and an 'innocent' end to the stanza. 'Subah ko leti hai, shyam ko leti hai' is a new song in the 'Choli ke peeche' mould. Another recent addition to song picturisation is the folksy orientation of music. Hindi films have in the past, too, drawn on folk tunes; but the representation has always been appropriate to the music. This is no longer so. Advertisements, particularly of leading textile mills, have for several years now combined a pseudo-folk ethos with ultra-modernism: a top model, exuding sophistication, for instance, will dance the *garba* very lightly. Several directors are following suit, drawing their images unabashedly from the advertisement world.

The Return of the Family

With the end of the notion of the unified will and intent that goes into the making of the persona has ended the fight between good and evil, in black and white terms, a characteristic of the melodramatic imagination. Several of the main and secondary characters are now subjected to many shades of differentiation. The family as the basic social unit was made up of members whose characters were in stark contrast to each other: one son could be 'good' (usually a police officer) and another 'bad' (a smuggler, maybe). The mother would represent, more often than not, the *insistence* on a life lived with moral values. The image of the mother has undergone sea change in direct proportion, it seems, to the viciousness of the villainy. Compare, for instance, the mother in *Deewar* who chooses to leave the elder son's house to stay with the younger son, a police officer, because she finds out that the elder works with smugglers, even though it is her first-born she loves more — to the mother in *Jigar* who thrashes her son, pronounced clinically dead, back to life, inciting him to take revenge for the public molestation of his sister which has led to her suicide. *Gardish*, in fact, has a variety of attitudes that police officers may have on display. There is the upright policeman who will brook no deviousness from anyone, even his own son (Amrish Puri, who plays the protagonist's father); there is Suresh Oberoi, a police officer, who too is upright but understands the importance of moulding rules to suit one's purposes, if it means getting the better of the enemy; there are the other police officers who are indifferent to their work and to the values involved in it....

Even the hero, in this new narrative, seems to act against his wishes. *He* does not want to be a criminal, but is constantly being pushed to the wall. This nuance of self-doubt, of aspiring to the security of a 'normal' middle-class life and instead getting criminalised, is rare if not non-existent in the cinema of the seventies and eighties. The hero in *Gardish* after every skirmish with the law insists he did not want to be a criminal. His law-abiding father, who has opposed him throughout, finally tells him when he protests (after killing the villain) that he had not wanted to be a murderer — that he had in fact accomplished what the police force could not do and should be proud of himself.

The family has returned with force as the central theme of commercial cinema. It is the attack on the family by the villain, a physical and disruptive invasion, that 'makes' the vigilante. If in the '70s the hero moved away from the family — as in the Amitabh Bachchan films — the protagonist is now definitely enmeshed in it, even when he is a rebel. Acts of violation committed against the father, sister or mother are what are responsible for the rebirth in violence of the hero. The social space that the protagonist of the films of the '50s and '60s entered, whether they dealt with romance or gangsterism, often rested on a tension between familial and social relationships. The family has for decades stood for positive moral values. In the films of the '70s, the family showed signs of breaking up, with the father getting lost either morally or physically. This loss defined the hero's being. Today it is the family and by extension the community, as *territorial* notions, that are to be defended at all cost. This is borne out by the kind of sets that the film is shot in. Two types predominate: the big mansion-like house, complete with the mystique of stairs and floors, or the house in the *chawls*. The family has assumed such thematic centrality that sometimes even treachery and villainy, particularly with regard to women, are measured by this yardstick (I have already referred to *Tezaab*). Even in a film with a 'nationalist' theme like *Roja* nearly half the film is devoted to the hero and heroine getting bound into a family relationship.

It is in this context that the hit of the late '80s *Phool aur Kaante* is interesting. It deals with the 'lost father' returning very decisively to reinstate himself emotionally and physically into the 'family'. This inversion of the popular '70s theme possibly was as much a factor in the film's success as the new type of violence it ushered in. Nageshwar Rao, the city's leading underworld don, kidnaps his own grandson to force his estranged son and daughter-in-law to come and live with him.

He is finally killed in an encounter with a rival gangster and his 'surrogate' son, who has been with him through thick and thin and expects to inherit the 'empire', and is now incensed at Rao's affection for his biological son. In the gangster films of the '70s it is the hero, who estranged from his real father, gravitates towards a surrogate one from the underworld.

Post-Sacred World

The breakdown of institutions is what is most characteristic of this *our* post-sacred world. The belief in the ability of institutions to dispense social justice was a given of the narrative of the cinema in the period immediately after independence. The man on the margins, the outcast, the vagabond, the petty criminal — all served to *affirm* the power of institutions, their ability to transform and mould character into positive social values. Whether it was Raj Kapoor with his diffused socialistic, globally benign outlook (as expressed in the 'Mera joota hai Japani' song in *Shri 420* or Dev Anand, a light and easy man on the margin, or Dilip Kumar, rhetorical, heavy, with a tragic vision of love — all these varied persona had the romantic element in-built strongly in them. One of the most significant examples of transformation in the cinema of this period is the song sequence in *Awara* (1951) where Raju, the protagonist, decides to stop being a criminal. It is a rare example where a song charts this change in mind and attitude and conjures up a religious-moral universe under the sway of love.

Sholay and *Deewar,* both released in 1975, represent the irreversible turn the narrative of commercial cinema took: the impossibility, or at any rate the difficulty, of being honest when the state and its law-enforcing agencies could not guarantee social justice, now suffused the logic of these narratives. It is highly symptomatic that in *Sholay* it is an *ex-police officer* and a *thakur* (one who wields power in the hierarchy of the village) who, convinced that he cannot mete out justice to the dacoit Gabbar Singh either through the police force to which he had belonged, or through the economic and social power he wielded in the village, hires petty criminals to catch the dacoit. From then to the current decade, the police officer, the lawyer, the judge and the minister have become central to the weaving of the logic of villainy in the narrative. It is this crisis of faith in institutions that has paradoxically led to the growing complexity of the representation of villainy: villainy today, as pointed out earlier, is no longer involved with an ethics of money or with innate evil. It has to do, of necessity, with being involved in a corrupt nexus of power that extends to the police force and often even to the law and those responsible for governance — the ministers. This accounts for the changing role of the penultimate narrative segment, where the police arrived — invariably late — to dispense Justice and restore Order. The police still arrive (though there are films in which they do not, and justice is dispensed by the warring parties themselves as in Vinod Chopra's *Parinda* (1988), but they no longer have the Order-restoring power that they had earlier (I have already referred to the end in *Gardish* and the dialogue between father and son). In consonance with this new status of villainy, we also have fewer final sequences where the villain tries to leave, presumably for some foreign land, in a helicopter. This is in keeping with the collapse of the threat of the Foreign Hand, integral to the nation's political perception of the forces out to destabilise it. The helicopter, the technological gadgets that were as integral a part of villainy as the vices — drinking, smoking and lust — were also possibly expressive of the distrust of a technological modernisation of a society still largely feudal and traditionalist. Our villains today are earthy, for most part uneducated, have little to do with technology and are often almost pious. In *Gardish*, the villain who had kidnapped the upright police officer's daughter assures him that he is not interested in women; he would, however, be forced to parade her naked if the protagonist, the girl's brother, did not give himself up to the villain. This is an absolute break from the villain of yore, who had of necessity to attempt at least one rape.

This brings us to the question of religion as a subtext of narratives. The protagonists often have names of gods (Jackie Shroff in *Gardish* is Shiva, one of the three most important Gods in Hindu mythology). Jackie Shroff and Anil Kapoor in *Ram Lakhan* play out roles of Ram and Lakshman (from the Indian epic *Ramayana*). Thematically too, mythical narratives are simulated: *Khalnayak,* also by Subhash Ghai, has references throughout to the triadic figures of Ram, Sita and Ravana (from the *Ramayana*). But the communalisation of politics and social being have made other insidious entries into the narratives of commercial cinema. That communities are now charted out, with a definite sense of siege, as well as of aggression, is symptomatic of the growing communalisation of the body politic. The villains often have Muslim names: in *Angaar*, the dons are a Khan family; in *Gardish* the villain is Billa Jalani, a Sindhi Muslim. *Tezaab* was a 'trail blazer' in this respect too: the villain is Lotia Pathan. Pathans have traditionally been friendly characters in Hindi cinema, an ideological off-shoot, possibly of the positive role they had played during the struggle for independence against the British. (One of the most popular Pathans in Hindi cinema was Pran in *Zanjeer*. An index of the importance of the character in the narrative scheme is whether he/she is accorded a song sequence or not! The song that Pran sang in this film 'Yaari hai iman, yaar meri zindagi' was a chartbuster of the year the film was released in. A recent film on a 'positive' Pathan from Afghanistan was *Khuda Gawah,* with Amitabh Bachchan in the lead.)

Tezaab not only ushered in the villainous Pathan, but also, more importantly, charted his community. The shift from the family as the basic social unit against which values were tested to the community, therefore, has ominous significance. It is a silent discourse on what constitutes the national.

Nationalism is very much on the agenda of commercial cinema in thematic terms, whether implicitly (through the delineation of community), or explicitly (where patriotism is combined with a peculiar regionalism). The success of films like *Roja* and *Tiranga* is evidence of the latter mode. The latter exhibits all the symptoms of narrative dispersal spoken of earlier. The love theme is almost non-existent; the film has several narrative threads and is indifferently made in terms of technique. But the film clicked because of its fervour against traitors to the nation including ministers, policemen and the arch villain, Gendaswamy, who kidnaps scientists to get them to activate missiles to blow up the country on Independence Day. (This is one of the few recent Hindi films that makes use of sets that evince 'Technology' — but the attempt is rather crude). Names in this film are politically significant. The villain is obviously a South Indian (Gendaswamy invokes a common name from the south like Gunduswamy). Its transformation to 'genda' (a rhinoceros) is itself telling: The term is often used in Hindi for people who are fat and dark. The two 'liberators' who are answerable only to the highest in the land are Commander Swaroop Singh (Raaj Kumar), a North Indian Thakur, and the policeman Shivajirao Wagle, a Maharashtrian (Nana Patekar). The tension between the north and south, particularly as it is evinced in communal ideologies of the right, is in evidence here. Mani Ratnam's *Roja*, on the other hand, is the South's answer to this problematic of nationalism! Technically slick, it makes effective use of contrasts and combines a 'documentary' form of realism (the capture of the dreaded Kashmiri militant in the 'prologue' of the film) and extreme 'unrealism' (the attempts of the wife to get her husband released by enlisting the help of an army official and a reluctant priest!). The first half of the film is enmeshed in a story of love and misunderstanding, the family and the benign community. The second which deals with the kidnapping of the engineer by militants and escape is riven with improbable moments. The militant chief is shown to be capable of compassion. This delineation of

Shakti, 1982, Ramesh Sippy
Raakhee, Amitabh Bachchan and Dilip Kumar

character in fact serves to highlight the chasm between religions: when the Indian flag is being burnt the hero rushes to save it; but the chief who is doing *namaz* does not interfere one way or the other in the ensuing fight between the terrorists and the protagonist. The insidious point about religion being ultimately sacrosanct for a particular community and hence their being 'different' is made forcefully.

This crisis of institutions, their break-up, the communalisation and community-isation of politics, the regional tensions, all of this is reflected, even if in a distorted way, in the narratives of commercial cinema. In the films of the preceding decade, particularly those featuring Amitabh Bachchan, the emphasis was on the search for, or rejection of, a father, the symbol of Order, and the adopting of a surrogate father, who would operate outside the pale of law (*Deewar, Trishul, Laawaris, Shakti*, to name a few). In the films of this decade, the protagonist is seen as a liberator of his community, a passive community.... This, commercial cinema seems to state, is the only mode of social being for a middle class being pushed to the margins.

It is in this context that a film like Kundan Shah's *Kabhi Haan, Kabhi Naa* (1993) is a welcome break. It practises a deliberate 'innocentisation' (I am coining this word for the lack of a better one) of the subversive elements of commercial cinema predominant today: the don who is a romantic 'softie' at heart, and whose only villainy within the precincts of the film is in procuring a false marksheet for the hero, the no-good protagonist who can make up the most impossible lies to win the triangular contest of love, the joyous, non-aggressive picturisation of songs, the gentle humour and the very invoking of a (stereo) typical Christian family in Goa...

Note: This is an expanded version of the article that appeared in *Cinemaya* 23 (Spring 1994)

15

Who is the Bad Guy? Commercial Cinema in the South

— *K Hariharan*

In whatever manner the camera decides to gaze there is only one way that cinema and its spectator can see the world — as the image that brings the total reality on the same plane. Whether the filmmaker likes it or not, in the words of Sam Rohdie, 'Movies are not two-tiered, mass culture masking minority culture, but multi-tiered whose levels are expressed at a single level — primarily that of concrete visual images'. The realism of the image is actual, physical, inescapable; and all film stylistics merely dull or enhance the 'real sensous world'. Either they stir the audience or bore them to tears or sometimes do a little of both! The sum total of the audience manage to see everything in one film, if they get to see the film at all.

In the process of 'mistaking the trees for the forest', as quoted by Andrew Sarris, socio-moralistic forces have of course always shunned the sensous (commercial-exploitative) in preference to a pseudo intellectual plane of cognition (art-autueristic) until the 'flood of time' wiped away such distinctions. John Ford, Alfred Hitchcock, Chaplin, Kurosawa, Guru Dutt have all been knighted as 'classic' filmmakers, a delayed reflection of a sick intelligentsia who decide to make a fetish of all that they were told to keep away from when they were young and spirited.

If there is one film that can nail '1994' to a Tamilian's memory wall, it will be *Kadhalan* (The Lover) directed by Shankar and produced by K.T. Kunjumon. It will be remembered as the film which the 'intelligentsia' in South India would like to forget about and as the pulp fiction which every distributor wished he had the rights to but ended up waging an open war with its producer who decided to keep the booty all to himself.

Written off as a sure failure in its first two weeks by forecasters, *Kadhalan* literally rapped its way to the box-office all over South India and slaughtered every competitor in its path. Highly stylized and yet sensuous, the form manages to develop a 'totem pole' from several levels of contemporary South India today. The on-going battle between the Governor of Tamil Nadu and its Chief Minister; the complex culture war between 'good' traditional classical dance and 'bad' western rap gyrations as seen in every household; the breaking down of the 'generation gap' where elders now appear more spoilt and corrupted than the younger generation; the sudden spurt in the presence of technological gadgets as manifested in the film by its plethora of special effects, pyrotechnics in some superb imagery by cameraman Jeeva and its highly innovative music track by A.R. Rehman.

Certainly *Kadhalan* does manage to pack in a lot of the contemporary, as it develops a familar lovelorn mythology, of a scraggy 'Krishna' (played by a fabulous rap dance artiste called Prabhu Deva, who is also aware that he cannot act!) who is prepared to do anything, even something as bizarre as eating cockroaches, to get his politically correct and emotionally distraught 'Radha'!

This film is not going to win any national award but two other films made by previous national award winners Sethumadhavan and Bharatirajaa leave a lot to be desired. Sethumadhavan's *Nammavar* (Our Man) and Bharatirajaa's *Karuthamma* also try to pick up threads from contemporary subjects but get lost in trying to be serious and preachy about their opinions about it.

Sethumadhavan's film stars Kamalahasan as a goody young yuppie professor who wants to change the hearts and minds of his students in a dreary college campus and ends up giving sermons even when beaten up by rowdy students. Although the film tries to portray the megastar like a common man, the idiom is one of a battle between 'good and evil' which is essentially melodramatic and heroic. Trying to roll films like *To Sir with Love*, *Sister Act* and *Dead Poets Society* into one, it ends up looking like a dismembered idea scrap book.

Even in a film released earlier this year *Mahanadhi* Kamalahasan seems to be displaying a fetish for a Christlike martyrdom, the 'simple' man victimised in his search for a simpler 'honest' lifestyle. All said and done he remains one of the most consummate artistes in India today. His fascination for the epic form has produced memorable films like *Nayakan* and *Thevar Magan* but in *Mahanadhi* he is completely without any proper supporting cast, an essential prerequisite for an epic drama. The 'down to earth' hero has his limitations too when he decides to carry the whole on his shoulders as an actor.

Kamalahasan in Mani Ratnam's *Nayakan*, 1987

Karuthamma picks up female infanticide to be used purely as a starter and then goes on to narrate a conventional love story where the hero is trapped in a love triangle — with one girl that he loves and another girl who loves him. The two girls are sisters who have escaped being poisoned to death at childbirth. The horror of female infanticide remains a mere topic for the first and the last reel as Bharatirajaa continues in his usual style replete with irritating jumpcuts, inept handling of amateur actors and absurd slogans all through. Casting non-actors for the sake of 'new faces' had some relevance fifty years ago and for a different kind of cinema. But stories like *Karuthamma* need powerful artistes and any amount of voicing over and rapid cutting is not going to detract the attention of the audience from poor performances.

At the end of every year, when you look back at the events in the Tamil film industry, you can smell a depression swelling up, the earth cracking, and imminent disaster written all over. You wonder how this *idli-vada* industry is ever going to survive; with so many flops, just two 'heroes', too many vamps, and the video/cable gangs waiting like hyenas to scavenge on the remains of a season's kill. With liberalisation and a number of tax reforms the film industry, which used to be the black money man's haven, is slowly being shunned like the plague and most financiers are now training their sights on the real industrial world. Film releases dropped drastically to around a mere 70 in 1994 and the average first run for a film is just about 3 weeks. Where are the films?

Apart from the few films mentioned above, there were others like *Veera* (Rajnikanth), *Veetila Visheshanga* (Bhagyaraj), *Amaithipadai* (Satyaraj), *Magalir Mattum* (Revathi) released to great expectations, but excited only a few. Certainly all of them do need major sociological analysis. It is worthwhile looking beyond the silver screen for some explanations to understand this unhappy situation.

The frustration of the thousands of people in this film capital of the South employed somehow or other in the film trade can be imagined. The first and easiest thing to do is to put the blame for this pathetic situation on the 'quality' of films that are churned out. But how different are they from the films made in the mid-'80s which could be called the peak point in film production?

Certainly, the films made today look better, sound much better but they seem to leave a bitter taste at the end of it all. Does it mean that the audiences are not really getting what they want? Are the filmmakers confused or careless in judging audience reactions? Or is the total environment becoming non-conducive to a healthy interaction between filmmakers and their viewers? Are there no more stories emanating from the social milieu for filmmakers to fabricate their myths upon? Or are the dividing lines between 'good' and 'bad' in social values slowly fading out, making it difficult for scriptwriters to work out their archetypes? When you look at it in this perspective the answer seems to lie somewhere in this complex maze.

This blurring seems to be a phenomenon happening to filmmakers all over the country and the world resulting in major archetypal shift and the emergence of the 'flawed yet valiant hero', the bizarre comic villain, the 'seductive good heroine', etc. More than half the film gets filled with lengthy and elaborate song, dance and fight sequences as a strategy to avoid proper characterisation, thus distracting the viewer to a non-narrative, purely voyeuristic preoccupation. Most Indian mainstream films seem to have fallen into this 'musico-emotional' form and the trap obviously shows in the sudden rise in sales of music cassettes and the domination of the song/music director.

This trend is certainly represented in Tamil cinema by the highly imaginative A.R. Rehman whose music can easily compare with any international 'rock-rap' standard. But Tamil cinema has always been unique and different in its evolution of archetypes. Writers who believed that they had to be 'socially responsible', actors who practised what they preached on the screen and audiences who thought the world of their film heroes and heroines. It was one grand 'cine-lila'.

Being born in a highly volatile culturo-linguistic atmosphere, the Tamil cinema always carried on its shoulder the cross of 'giving a message' (*karuthu*) social purpose and good morals. The Dravidian secessionist movements of the '30s fused with the nationalist spirit and gave rise to a kind chauvinistic awareness which was to be carried right through the '70s. Even after the retirement of stalwarts like M.G.R. and Sivaji Ganesan, the mantle was carried on by the post-Emergency generation ushering in a fresh supply of energy to an anaemic Tamil film movement with directors like Bharati Rajaa, Bhagyaraj, T. Rajendar and Mani Ratnam.

But the second generation could not counter the larger feeling of disillusionment with the political process which was so strong among the people. The 'cine-lila' was betrayed by the very entertainers they had trusted so much. Rampant corruption and an unscrupulous administration system was something which the masses never dreamt would ever touch the soil of Tamil Nadu. For example, thanks to the compounding tax structure for cinema theatres in the *mofussil* areas, for example, theatre owners have now resorted to selling tickets at black-market prices across the counter itself. Today, an audience bent double under this corrupt system has accepted it without complaint and has even accepted such a practice as normal. It is a virtual free-for-all at the moment, with producers and distributors waging a relentless war with each other on how to share the spoils.

In the midst of all this the censor board imposed a fresh set of guidelines to curb the growth of sex and violence. The clean-up campaign ruled that films should not show ministers, Members of Parliament or of the State Legislative Assemblies, senior officials of the judiciary, military, the police and the administrative secretariat as 'bad' people. The censor board hereby decrees that they are all 'good'! The other impositions of decency are such as to embarrass any intelligent Indian citizen. Producers fret and fume at the harassment, even carry out a *morcha* to register their right to freedom of (s)expression, but when you finally see the film, your eyes pop out. Was the censor board sleeping or was the 'greasing' so strong that the scenes just slipped by? Just go and see a recent blockbuster called *Kadhalan* (The Lover) and one will realise the absolute mockery at work again.

When a viewer had become party to a corrupt system at large, what kind of roles (*vesham*) is the filmmaker going to give to his protagonist and antagonist?

16

A Bit of Song and Dance

— Partha Chatterjee

WATCHING SONG AND dance sequences from contemporary Bombay films is both painful and amusing. Painful because song, that once reigned supreme in this cinema, is now only programmed sound made barely acceptable by the miracle of modern electronics and meant only to be danced to; amusing because what passes for dance is a very creditable imitation of St. Vitus' Dance. In the good old days, dancing was not considered a masculine pursuit and the likes of Dilip Kumar, Dev Anand and Motilal, of an earlier generation, would have taken exception to the very suggestion that they did more than a few rudimentary steps in their films as an accompaniment to the songs they picturised. Stars were gauged by their ability to make the songs come alive on the screen so that they became a part of the viewers' psyche — thus guaranteeing financial success. Through sheer force of personality the stars of those times could mime a whole *antara* or verse on camera, without falling back on quick changes of camera angles and trickeries of fast cutting.

The art of song picturisation is unique to Indian cinema. It reached its apogee in the '40s and '50s when masters like Jayant Desai, Zia Sarhady, Master Bhagwan, Mehboob Khan, Guru Dutt, Bimal Roy and Raj Kapoor actually used the song within the film to pass on the real intent of their scripts through telegraphic audio-visual signs to the viewer. We do not know if such guerilla tactics became necessary when the producer-distributor-exhibitor nexus became all powerful after the Second World War with large amounts of black money suddenly flowing into film production, upsetting the economics of established studios where popular films with a certain aesthetic quality were produced. The rise of the war profiteer-turned-producer, alongside the advent of the traditional money-lender as film financier, no doubt adversely affected the quality of film production in India, particularly Bombay, the home of the Hindi film after the partition of the sub-continent in 1947. They were only concerned with quick and substantial returns on their investment and would go to any lengths to achieve the aim — including corrupting public taste. It is all the more commendable that ingenious filmmakers found both an artistic solution to their dilemma and a means to placate their conscience on the issue of the larger compromise on the script and the final film, through the uplifting art of song-picturisation.

In the beginning, that is, around 1933-34, allowing for two or three years for people to discover the potential of sound after 1931 — including song and its picturisation — the song very naturally became an integral part of the script. Any New Theatres film from the period will bear this out, although the picturisation remained quite straightforward. The real possibilities of song-picturisation became apparent in Fatehlal and Damle's *Sant Tukaram* produced by Prabhat Studio, Pune, in 1936. Vishnupant Pagnis played the title role and song in his voice 'Panduranga Mani...Dhyaani...Gyaani' (The dark god Panduranga is aware...meditative...omniscent). The picturisation was direct, spartan. The niceties of rhythm created through camera movement, frequent change of angle and clever variations of pace in the cutting were eschewed in favour of an austere, almost unflinching camera gaze, that in a very few shots 'took in' the song and assimilated within its meagre framework an aesthetic (of song picturisation and, in our Indian context, of cinema itself) that would, by its very transparence, make enormous demands on the talent and integrity of the director. Variations on this approach continued to exist through the golden period of the Hindustani film song and picturisation that lasted from the late 1930s to the early 1960s, and in which period enormous strides in real and cosmetic technique were made.

The song in Indian films was quite different in its use and purpose from the song in the Hollywood film, where it normally served the purpose of taking the story forward and/or helped, on rare occasions, to bring out certain traits in the singer's character unknown to the audience. This is best illustrated by Ava Gardner singing 'Coming through the Rye', an old Irish love song, in John Ford's superb entertainment *Mogambo* — a non-musical adventure yarn. Gardner, supposedly a peripatetic nightclub singer and tramp suddenly expresses her desire and anxiety in song when the man she loves (Clark Gable) is seen in the company (off-screen) with another woman (Grace Kelly) who covets him despite being happily married. Similarly songs in *bonafide* musicals like *Roberta, Flying Down to Rio* (starring the legendary duo of Fred Astaire and Ginger Rogers); *Gilda* (with Rita Hayworth erotically singing *'Put the blame on me, boys'; Band Wagon* (also featuring Astaire) and *An American in Paris* (dancer — choreographer Gene Kelly's gorgeous, if a trifle self-indulgent-exploration in song and dance of an artist-in-search-of-the-self!) always served to take the story forward and occasionally reveal character.

Perhaps only in *Lili* does the use of song approximate the aesthetic of film(ed) song in Indian films. The story set on a carnival is about the unspoken love of a handicapped puppetteer (Mel Ferrer) for Lili (a child-like beauty played by Leslie Caron) who also works there, despises him and is foolishly attracted to a rogue. The lyrics: *'The song of love is a sad song'* are poignantly brought alive by the rendering (not by the puppetteer!) and help to underline and enunciate the meaning of the film's theme and also mirror the feelings of the hapless puppetteer for Lili — who will, in a fairy-tale like transformation, discover the generous heart that beats inside the ravaged body of her true suitor.

To come back to song-picturisation in Hindustani or Hindwi films, it would also be necessary to include dance which formed a part of our cultural life in pre-industrial India and till much later. Men and women danced together in rural and tribal India during seasonal festivals. It was with the building of towns and cities that such communal celebrations involving men and women stopped. Cinema with its ability to go back and forth in time revived these social customs in the stories that were filmed. Dances in the early films were rudimentary and the movements derived from folk dances (often as remembered by urbanised filmmakers from their childhood in rural India) with a smattering of Kathak grammar gleaned from out-of-work dancers from the smaller, money-less feudal courts on the verge of collapse in the 1930s, who were trying desperately to get a foothold in the burgeoning film industry. The choreographer, who was to rise to such (undeserved) power in the late 1970s to the present times, had not come into existence. Although he was there as a behind-the-scenes figure he was not acknowledged in the screen credits for a long time.

Dance was not a requisite of song-picturisation in those days and was of minor importance — unlike the Hollywood musicals that revolved mainly around dance and had songs only in rare cases like the films starring Judy Garland to augment its charm. The stars in Indian films were not required to dance really, but to move with a passable sense of rhythm when required; the song sans dance was the dominant feature of Indian films including the ones in Hindustani.

Jayant Desai from Bombay was the first master of song picturisation in Hindustani to be sure and possibly in Indian films as well. His mastery over the language of cinema in its range and subtlety easily surpassed the accomplishments of V. Shantaram under the aegis of Prabhat Talkies, Pune, and P.C. Barua operating from New Theatres, Calcutta. Desai's musical *Tansen* (directed for Ranjit Movietone, Bombay) has an all-emcompasing loveliness unapproached by any Indian film, including the successes Fatehlal and Damle, Shantaram, Barua, Nitin Bose, Hem Chandra Chandra and Debaki Kumar Bose. In its lighting, composition, camera-movement, set-design, mise-en-scène, cutting and music, *Tansen* is a truly sophisticated achievement. Made in 1943, it wears its years lightly and still enthralls the viewer. K.L. Saigal's superb singing, very well supported by Khursheed's, the charisma of their individual presence, and of them together easily cuts through the barriers of race, language, culture and time. *Tansen* is a film of its time and for times to come.

Remarkable is the first meeting between Tani (Khursheed), the peasant woman, and the young Tansen (K.L. Saigal) just returned from his music Ustad's home after years of dutiful riyaaz (practice) under his guidance. Tansen is introduced as a great classical singer to the disbelieving Tani who promptly puts his singing to the test by asking him to call back (in song) her cattle that have strayed far afield. Tansen, with all his knowledge and musical prowess, tries and fails and Tani succeeds singing a simple folk-song 'Aao Gauri, Aao Shyama, Aao'. (Come back Gauri, Come back Shyama... Do come back). The astonishment on Tansen's face, the matter-of-fact girlish triumph in Tani's eyes, the cows coming back as if on cue add up to a perfect bucolic comedy and enhance our respect for Tansen, as he comes across as a very nice, vulnerable human being, and also for the director for showing such good sense. All this is accomplished mostly with simple, beautifully framed fixed shots with subtly varying depths-of-field; slow, quiet camera movement through tracking sideways and diagonally and fine blending of studio settings with outdoor locations and the lighting that emanates from each. Sensitive use of black-and-white, aided by high-quality processing in the laboratory, made this possible. It is impossible to film this song in colour, use zoom lenses and achieve the same magical effect.

Tansen had two other songs where Jayant Desai showed his high artistic calibre. The first: 'More Baalepan ke saathi, chaela bhool jaiyona' (Companion of my tender years, don't forget me !) a duet sung by Saigal and Khursheed with dignity and great depth of feeling and composed by Khemchand Prakash (as with all the songs in the films) with consummate skill and understanding of things supra-musical. Tani's request to her sweetheart Tansen leaving for Akbar's royal court not to forget her and by implication retain his musical and personal integrity, is filmed largely in medium and mid-close shots cut to a gentle but insistent rhythm to heighten the meaning or, really, the message of the song as embodied in the tune and the words.

'Barso re' (Rain in torrents, you clouds) is the other song based on the Raga Malhar that with controlled intensity brings out with economy and telling detail the necessity of pouring rain to cool the near fatal heat generated in Tansen's body after he has been tricked into singing 'Jagmag jagmag diya jalao' (Light the bright lamps) in Raga Deepak that, according to legend, sets aflame both the singer and objects within close proximity when rendered correctly. The Malhar brings in its wake rain to cool, cleanse and ultimately save Tansen the court musician's body and soul and unite it in flesh and spirit with his guiding force Tani who is, in every sense, of this earth. The filming of this song is done with surprising restraint and implied power. The vision of the director here and in the other songs is meant to approximate ordinary, normal vision, that is, the image seen through a 50 mm lens. Jayant Desai's cinematic technique was as refined as it was elegant and helped to set standards for others to aspire to.

The film song in Bombay and the rest of India had begun to mirror life and the fantasy that grew out of it. A little before *Tansen* the camera had ventured briefly outdoors to film a song called 'Sawan ke nazare hain' (The splendours of the monsoons are here) in *Khazanchi*, made in Lahore by Dalsukh M. Pancholi. The melody that had the encompassing sweep of showers flung about by wayward winds, was sung with a tinge of girlish eroticism by young Shamshad Begum, the discovery of Master Ghulam Haider responsible for the masterly compositions in the film. The daring was in photographing a group of girls led by the heroine riding bicycles across a rural landscape in so cleverly choreographed formations as to simulate spontaneity. By marshalling every trick of editing, sound and image at their disposal, the editor and the director made the audience believe that it was the most natural thing in the world for the girls to burst into song! The filming, in retrospect, was quite simple.

Song-picturisation in the next few years was to get progressively more intricate as the varied subterranean messages contained in the songs themselves. A notable exception was the songs in the films of Master Bhagwan, a portly, slightly inebriated comedian who danced with surprising rhythmic ease. His films were a pot-pourri of song-dance-romance and a simple desire to caress the moon. In *Albela,* an all-time favourite of filmgoers, his clarity of vision helped to express complex ideas simply. It is quite likely that he himself was blissfully unaware of the hidden implications behind his artistic intentions since he was wary of theorising and bookish learning.

Four songs need to be seen with passion and intelligence in order to partake of the genuine pleasure they offer while telling us about the many themes that are there within this simple story of a young dreamer's hope of being a celebrated singer-composer. The most compelling one comes quite early in the film. The impecunious musician (Bhagwan) fantasises about his chaste inamorata (Geeta Bali) who is also his inspiration and the keeper of his conscience.

The cardboard cutout set of different clocks with moveable parts to facilitate smooth camera choreography speaks volumes for the director's ingenuity in turning a budgetary restriction to his advantage. While Bhagwan and Geeta Bali sing to each other 'Meri dil ki ghari kare tik tik tik' (My heart goes tick! tick! tick!) as an illustration of their dream(s) of the future the dark night outside bears witness to their aspiration. Lata Mangeshkar in a rare moment of self-awareness sings with amazing adult perception and in spirited counterpoint Chitalkar (C. Ramchandra, the composer of the marvellous songs in *Albela*) responds with considerable insight and wit. Geeta Bali, by being in turn witty and emotional — in a creative sense — on screen provokes a musical acknowledgement of her screen personality by Lata

Mangeshkar; similarly Bhagwan's laid back yet assured and ethically informed film-presence is befittingly etched by Chitalkar. The idealist seekers looked upon as a fool by most of the world guided by the moral and erotic impulse of his lady love goes out to find happiness and after many travails succeeds. This simple faith in the purity of the human spirit made the film a great hit with the post-Bengal famine, post-partition audiences battered by fate and man's bestiality in the face of economic greed.

The second song — 'Shaam dhale khirki tale' (Don't you whistle under my window while the sun goes down) despite its implied sexuality or perhaps because of it has an undeniable appeal that is enhanced by its child-like innocence and a touch of Chaplinesque pathos. Photographed and edited with exemplary grace and simplicity stands for Geeta Bali's feminity rendered plastic by her face and body catching and reflecting the myriad fleeting moods suggested by the lyrics and Bhagwan's lovely, slow floating dance movements activating and confirming her actions.

'Dheere se aaja ri akhiyan mein' (Come softly in my dreams) the third song from the film performs different but vital functions germane to the story on the three occasions it is used. The first time the lullaby (rendered by the young Lata Mangeshkar in dulcet tones under the loving guidance of C. Ramchandra) has Bhagwan's little sister as the point of focus. She sings her restless brother to sleep; he, who has not yet had the opportunity to prove his very real musical talent to a large audience. The second time the song is rendered even more significant because the story has progressed. The hero has found an avenue to express himself in a musical-theatre company along with his lady love. But there is opposition from within. Lata Mangeshkar sings for Geeta Bali too but her delivery is different. Ramchandra gets her to express more adult perceptions than he did when she sang for Bhagwan's sister, whose prayer is that her brother be soothed and calmed in sleep and spared the anxieties of life. The second time around he is in the thick of life's battle, Geeta Bali in song clearly wants him to find himself after the welcome respite of sleep. The third and final time the melody is rendered by Chitalkar (actually a part of the composer's full name) as an offering of thanks on a moonlight drive, after he and his loved ones (father, sister and sweetheart) have been severely tested by fate — mercifully for the last time in the film.

The fourth song 'Bholi soorat dil ke khote, naam bade aur darshan chhote' (With guileless face and perfidious heart!) also has enthusiastic if slightly clumsy dancing in it and is a critique of existing social mores that stifle decency and originality and uphold dishonesty and mediocrity. The two aspiring musical artists — Geeta Bali and Bhagwan — find unscrupulous rivals styming their best laid plans.

The entire artistic thrust of *Albela* is contained in these four songs and have us believe that the rest of the script and film are necessary formalities that are there to ensure the film's commercial release. Although this film was for ninety per cent of its length well paced and more than adequately structured songs played a pivotal role in energising and illuminating its major concerns namely the artist's responsibility towards himself and his role in society in a given historical moment. Bhagwan, to be sure, would have been flattered and startled by so much attention; he would have laughed everything away by saying — 'Oh ! we made the film to have some fun'.

Dance till then had not become a necessary ingredient in song picturisation. A star did not have to gyrate at the drop or non-drop of a hat to borrow a (James) Thurberism. Amongst the actresses Vyjayanthimala and later Waheeda Rehman were accomplished dancers trained in Bharatanatyam, so were the Travancore sisters Padmini and Ragini who had joined films to improve their fortunes. But these actresses were rarely called upon to perform full throttle like the present-day stars who have to twist, turn and contort themselves into impossible shapes all the time. As a matter of fact their psycho-histories are largely dominated by greedy parents and clueless, unsightly choreographers!

The man who started it all was Shammi Kapoor, matinee idol Raj Kapoor's younger brother, a man of intemperate habits and a constant weight problem who, having failed as a leading man, made a successful comeback by deftly manoeuvring his ever-increasing bulk to various dance beats, much to the delight of the young. He also shrewdly promoted to his benefit the image of the cave man whom women found irresistible from 'Tumsa nahin dekha' (Never seen anyone like you) under Nasir Hussain's careful tutelage to films like *Professor, Junglee*, *Janwar*, *Raj Kumar,* and others! Shammi Kapoor through unintentional absorption, brought the ethos of black rock 'n' roll as exemplified by the bump and grind sexuality of artists from the

American south like Little Richard, Bo Didley, Chuck Berry and others, along with their extremely famous white imitator Elvis Presley, to Bombay films; to this he added a dash of Punjabi bhangra and made a lasting contribution (if not an entirely constructive one) to the dance vocabulary of the Bombay film choreographers.

Disillusion started setting in a decade after Independence. The economy failed to take off despite the fond hopes of its custodians and the literacy programme moved much too slowly to make a dent on the body politie of firmly entrenched conservatism. Cherished values of filial piety and selfless friendship began to disappear quickly. Along with jingoism hypocrisy in personal and professional life slowly but surely took over. These negative developments, and the values they perpetuated willy-nilly found their way into popular films — more readily into dance choreography that stayed in memory because of its visual content rather than banal dialogue that was soon forgotten like the announcements in a railway station drowned in a sea of accompanying noises. Dance or, shall one, say spasmodic shudders gradually took over the function of the song over the last two and a half decades as melody slowly but surely went into oblivion, thanks to the ever-increasing noise in our daily lives as a result of a so-called technological revolution that has played havoc with the environment, raised the level of atmospheric pollution to alarming levels and in general desensitised people at least in the urban and suburban areas where fumes from the lead-based petrol used throughout India have definitely affected the brains of millions of people.

In the days of hope, immediately after Independence to another fifteen years on, melody was king in film song, and its picturisation considered a sacred duty by directors of talent. Among those who understood the value of song picturisation was Mehboob Khan — an unlettered man but nonetheless a filmmaker by compulsion. In *Andaaz* (Mehboob's only attempt at trying to understand the world of the sophisticates) he brought his native skill and elemental passion into play to picturise the song 'Hum aaj kahin dil kho baithe' (I lost my heart today) sung hauntingly by Mukesh for the rising tragic hero Dilip Kumar. Low-key, contrastive lighting to heighten chiaroscuro, white curtains billowing in the wind suggesting myriad psychological undertones, a dark baby-grand piano and the deceptive face of Dilip Kumar — transparent and opaque at the same time — all added up to

Raj Kapoor, Nargis and Dilip Kumar
in *Andaaz*, Mehboob Khan, 1949

'announce and predict' the tragic outcome of the film twenty minutes after its beginning.

Mehboob was capable of calling a cheating accountant a Freud instead of a fraud, in a burst of mercurial temper. He was also equipped to get past intellectual and emotional facades, despite his lack of formal education, more quickly than most directors — including Ritwik Ghatak and G. Aravindan, two great artists who followed him. His filming of O! Mere Devta.... in *Amar* is quite astonishing. Nimmi, a peasant girl, dances in honour of Dilip Kumar, a lawyer, and Madhubala, his betrothed. Everything is chaste and proper until a certain point in the song when she walks or rather floats backwards on beat. Suddenly a kinetic force envelopes the image and in a flash her longing for Dilip

Kumar comes to the surface and also prepares the viewer for the moment when he in a moment of elemental recklessness will seduce her and get her with child. Thus in an instant cinematic revelation, Mehboob playing story-teller and sooth-sayer simultaneously predicts an impending event and sets the stage for it.

In contrast Bimal Roy's approach to filmmaking and song picturisation was a shade too modest: as if he echoed simultaneously the sentiments of the great Scottish director Alexander McKendrick ('Trust the tale, not the teller') and the major English novelist E.M. Forster ('The author should be everywhere implicit but nowhere in evidence'). Roy too was interested in people and their behaviour when alone, in a group, or with someone they cared deeply about. He was fed up with the subterfuges he had to rig up as a cameraman in New Theatres, Calcutta. On becoming a director he turned instead for inspiration to neo-realist masterpieces from Italy including Vittorio De Sica's *Bicycle Thieves*. His approach to song picturisation was matter-of-fact, austere, but behind this mask of near-Gandhian rectitude was a deeply romantic temperament. For example, the song 'Gore gore haathon mein mehndi lagaike' (Fair hands... on them bridal henna) from the film *Parineeta* (1951-52) is rich in social and psychological reverberations in its content but spare and grand in its presentation. The sensitive mixture of the song in the background and the overpowering emotion only hinted at in the sparse dialogue between the lovers (Meena Kumari and Ashok Kumar) has a parallel in the song 'Priya praan kathore...' an adaptation of a traditional composition from *Nagarik* made in 1952 by Ritvik Ghatak, a future associate of Bimal Roy. Ghatak was to distinguish himself as a director very soon.

Do Bigha Zamin (1953), a deeply-felt naturalist essay on the migration of the poor peasantry to the cities only to have their hopes dashed, also had very moving songs composed by Salil Chowdhury, a former member of IPTA (Indian People's Theatre Association), the cultural wing of the Communist Party of India. With his penchant for accurately depicting the needs of the script Bimal Roy visualised songs like 'Hariyala sawan dhol bajata ayaa' (Nature responds in myriad hues of green) with its message of hope, infectious rhythm and melody; 'Mausam beeta jaaye' (time flies), a plaintive reminder of our mortality, and 'Aaja ri aa nindiya tu aa', a lullaby of great poignance and intensity, through which he tried to convey the desire for a happy future for his protagonists.

His cutting on the off-beat in 'Mitwa naahin aaye' in *Devdas* (1955) has to be seen to be believed. The song in its photographed form is meant to suggest many things and it does. Devdas's alienation from his world after losing his beloved Paro in marriage to another; the hide-bound society that makes this possible; the indifferent landscape on a hot afternoon that bears witness to Devdas, gun in hand, searching in utter futility for birds to shoot! Talat Mahmood's soulful *legato* makes the tragedy vivid, uniting all its different strands in its course. It is the guile in the song's tempo which makes this possible.

He photographed nature with the same respect and directness that he did everything else. The sensitivity with which he captured landscapes in the 1958 fantasy romance *Madhumati* (scripted by Ritwik Ghatak) in black and white is yet to be equalled. Despite the use of the 25 mm wide angle lens in many key song and dance sequences there is virtually no distortion in the image and the psychological impact of the story on the viewer is considerable. Bimal Roy and his excellent cameraman Dilip Gupta achieved the impossible of making a ghost story seem a romantically tenable proposition. What was said of Roberto Rosselini can also be said of Bimal Roy — his frames were beautiful because they were right.

The possibility of achieving beauty and knowledge through austerity and sacrifice as embodied in Fatehlal and Damle's *Sant Tukaram* had its adherents in the early '50s as well. Two films, quite different in content — *Sangdil* and *Daag* — come close to achieving the aesthetic goals of Tukaram. In the first film *Sangdil* the director, R. C. Talwar, picturises the duet 'Dil mein sama gaye sajan' (You melt into my heart, beloved) with deceptive simplicity and skill, though at first glance it appears to be amateurish. The camera pans over an almost scrawny landscape with peasants in the foreground, accompanied by Lata Mangeshkar's slow enunciation of Rajendra Krishan's words over Sajjad's melody. Then the camera takes in Madhubala and Dilip Kumar in mid-long shot sitting amongst rocks and shrubs in three-quarter profile in the morning light. The song begins and Madhubala very quickly builds such a nimbus around everything, (with some help from Dilip Kumar) that when it comes to an end we are mesmerised. The camera appears to have been transfixed (to exaggerate a bit) in the same place as us, the viewers! Through the song both Madhubala and

Dilip Kumar appear to become a part of nature.

In Amiya Chakravarti's *Daag* the anguish of the alcoholic toy-maker (Dilip Kumar) is vividly brought alive as he sings 'Aye mere dil kahin aur chal' (Come let's go elsewhere dear heart) walking briskly across an unyielding landscape. The song is shot in extreme long, long, mid-long and mid shots. The director very grudgingly allows the camera to catch the actor in a fleeting mid-close shot once. The spiritual despair of a good man held prisoner by an addiction could have scarcely been filmed with greater empathy. A curious dichotomy is achieved in the picturisation as if to mirror ordinary people's ambivalent attitude towards helping alcoholics in a positive way. Nature, photographed in semi-silhouette, seems to embrace and reject the hapless toy-maker at one and the same time.

Raj Kapoor and Guru Dutt were the two flamboyant filmmakers of Hindi cinema. Raj Kapoor's personality was like his work — an open book. Guru Dutt on the other hand conveyed different impressions to different people. His work like his life was contradictory and brought to surface his world-weariness and his love of life in turns. From the beginning of his career Raj Kapoor had shown a love for marrying movement (dance) with song. 'Mudh mudh ke naa dekh, mudh mudh ke...' (Stop ! don't look over your shoulder) from *Shree 420* (1955) is a marvellous example of song and dance coming together in unison to echo the sentiments of the unprincipled go-getters participating in the revelry and, who shall embroil and try to ruin for their own ends the innocent hero (Raj Kapoor) who is, through his actions and ideas, the symbol of everyman. The song is picturised with a verve and mastery seldom seen on the screen. The mise-en-scéne (inclusive of lighting, camera, editing, sets, music, and acting) is absolutely dazzling. Nothing that Raj Kapoor did before or after approaches this song.

In altogether a different vein is 'Pyaar hua iqraar hua hai' (Why is the heart afraid, when love has come) from the same film. *Shree 420* shot at night in pelting rain, on a ninety-foot studio set made up to look like a quiet part of suburban Bombay of the time, this song in its recorded as well as picturised form has a most affecting lyricism. It affirms the life force and celebrates man's desire to marry, have a family and live on through his progeny. Never has sex in our films been treated with such sublime beauty. Nargis, one of the most charismatic actresses in Indian films, appears both ethereal and divine in a few close shots and evokes the image of the traditional Bengali clay idol of the goddess Durga. It is immaterial whether this visual effect is achieved through accident or design; the film and the viewer are enriched by it.

Guru Dutt Padukone is the most problematic of all Indian filmmakers. At its best his work seems to suggest a genius amongst philistines; he was after all forced to work amongst the crass financiers of Bombay. His gift for song picturisation and visual condensation surpassed that of his contemporaries and quite certainly his successors. Most of the songs he picturised were perfect little films in themselves: ambiguous yet pregnant with meaning, utterly transparent but with hidden nuances. His most famous song picturisation is of 'Waqt ne kiya kya haseen sitam...' (Beguiling were the tricks played by time) from *Kaagaz ke Phool* (1959), a work about the rise and fall of a director. In retrospect, Kaifi Azmi's lyrics and S.D. Burman's score fuse into Geeta Dutt's voice to emerge as a cry from the heart and a prophesy of doom. The filming in black and white and cinemascope on a set lit to suggest absolute desolation (of the soul) exhausts all superlatives for it has a ring of truth that cannot be ignored. The tragic love between the director/svengali (Guru Dutt) and his Trilby (Waheeda Rehman) is literally played out before our eyes with remarkable restraint and absolute fidelity.

Guru Dutt and Waheeda Rehman in
Guru Dutt's *Kaagaz ke Phool*, 1959

In complete contrast is a duet from the comedy *Mr. and Mrs. 55* (1955) — 'Chal diye banda nawaz' (After tugging at my heartstrings) picturised on Madhubala and Guru Dutt. Filmed with great abandon the song fairly bubbles over with fun and mischief. Madhubala's beauty and effervescent presence complements the comic qualities mingled with the ever romantic in the song and, in the process, draws out the sunnier side of the twenty-nine-year-old Guru Dutt's personality. To think that *Kagaz ke Phool* was only four years away and the manic depression that was to ultimately destroy him in 1964 would set in then, is a deeply saddening thought. At his best Guru Dutt's technique had the resource of an Edgar G. Ulmer and the elegance of a Max Ophuls. His song picturisation too had the quality of blending the erotic with the spiritual to achieve a delectable flavour that was completely his own.

After the passing of Bimal Roy and Guru Dutt and the eclipse of Raj Kapoor the one director who began to be noticed for his singular song-picturisations and well-scripted films was Vijay 'Goldie' Anand, kid brother of director Chetan Anand and matinee idol Dev Anand. His films were robust, humorous and a trifle sentimental at the same time. He showed a marked aptitude for blending the poetic with the commonsensical in his song-picturisations. A natural sense of rhythm and a flair for re-creating through the camera lens beautiful equivalents of what the human eye could comfortably see or do made him an exceptional craftsman surpassing on many occasions the old Czech master of classical technique — Otakar Vavra. When still in his middle twenties his visualisation of a song from the film *Kala Bazar* (1960) — 'Rim jhim ke tarane leke aaye barsaat' (Pitter patter falls the rain...) showed his originality. The film's two lead characters, Dev Anand and Waheeda Rehman, meet at a bus stop in the rain after a fairly long time. They share an umbrella walking to her home, remembering. Past experiences with each other in different seasons and locations come flooding back and the images of happily shared memories are superimposed (in the best tradition of European romanticism as exemplified in the work of Dimitri Kirsanov in the late '20s and early '30s) over flowing shots of the present in the monsoon. The choice of Geeta Dutt and Mohammad Rafi for the playback voices for Waheeda Rehman and Dev Anand is apt because they musically confirm the visual states of their hearts and minds so eloquently captured by the director.

All the songs cited so far had been shot in black and white. Vijay Anand is the only Indian director apart from Kamal Amrohi (two songs from whose *magnum opus Pakeezah* have a patrician grandeur) to have used colour successfully in photographing songs. In *Tere Mere*

Meena Kumari in *Pakeezah*, 1972, Kamal Amrohi

Sapne (Our dreams, 1973), he uses colour and movement gorgeously while filming the duet 'Hey maine qasam li' (I resolve again). The bicycle ride through a road flanked on either side by fields of bright poppies is amongst the loveliest moments in Indian cinema, as all of nature seems to clasp to her bosom the loving couple who pledge eternal loyalty to each other. Earlier in *Guide* also in colour, his song picturisation showed rare dynamism, particularly in the outdoor sequences. 'Tere mere sapne ab ek rang hain' (Your dreams are mine...) is a fine example of expressing the feelings in the hearts of the protagonists (Dev Anand and Waheeda Rehman) by placing them in the lap of fecund, lush green nature. Subtle, gentle dolly shots cut to a deceptive editing rhythm make for the magic. Vijay Anand, like most of his illustrious predecessors, with the exception of Raj Kapoor, felt ill-at-ease in including dance in his films unless the script called for it. This may have been because the dance directors, as the choreographers were then known, tended to usurp the director's privileges behind the camera whenever dance had to be filmed. The practice continues to this day. It would have been anathema to Vijay Anand who would rather call the shots literally.

Although many classical dancers, including the legendary Kathak maestro from Rampur, Acchan Maharaj, tried their hand at choreography in films, Uday Shankar, the cosmopolitan showman, seems to be the real inspiration for most choreographers. Shankar had imperiously appropriated movements and gestures from classical dance forms like Bharatnatyam, Kuchipudi, Kathakali, Kathak and also from folk dances he had seen as a child to create a pastiche ballet-style that made him a rage in Europe in the 1930s. Even classically trained choreographers like Sohanlal and Surya Kumari fell back upon the clichés that Uday Shankar's dance language had to offer. Only Gopi Krishna, Kathak virtuoso and choreographer of 800 films, tried valiantly to stick to his classical and folk roots — after making many compromises. Viyjay-Oscar in the '70s and '80s created a highly vulgarised style that made them very popular in the changing times. Saroj Khan went several steps forward and absorbed the overtly sexual movements from break and flash dance, and Chinni Prakash followed suit — with a little more skill and judgement. The net result was the banishment of the song as a perfect balance between melody and rhythm.

The startling near-pornographic audio-visual experience that song-picturisation has become today in the mid-1990s with tunes lifted en-masse from western pop sources (Michael Jackson of 'crotch-clutch' fame being a great favourite) and words to match, not to forget the frantic, carnal dance movement, has its roots in the late 1960s. Bela Bose in a film called *Fareb* did a finely executed dance with body breaks, shudders, quivers anticipating the choreography of the '90s film, suggesting the sexual act. The picturisation got past the stringent Censor Board of the time because the innocent manner in which the song was sung (in playback) and also the fixed, silly grin on ex-policeman-turned-actor Dev Kumar's face — frequently in frame — that inadvertently served to deflect the message so clearly present in the tall, shapely dancer's movements.

Within a couple of years Raj Kapoor in *Mera Naam Joker* tried to 'open things up' for Indian or Bombay filmmakers by photographing a scene, sans song or dance, in which actress Padmini was seen pressing her nude body against a translucent white, sheet much to the titillation of the audience. The outright libertine intent of this scene must be measured against the chaste eroticism of a similar moment from a much older film — Zia Sarhadi's *Footpath* in which Meena Kumari warbles, while bathing, *Sama hai pyaara pyaara ye ruth hai suhana.* Khayyam's exquisite composition has done full justice to Asha Bhosle's playback singing.

Sensuality and eroticism have always been a part of Indian films but they have been presented with grace and style by filmmakers like Kidar Sharma, Mehboob Khan, Zia Sarhadi, Guru Dutt and Vijay Anand. The lesser elements in the film community had correctly gauged the fast deteriorating public taste and inserted into their films titillating song and dance numbers picturised on vamps who, by virtue of their screen role, could get away with a fair amount of mischief ! Helen was the most successful of the tribe. An exceptional dancer, she might have found fame and fortune with Martha Graham's modern dance troupe or as a soloist in the nightclubs of Copacabana had her life taken a different course. She danced in various styles (that were in themselves a mish-mash) in Bombay films. From 'Mera naam Chin Chin Choo', a lovely, snappy come-on in *Howrah Bridge* in the late 1950s to 'Aaja aaja mein hun pyaar tera' in *Teesri Manzil* ten years later with its stop time precision in playback and dancing, and the mid-1970s knock-out, 'Mehbooba-o-Mehbooba' in *Sholay*, Helen proved conclusively that in her chosen field she was unrivalled, equal to the task of bearing an entire film's load of sensuality in song, dance and often dialogue on her shoulders as the vamp. The heroine(s) then were expected to preserve their chastity and look to the hero for protection and the stork for salvation !

Mumtaz followed on Helen's heels and did honour to her calling. Beginning as an extra she fought her way up to lead roles in stunt films, often with champion wrestler Dara Singh. From there she graduated to vamp roles in big-budget films because of her very attractive looks, curvacious figure and fine sense of rhythm. She finally made her mark as a leading lady of substance. In her days as 'the wicked one' she made her presence felt as no one had done since

Helen. 'Yeh hai reshmi zulfon ka andhera na ghabraiye' in *Mere Sanam*, composed by the irrepressible O.P. Nayyar on the comeback trail twenty-eight years ago and picturised on her, had a zing and amorous ardour not seen in a very long time. But neither song nor picturisation had anything in them that could be called obscene. Her winning screen presence and talent as a dancer were put to test in 'Dharka to hoga dil zaroor' (Your heart must have gone thud...) from a pot-boiler policier called *C.I.D. 999*. O.P. Nayyar with his flair for tricky time signatures and darting melodic lines composed a song that would try the skills of a seasoned dancer.

The scripts of even a few years later had neatly compartmentalised roles to deal with the forces with good or evil. When Bindu coaxed her amazon frame successfully to obey the dictates of R. D. Burman's superbly syncopated — 'Mera naam hai Shabnam' (My name is Shabnam) from *Kati Patang* in the mid '70s, it was the beginning of the end. Although she danced with energy, humour and healthy sexuality with Vijay Anand on the bonnet of a limousine during the picturisation of 'Main jo hota ek toota tara teri raaton ka...' (What if I were a broken star in the firmament of your nights); in Chupa Rustom by herself with great fervour in *Do Raaste* and in over a hundred other films, her screen personality (as built up the script writers and directors at hand) often spilled over onto the vulgar.

By the time Madhuri Dixit came to play the lead in *Tezaab* in the mid-'80s the vamp had been banished from Indian films. The heroine, in her new incarnation, was a over-sexed Jackie Collins-type woman crossed with pseudo Kung-fu training, a murderous, vengeful temperament to go with it, and the hypocritcal eloquence of the religio-social feminist crusader found only in India. Madhuri's innocence, vulnerability and girlish sexuality all come out as she slides, writhes, slithers, grimaces and shakes to the inane lyrics of 'Ek do teen' (One, two, three) set to a quickly forgettable tune. The story, need one add, was of great violence, where arson, rape and murder were looked at, so to say, from a mole's point of view by director N. Chandra. After this film, the Bombay product, became more and more violent and vulgar under the pretext of reflecting contemporary reality !!

Just into the '90s *Hum* was made and a song in it: 'Jumma Jumma lele chumma' (A kiss ! Friday upon every Friday) was picturised with hitherto unprecedented vulgarity on screen. Kimi Katkar is seen flaunting her explosive sexuality in a Flamenco dancer's garb (*à la* Ava Gardner from the 1954 master work — *The Barefoot Contessa*). She dances, or tries to, on a make-shift stage, egged on by a group of louts led by the one and only Amitabh Bachchan. At a crucial point she is sprayed with water from a hose-pipe. The suggestion of sexual intercourse is clear even to the most obtuse viewer in the theatre !

The Song/s have reached a nadir from where it will take a long time to come back. A hammering, insistent beat with raucous vocals given some shape and form by the miraculous forces of modern electronics during recording has resulted in a sound that is accepted as music in the absence of the genuine article — and to it is added doggerel of the worst kind. The final product for some inexplicable reason is called a song — a film song. Its musical qualities are of no consequence either to the director of the film or its veiwer; it is a sound to which the over-sexed young hero and heroine will dance — or is it gyrate? They look like boy and girl despite being in their twenties. Dilip Kumar, Dev Anand, Raj Kapoor and Guru Dutt looked like men at a comparable age. Madhubala, Nargis, Nalini Jaywant, Meena Kumari, Geeta Bali, Nutan and Waheeda Rehman looked and behaved like full-grown women by the time they got out of their teens! — O ! Tempora O ! Mores ! etc.

Today's urban Indian boy and girl, as exemplified by the lead pair in any Bombay film, know all about sex and the 'kick' it gives but do they know anything about its psychological, spiritual implications? It seems not judging by the animal-like grunts coming out of lax, hanging jaws in a face out which stare glassy eyes as the body threatens to collapse under the wanton animal energy summoned by the song (why not call it dance data?) on the sound track.

When Madhuri Dixit, hips swaying seductively, responded with inviting yet shy eyes to 'Choli ke peechey kya hai' (What's inside my blouse?) in Subhash Ghai's *Khalnayak* in 1992 there was a furore in Parliament that guaranteed the film's great success at the box-office ! The song, for all its implied vulgarity, is picturised with a fair degree of craftsmanship, and is remarkably tame in comparison to the hell-bent-for-leather efforts of the most successful star pair today — Govinda and Karishma Kapoor who together have brought the Indian cinema to the limits of vulgarity and are helping to consolidate its position.

Govinda and Karishma Kapoor in full flow can adversely affect the libido of an ailing pigeon, leave alone human beings. The coital heaves and hos suggested in their dance movements in *Beta* are at first shocking and then downright obscene. There is something frantic and marionette-like in their dancing. What takes the cake is the duo's 'Sarkai leyo khatiya' (Move the bed over) from *Raja Babu*. Clothed and groomed after a fashion, the two go through all the motions of the sexual act except actually committing it physically. It is difficult to imagine a more obscene song-picturisation. Govinda, son of the very talented, light-classical singer of yesteryear Nirmala Arun, has seen too much struggle to bother about how he earns his money.

Karishma Kapoor, the famous Raj Kapoor's granddaughter, quotes an old Punjabi saying in self-defence — "You must never refuse any work that comes your way !" What she seems to forget is that what was true of Punjab under British rule at the turn of the century is no longer so because the context has changed. Quoting today the old saying to justify one's working in dubious conditions is like avoiding out of fear an important responsibility.

Govinda and Karishma Kapoor are not the only ones among the Bombay stars to toe the line of least resistance. Among the others are Akshay Kumar and Kajol — both young and impressionable. 'Dekho dekho aayee barkha ki jhadi' (There ! There comes a splash of rain) picturised on them in *Yeh Dillagi* (an unforgiveable adaptation of Billy Wilder's immortal *Sabrina*), is soft pornography photographed and edited by a competent advertising filmmaker. The girl, sighing as she moves her legs seated on the ground with the rain falling on her, sends an absolutely clear message.

The dominant force in Indian films is money, and in Bombay its colour is mostly black. It has the power — or so it seems — to change the aesthetics of cinema for the worse and even get the very people responsible to justify their act! It is time to turn the tide and once more make films with abiding human values and lilting melodies.

Song and not dance was the mainstay of the Hindustani or Hindwi film in its days of glory. It is difficult to think of a really memorable film without melodious songs filmed befittingly. The song and all its components — words, tune, rendering and recording become the most expressive single element in our films. And in the finished film its visual expression became crucial to not only its commercial success but also in establishing its artistic credibility. Now that the film song has gone into a decline one can pray for its triumphant return by quoting from Master Ghulam Haider's 1945 masterpiece in *Humayun* — 'Naina bhar aaye neer, mere hathile raja aaja, aaja' (Mine eyes well up with tears...return, my haughty king, to thine domain).

17

When Stars Become Tsars

— Dr. S Krishnaswamy

Introduction

The Indian Parliament was discussing the abolition of privy purses to the erstwhile rulers of over 500 states. By way of an oversimplified backgrounder on the issue, one would say that these states were ruled by Maharajas and Nawabs until 1947 while the rest of the Indian sub-continent was directly under the British Crown. However, by an agreement between the British rulers and these princely states, these states were effectively under British control. A nascent emerging Union of India, in a remarkably swift diplomatic operation, integrated all these five hundred-odd princely states into the Union of India offering hefty privy purses, payable annually without tax, to the rulers of these states and their descendants, in return for their gesture of voluntarily abdicating their political authority and merging with the Indian Union. However, there was persistent, popular pressure, in particular from the leftist forces, to abolish this special status and the privy purses for all the erstwhile rulers by a constitutional amendment. The princes argued that it would be unethical to unilaterally cancel a binding legal agreement without the consent of the beneficiaries. Our concern in this article is not the arguments and counter-arguments for and against the abolition of the purses. This is merely to emphasise that one film actor eventually decided the turn of events from the day the matter came up for vote in Parliament. S.S. Rajendran, Member of Parliament representing the DMK party in Tamilnadu, is alleged to have had an upset stomach at the time the privy purses amendment came for vote. Although there was a whip issued by all political parties to ensure that every MP was present, Mr. Rajendran was the one absentee. The constitutional amendment was lost for want of one vote. The DMK had pledged itself to support the amendment. If only Mr. Rajendran did not have his alleged diarrhoea the political history of India from then on may have been different. Angered by the fact that her amendment was defeated in Parliament, Mrs. Indira Gandhi dissolved Parliament and ordered fresh elections. She returned to power with greater majority and successfully put through her amendment abolishing privy purses. It is indeed difficult to prove, disprove or substantiate that the powerful lobby of Maharajas had enough resources to ensure that one MP could absent himself and they probably found that the weakest element in the entire elected House of Parliament was a film actor. Those were the nascent days of film personalities in Indian politics. In the Lok Sabha today, we have over a dozen MPs who faced cameras and lights with make-up until the other day. They represent every major political party in the country. They come from films as well as television.

Early Days

The first Indian silent feature film was made in 1913. The first Indian talkie was produced in 1931. Indian films inherited two traditions: first, the tradition of silent cinema representing a new international non-verbal visual style of presentation; secondly, the style of the ancient Sanskrit theatre going back to a tradition of over 2000 years. Indian cinema also acquired two Indian characteristics; first the subject-matter of a large percentage of films was drawn from Indian mythology. Secondly, a cinematic style became unique to India in the sense of being a combination of opera, ballet and drama fused with a new technology. The Indian film became insular, in terms of its style, from the rest of the world. I strongly believe that the Indian film became a political tool by just being Indian. The strict political censorship enforced by the British administration could only prevent direct propaganda on the Indian screen. However, the Indian film as a whole had a subliminal value, projecting Indian mythology, glorifying ancient Indian themes, resurrecting in the native memory of a people, their glorious past and tradition. In addition to these films based on old Indian themes, there were several films which portrayed contemporary Indian life. Some of these films began to tackle social problems such as removal of caste and untouchability, widow re-marriage, women's emancipation in general, presenting a new cosmopolitan environment and encouraging individual liberty. Occasionally, despite strict censorship, filmmakers indulged in introducing political imagery. Several of them introduced images of the freedom movement, such as the spinning wheel, the Congress party flag, or the portraits of national leaders like Gandhi and Nehru. These images were incidentally introduced in the backdrop of films. But they underlined the fact that the central characters of the film identified themselves with nationalist aspiration. Some film makers went several steps ahead, and introduced direct political ideas in their films. The most important of these films with direct political messages during the era of the freedom struggle were K. Subrahmanyam's *Thyaga Bhoomi* in Tamil and V. Shantaram's *Dr. Kotnis ki Amar Kahani* in Hindi. Anyone specifically interested in this subject may like to see my compilation titled *Through a Different Lens*, a 20-minute documentary on the politically significant films of India before Indian independence.

After independence, certain circumstances developed which resulted in special relationship between cinema and politics in the state of Tamilnadu more than anywhere else. There were at the time of independence (there are even today) more cinema houses in Tamilnadu than in any other state in the country. According to statistics of the early 1970s, Tamilnadu had one cinema house for over 30,000 people, as against Uttar Pradesh which had one cinema house for over 200,000 people.

If we look at the motivations of all the communicators in all the media available, there were not many people interested in communicating with the rural man in India. The print media was least interested in the rural man, because of the high rate of illiteracy in the rural areas of India. Hence, journalism became almost exclusively urban-oriented. The advertising man was (in the first three decades after independence) not interested in the rural man, because the Indian farmer had no purchasing power. Television was just starting out. There were thus only three kinds of communicators who were interested in the rural man. First, the radio broadcaster: his time, however, was more devoted to music and developmental communication. Any political message was inhibited by the fact that broadcasting is a government-owned medium in India. We are left with two others: politicians and filmmakers. To the politician, the rural man was a prospective client — a consumer, because he had a vote in his hand. To the filmmaker, the rural man was an important client, for his profits came from the rural cinemas. Thus, the only two kinds of communicators for whom the rural man became important in the first three decades of independence were the politician and the feature filmmaker. This combination became more valid for Tamilnadu than elsewhere, because of the deep penetration of cinema in that state. An unintended social engineering began to take place, with tremendous political consequences. In fact, the relationship between cinema and politics in Tamilnadu since independence has been such that it is difficult to discuss the history of either, without bringing in the relationship between the two.

Stars Turn to Politics in Tamilnadu

Annadurai, the founder of the Dravida Munnetra Kazhagam (DMK) was himself a dramatist and one-time actor, who began to write screenplays in Tamil, more or less from the time he founded the party in 1949. Annaduari attracted a few other writers and a large number of performing talents to the fold of DMK. Several symbols of the DMK movements, such as its party colours and its party election symbol, as well as dialogue either directly or obliquely referring to the domination of the north over the south, and the need to liberate the Tamils were all introduced in feature films, which were otherwise mediocre, if not aesthetically sub-standard, with no specific political themes as such. Throughout these years, film actors played a role in party rallies. These rallies were usually advertised as occasions for meeting film stars.

The star who dominated the whole movement was M.G. Ramachandran. MGR, as he came to be worshipped by his fans, began to specialise in stunt roles. He appeared as folk hero, battling royal usurpers and their henchmen, fighting against incredible odds. Critics considered the stories purely escapist. However, Ramachandran expressed the opinion that they were not escapist. To his public, he explained that the long entrenched leadership in New Delhi had become a species of royalty and the folk hero symbolised the southern Dravidian struggling against odds to establish justice. In fact Ramachandran had begun to perform one archetypal role in all his films. In the nearly two hundred films in which he played the hero's role, he had met with death only in one film, in the early 1950s, now long forgotten. In all the other films, he was the idomitable and indefatigable hero. The dream image that he built for himself in the sub-conscious mind of the people is unique. In simple terms, the character which he always performed combined the strength of a Hercules, with the love and compassion of a Jesus Christ and the modernity of a James Bond. Girls always fell in love with him in every film and it was up to him to respond. Yet his character could be indentified with the conservative morality of Rama, the Indian mythical hero. While building up a specific conscious screen image, in his real life, MGR took an active part in the politics of the DMK evolving an extraordinary public relations organisation. MGR fan clubs all over Tamilnadu became active units of the political party, with much publicised charities from his personal income for such causes as relief after flood and other natural calamities. Gradually, a stage was reached by which the on-screen image and the off-screen image of the man merged, creating a fusion of dream and reality, fact and fiction, transcending the elements of entertainment and culture, to perform major political role in real life. Looking at the DMK popularity based on fan rallies of film stars, respected Congress leader and Chief Minister of Tamilnadu, K. Kamaraj asked in the late 1950s, "How can there be a government by mountebanks?" The contempt rallied the screen world to the DMK. Indian film tradition has been closely meshed with a hero-villian pantheon. Most of MGR's films had villains and prominent among the villains was M.R. Radha. Shortly before the 1967 Tamilnadu state elections, Radha visited MGR, who was then a candidate for the state legislature representing DMK. Radha was alleged to have shot MGR in the neck, and then shot himself. This was an extraordinary event, when common film situations were re-enacted in real life. Radha was convicted and sentenced to jail. MGR was critically wounded and hospitalised. As millions of fans prayed for him all over Tamilnadu and thousands of them arrived in the hospital compound, Ramachandran survived reaffirming his demi-God image, as he had survived any number of attacks of the same "villain' in any number of films.

The DMK used posters with MGR in bandages as part of the election campaign. The elections to sate legislatures all over India came up with a confused political picture, with no party obtaining clear majorities in several states. In sharp contrast, the DMK swept to power in Tamilnadu, capturing a majority of seats in the legislature, defeating the Congress party. Having moved from the region to the centre-stage of national politics as President of the Indian National Congress, Kamaraj had to accept defeat at the hands of the mountebanks. Annadurai was sworn in as Chief Minister. Within a few years of the death of this founder of the party, the DMK broke up. MGR founded his own party called Anna DMK which he later renamed All-India Anna DMK to remove the parochial stigma. He proclaimed "Annaism" as his central doctrine in memory of Annadurai. MGR defined Annaism as "the best of capitalism combined with the best of communism". The large electorate was in any case not interested in the subtle details of ideology. They would back their hero. In 1977, MGR became Chief Minister and held the position until his death in 1989.

N. T. Rama Rao in *Mahamantri Timmarusu*, 1962

The success of one film personality in the political realm provoked several regional and national film actors and actresses to enter politics.

Meanwile in Andhra Pradesh N.T. Rama Rao performed an extraordinary feat. It is doubtful if any other political party in any part of the world equals the record of coming to power in a state within one hundred days from the date of formation. That is what Rama Rao's Telugu Desam party achieved. NTR had performed the roles of the mythological Gods, Rama and Krishna, in over 100 feature films. In another extraordinary merger of the image with the man, people deified him as the Omnipotent, the Ominiscient and Omnipresent. He has the distinction again of being the first film actor in the world for whom a temple was built in his lifetime on the outskirts of the port city of Vishakapatnam. It is a temple complete in all respects including a sanctum sanctorum with a statue of Rama Rao, with priests performing pujas and offering camphor. The temple existed before NTR started his political party. To his credit, it must be admitted that he used a politically opportune time to whip up regional sentiments and dislodge the party in power in the state in one of its weakest moments. While MGR remained in power for the rest of his life, NTR was voted out, but he had emerged on to the national political scene as the Chairman of the National Front which helped to instal V.P. Singh as Prime Minister. The media projected NTR as a potential candidate for the highest office of the land. Unlike MGR who had a parallel political background throughout his film career, NTR was a newcomer to politics but was able to perform the magic of converting his fan-following into a vote bank. Major political parties across the country began to feel it was essential to have film personalities on their side. With the success of the mythological *Ramayana* on the small screen in India, three artistes of the serial got elected from different political parties to the Lok Sabha.

Technologically, Indian cinema has progressed in leaps and bounds. Cinematographers, sound recordists and editors have contributed a lot more to the art of cinema in the last four decades. Colour and the use of colour has added glamour on the one hand, and a touch of physical reality on the other. But more often than not, the writers and directors of Indian cinema have created characters who are not only colourless but even devoid of any shade of grey. With honourable exceptions, the characters remain black and white — heroes and villains. They are crude archetypes, far removed from human reality, perhaps betraying a lack of grey matter to create that shade.

A parallel cinema movement developed in India, with a few inspiring names hitting the headlines of world cinema. The committed filmmaker made films for an elitist audience with much vigour and aesthetic vitality. Beauty and elegance of form married to a mature reflection of the reality of contemporary Indian society became the hallmarks of this parallel cinema. Even though several of these films were in black and white, their characters were of many colours and shades. However, to face a bitter truth, they have hardly had any impact on a majority of the Indian audience. This is not to find fault with the parallel cinema, but to dramatise its limitations against the onslaught of the devastating predominance of the Indian commercial film milieu, and its political nexus.

Since Independence Indian politics has been very substantially personality-oriented where every major political party is largely dependent on the charisma and public image of its individual leaders rather than on any ideology, economic or political philosophy. It is elementary that personalities can be built up due in large measure to their visibility. The hero-villain mesh of Indian cinema fits in ideally with the cult-dominated Indian politics to promote such personalities. Thus, the style of the popular commercial Indian cinema is perfectly suited to the style of functioning of the Indian political party, with common trappings, covering stars and Tsars.

Film stars of more than one generation have been closely associated with the politcial leadership at New Delhi. Nargis, a household name in many nations besides India (in particular the former Soviet bloc countries, co-starring with Raj Kapoor) became a close friend of Mrs. Indira Gandhi and was nominated a member of the Rajya Sabha (Upper House of Parliament). Her husband Sunil Dutt, also a celebrated star of the Hindi cinema, contested as a Congress candidate from Bombay and continues to be a Member of the Lok Sabha (Lower House of Parliament). While other film stars such as Rajesh Khanna, Shatrughan Sinha, Vyjayantimala Bali have entered the corridors of Parliament and have rubbed shoulders with the major political leadership, the person who came closest to power on the national scene is Amitabh Bachchan, the super-hero of the Hindi cinema. A childhood friend of Rajiv Gandhi, he burnt his fingers when he won an election to Parliament as a member of the Congress Party, and quickly withdrew from the political scene.

The archetypal hero of the Indian screen had, in the meantime, undergone some changes. The brutality of the hero in terms of violence became increasingly indistinguishable from that of the dark villain. Indian cinema had to mirror a growing insensitivity to crime and a cynicism born out of things that were going wrong in society

President Sukarno of Indonesia had once told a surprised Hollywood audience, "You are co-revolutionaries in post-war Asia". He went on to explain to an audience which was convinced that they had no role beyond entertainment: "By showing ordinary people refrigerators and automobiles and the good things of life, you have removed the contentment and apathy of our masses". In short, there was a graph of rising expectations motivating people to be ambitious and contributing thereby to a revolution.

If Indian cinema of the pre-Independence era in a selective way remained nationalistic, the cinema of the first thirty years after Independence contributed to a growing discontent without ever glorifying work ethics. For comparison not for emulation, the Soviet cinema of that period was loaded with motivational factors for work ethics. You almost felt that the girl fell in love with the tractor, rather than the tractor driver. This writer remembers a film in which the heroine changes her allegiance to a man who wins the Lenin Prize for higher productivity, discarding her lover who did not do equally well in the factory. On the contrary, the Indian hero hardly had any occupation except to sing a duet song in between shaving and eating. All social conflicts, whenever they were portrayed, were resolved in inter-personal terms of a relationship between a hero and heroine. A glaring example is one in which the labour dispute of a major factory is resolved because the union leader falls in love with the owner's daughter. The screen image of the hero always showed him as succeeding by an enormous factor of luck, maybe a lottery, or

Jayalalitha as a film star

marriage to a rich girl, after overcoming formidable opposition from the rich in-laws, or suddenly discovering that the 'poor' hero was indeed the heir to a major empire of which he was not aware. Indian cinema in that period hardly ever dramatised man's realtionship to nature or his struggle as a working human being, but constantly overlaid his struggle to win over villainy and win the hand of his sweetheart. The off-screen image of the Indian hero was that of a young man who walked to the studios and was driven out of the gate by the watchman, until one day suddenly, Dame Luck smiled on him and he became a super star with the luxuries that go with that status. Again, the on-screen and off-screen images merged in the public mind.

Hence, the revolution of rising expectations was turning into a revolution of rising frustrations nation-wide. The dreams were not fulfilled. The romance did not translate from dream to reality and the new hero of the last twenty years reflects this mood of frustrated and angry youth without any sense of direction. Amitabh Bachchan is the single most perceptible archetype of this image. This is no reflection on the unquestionably extraordinary histrionic calibre of the super-hero. It is just that a star is the product of his time. If there is a super star of India who has almost missed direct power (has he?) narrowly, it is this pleasant, suave, gentlemanly Amitabh.

This article started with a reference to the Maharajas and Nawabs of pre-Independence India. India has replaced them with a new species of royalty, the film star-turned politician. The direct relationship between politics and cinema began in Tamilnadu. We return to this in conclusion since at the time of writing this article, another star is the tsarina of Tamilnadu — M.G. Ramachandran's heroine of yesteryears, and his political successor, the all-powerful and charismatic Chief Minister, Jayalalitha.

M. G. Ramachandran in *Nadodi Mannan*, 1958

18

The Stars Call the Shots

— Deepa Gehlot

INDIA MUST BE THE only country in the world where film stars are worshipped as idols in temples; where stars who have played religious figures in films have won elections on the strength of their screen images; where a film shooting or the sight of a star can paralyse traffic; where cinema has an amazing grip on the day-to-day lives of the common people.

That is why counter-productive and destructive though the star system may be for India's sprawling film industry, it cannot but help bowing to the power of the film star. Because it is the star who brings in audiences, sells tickets and makes the money circulate from posh production offices to the dingy cabins and dank corridors of the film trade centres all over the country.

The way things work today, a star who has proved a success in one film can hike up his/her fee, dictate terms and demand unbelievable perks from producers who have no option but to obey every whim of the star. Because if the golden calf is displeased, it could mean no dates allotted to that producer's film, and even a possible abortion of the project.

This slavish dependence on stars is unhealthy for the film industry as a whole, because the unavailability of the actor/actress for any reason spells ruin for all the people who have put their money into the film. For instance, Vinod Khanna's sudden *sanyas,* Parveen Babi's disappearance, Amitabh Bachchan's near-fatal injury, Divya Bharti's tragic, premature death and Sanjay Dutt's arrest on a criminal charge, all caused the suspension of several film projects and caused unimagineable misery to the producer.

But this is considered just one of the risks in an already unstable profession of show business. Very few filmmakers have the confidence or the ability to make films with newcomers. Only those filmmakers whose success has made them immune to the vagaries of the trade can introduce new faces and see them through to stardom, either via sustained media campaigns or, of course, a successful film. When the newcomer becomes a saleable star, the whole cycle of indiscipline and exploitation of a weak producer and the perpetration of a chaotic system starts all over again.

With the film industry already weakened by the invasion of television, video and cable, distributors who invest their money in films and exhibitors who buy films for their theatres want the safety net of popular and recognisable names, be it a big star, a hit-making director or a chart-busting music composer.

In the disorganised and disunited Bombay film industry, proposals are made in a very peculiar manner. The signing of a saleable hero — it is still a very male-dominated field — is often the first step in the putting together of a proposal. The industry is also known for its herd mentality — so a star, director, composer, or writer who has been involved with a hit gets flooded with offers, which usually taper off.

The director, who is able to persuade a top hero to sign up, is for the time being a 'big' director. A top heroine who is available and affordable, a few recognisable character actors and the current best-selling composer completes the package that is presented to the distributor, who will then decide if he wants to back the project. Raising funds for a film is a painful and arduous process with interest rates being prodigiously high. The producer's survival often depends on the ability to sell the film for a high price and it is the current box-office rating of the stars involved that more often than not decides the viability of the proposal.

Very few producers are able to rise above the system and make films on their own terms, but it would take a consistent record of hits, or at least cost-recovery films, to come to this stage. Even stars consider it a privilege to work with top-ranking producers and directors, and leave their tantrums behind. Because a good director is more likely to deliver a box-office hit and enhance the star's standing. Which in turn gives the actor or actress more power and more money. Because the initial success of a proposal depends on them, stars milk huge signing amounts, fees and perks from smaller producers, while they are always willing to accommodate established filmmakers with priority dates and reductions in fees. That also explains why producers keep going to successful and popular stars in spite of the risks of dates, price hikes, extraordinary demands and no guarantee of completion of the film.

Star prices form a bulk of a film's budget, and a star who finds him/herself unable to meet the constant pressure for hits, or at least satisfactory earner for all concerned, is thrown out of films. It has happened in the last few years to superstar Rajesh Khanna, the demand for whom dropped almost overnight, and more recently to Salman Khan after he stopped churning out hits. Many actors and actresses found their thriving careers abruptly cut short when their box-office draw reduced — Randhir Kapoor, Kumar Gaurav, Dimple Kapadia, Rekha, Jayaprada, to name a few, all found themselves suddenly out in the cold with no new film offers coming their way. Madhuri Dixit, once number one, is struggling to retain her position because producers complain of date hassles. They did not mind the problems when she was giving hits, but after a few films flopped, nothing she does seems to be right.

Madhuri Dixit

Stars like Mithun Chakraborty and Rishi Kapoor, who have remained steady in spite of several flops, have done so because of their level-headed and pragmatic approach to their careers. They never charged astronomical fees, didn't vary them according to the fate of their last film, completed the projects in a reasonable amount of time, thus ensuring their films were not over-priced. If budgets are kept in control, it is possible for everyone connected with the film to make a respectable profit, and they have no problems repeating the star — even if he or she is not "number one".

From among the heroines, Hema Malini, Mumtaz, Zeenat Aman, Poonam Dhillon, Rati Agnihotri, Meenakshi Seshadri survived so long in spite of bad patches, because of their professionalism and cooperation with producers, when more talented actresses like Raakhee and Moushmi Chatterjee didn't last as long. Top stars like Amitabh Bachchan and Sridevi, because of market compulsions beyond their control, outpriced themselves, so that ordinary producers could not dream of making films with them.

Ajay Devgan, whose price at one point reached an impossibly high figure, had said in an interview that he wasn't the one who upped his fees, but after the success of his first two films, producers came to him with brief-cases full of money to sign him, and wouldn't take no for an answer. All successful stars probably face the same problem and end up signing films they regret later.

In the business of proposal-making, where the stars are signed first and then the music recorded, the script of the film is the least important part of the film. However, some of today's young stars have started becoming particular about the subject. Shah Rukh Khan insists on a complete bound script, and because he is successful and in demand, producers are prepared to oblige him. Aamir Khan and Sunny Deol have limited the number of films they accept and work only with the filmmakers they like. They don't wish to be "number one", they are content with doing good and consistent work. Anil Kapoor and Jackie Shroff had to do major rethinks on their career strategies when their films started flopping.

Anil Kapoor

Stardom is obviously not forever, and in the bid to hold on to it for as long as possible, stars make mistakes that cost them their careers. Power is obviously the major corrupter and actors who were well-behaved and humble when they entered the industry turn into nasty, irresponsible and greedy monsters when they became successful.

The contribution of the press in creating images of the stars and keeping them in the news cannot be denied. A negative story about a star planted in a magazine can cause terrible harm to a star's reputation and standing in the industry. It is very difficult to fight rumours and repair the damage. On the other hand, magazines keep promoting their favourities and keep them in the public eye when their careers are down. People like Chunky Pandey, Rahul Roy, Pooja Bedi, Sangeeta Bijlani, Sonu Walia, Somy Ali, owe their visibility entirely to their tactic of making themselves available to film magazines for spicy interviews and uninhibited photographs.

There was a time when the studio was king and stars merely salaried employees. Today people barely know who acted in the early hits, but the filmmakers of that period from the pioneering Dadasaheb Phalke to Himansu Rai, Debaki Bose, P.C. Barua, V. Shantaram, A.R. Kardar, Sohrab Modi, Kidar Sharma and others, are idolised by film students and historians. That is because the actor was subservient to the studio-owner, producer and director. If an actor misbehaved with a film-maker, he never got to work again. Like the great studios in Hollywood, India also had its New Theatres, Bombay Talkies, Ranjit, Prabhat, AVM, Gemini, and Filmistan, controlling the film trade, with stalwarts like B.N. Sircar, V. Shantaram. Himansu Rai, Chandual Shah, S.S. Vasan, A.V. Meiyappan, Shashadhar Mukherjee running them.

As various social factors led to the increasing popularity and social acceptance of films, stars started breaking away from the studio system. The transfer of power from studios to independent producers to stars took place gradually over the years.

K.L. Saigal, Sulochana, Prithviraj Kapoor, Chadramohan, Naseem, Kanan Devi, Devika Rani, Shanta Apte, Ashok Kumar, Leela Chitnis, Noorjehan, Suraiya are the stars of the '30s and '40s that people remember even today. Occasionally one comes across names like Master Vithal ("the Indian Douglas Fairbanks"), the Billimoria brothers, Jahanara Kajjan, Khurshid, in accounts of the pre-golden age cinema, but nothing much is known about them.

The star system started getting formalised in the early fifties, and later in the decade the immortal trio of Dilip Kumar-Raj Kapoor-Dev

Anand dominated the industry. Singing star Suraiya was probably the first actress to command a frenzied male fan following; according to film lore, men camped for days outside her house to catch a glimpse of her, and slashed their wrists in disappointment when their proposals were firmly turned down.

Still, in the nascent days of the star system, the actors knew there were certain limits they couldn't cross. Director Mehboob Khan was known to let loose a volley of abuses when any actor goofed, and great filmmakers like Bimal Roy, Guru Dutt, Nitin Bose, J.B.H. Wadia, commanded respect. The actors knew their place — even though the greatest and all-time favourite stars like Nargis, Madhubala, Beena Rai, Meena Kumari, Nutan, Bharat Bhooshan, Raaj Kumar, Nimmi, Geeta Bali, Premnath, Waheeda Rehman and Shammi Kapoor belong to that period; Shammi Kapoor was perhaps the first star with a mass following of young people.

The sixties saw the genesis of the ills that plague the industry today. The director started accepting a lower position than the star in the film hierarchy and the producer, even lower, though he was the one who paid the stars and crew and put the project together. The system of multi-starrers and multiple shifts started then, causing a complete turnaround in the working of the film industry.

The early seventies were to see the birth of a phenomenon called the superstar in the form of an ordinary-looking, minimally-talented Rajesh Khanna. After his reign was over, people couldn't believe that he could have won such a massive fan following.

By then the biggest star the industry had ever seen — Amitabh Bachchan — had made his appearance. According to Javed Akhtar who was co-writer of some of the films (*Zanjeer, Trishul, Deewar, Sholay*) that propelled Bachchan to "number one" position, the entry of the criminally-inclined, angry young man or anti-hero, coincided with the complete breakdown of a traditional lifestyle, legal system and society as it had been until then. His films mirrored the rage and disillusionment of the youth in the seventies. They saw themselves in his roughhewn screen persona, and fantasised about the power they never had.

Two decades later, the creation of a more evil and vicious anti-hero, personified by Shah Rukh Khan in *Baazigar, Darr* and *Anjaam*, caught the imagination of the public, because the intervening years had seen a deterioration of values and a shift in moral attitudes that made society and films glorify criminals and gangsters. These films made Shah Rukh the new superstar. Like Amitabh he has the talent and discretion to sustain his position longer than his peers and contemporaries did.

Both Amitabh Bachchan in the early part of his career, and Shah Rukh Khan today, represent the saner side of the star system. They are both tremendously hard-working, devoted to their profession and meticulous about their craft. Even though Bachchan has not done a film in three years, his following remains undiminished, his star aura intact.

Manmohan Desai's *Amar, Akbar, Anthony*, 1978 with Amitabh Bachchan as Anthony

There is a saying in the industry that a star must be good to people on his way up, because he will meet the same people on the way down. Not many of them remember that in their glory days.

The South Indian film industry, comprising films made in Telugu, Tamil, Malayalam and Kannada, has all the features of the Bombay star system minus the arbitratiness. For instance, the stars there, particularly in the Tamil and Telugu industry, are paid in crores, more than the budget of a medium-sized Hindi film.

However, by the adulation they get and the box-office success they guarantee, they more than earn their enormous fees. Rajnikant, Chiranjeevi, Nagarjuna, Vijayashanti, Khushboo and Naghma (the last two Hindi film rejects) can make any film work. Khushboo even has a temple built in her name in a suburb of Madras. And former matinee idols, M.G. Ramachandran, N.T. Rama Rao and Jayalalitha, turned out to be popular Chief Ministers of their states. In other parts of the country too, film and TV stars like Sunil Dutt, Rajesh Khanna, Vyjayanthimala, Deepika, Arvind Trivedi and Raj Babbar have successfully switched to politics.

But they are punctual and disciplined and dare not be otherwise. The South Indian film industry has always been a stickler for discipline and can keep erring stars in check by forming a united front against them. Recently, Rajnikant and Kamalahasan were threatened with a ban, because they had increased their fees by an unjustifiable amount. Stars there are not allowed to sign dozens of films at a time. The industry works methodically and films are completed within a few months, unlike Bombay where a normal film takes at least 18 months to complete. There is, of course, no upper limit!

In the South, stars treat their producers and directors with respect, honour their commitments and reach the set or location with make-up whenever they are asked to report.

In Bombay arriving hours late for shooting, or not turning up at all is normal; it is not even unthinkable for a star to allot dates promised to one producer to a bigger project than would fetch them more money. That is why, stars from other centres — like Uttam Kumar, Suchitra Sen, Kamalahasan, Rajnikant — who tried working in Hindi films from time to time gave up in disgust.

Hollywood has the system of giving percentages to top stars to ensure their interest in the welfare of a film, and also insurance to protect the filmmaker from risks that cover accidents and star caprices. Besides, there are so many stars available at any given time that finding a replacement at short notice is not difficult, though Hollywood also has its superstars like Sylvester Stallone, Arnold Swarzenegger, Tom Cruise, Bruce Willis, Kevin Costner — all male, incidentally — whose names sell projects and movie-tickets. But it is possible for an independent filmmaker to make a movie with lesser-known faces and emerge with what is known in Hollywood parlance as a sleeper (hit).

Also, movie stars have to share popularity with baseball players, rock stars and TV anchor persons. It might be possible for a Hollywood star to walk down the mall or do his own shopping without being mobbed, but Indians have no qualms about invading a person's privacy. On the negative side, stars there have to contend with lunatic fans who try to harm them, and live in heavily guarded fortresses. An Indian star can shoot on the street with no danger to his/her life.

In Hollywood, however, a successful director is as important and well-paid as the biggest star in Hollywood. Today, nobody would even ask who Steven Spielberg was signing for his film, the project would sell anyway. At the same time, Woody Allen can keep making small personal films and have them work on the strength of his loyal fan-following built over the years. Here Mani Ratnam, Subhash Ghai, Pahlaj Nihalani, and David Dhawan are among the few who can work on their own terms.

A legal system that offers quick justice also makes an American or European star answerable to the studio or the producer. The recent

Dimple Kapadia

case of Kim Bassinger being slapped with a multi-million dollar fine for walking out of a verbal commitment to do Boxing Helena must have sent a strong message to other stars to behave or else....

In India, producers hesitate to take a star to court for breach of contract or other misdemeanours, because of the notorious delays in procuring justice. In spite of some attempts by organisations like the Film Makers' Combine and the Indian Motion Picture Producers' Association, to force stars to honour their commitments, the rate of successes depends on how much in demand the star is. They can threaten Dimple Kapadia with a ban for walking out of *Kartavya* because her career is at a low, but they cannot make Sanjay Dutt finish the films he is acting in before he signs new projects. They can fine Govinda or Vinod Khanna for harassing producers, but they cannot make them pay up. Stars are protected from punishment by the sheer number of films they have on the floors at any given time. If producers want to ban a star, dozens of them have to agree to bear financial losses, or worse, abandon their projects. The Cine Artistes' Association is also a supporter of fickle stars.

The biggest point in their favour is that the industry needs them to survive in an increasingly precarious era. At one time, the Hindi film industry had a small but thriving parallel cinema movement that worked without the crutch of established star names. In fact, it created its own stars like Shabana Azmi, Naseeruddin Shah, Om Puri, Smita Patil, Amrish Puri, all of whom eventually found acceptance in the mainstream cinema. But today, a director who wants to make an offbeat film also needs star names to make it viable. That's why the parallel cinema approaches stars like Dimple Kapadia, Rakhee, Hema Malini, Mammooty and Mohanlal (the last two are both Malayalam megastars) to get financiers, distributors and audiences interested in their films. Today the names of Shyam Benegal, Govind Nihalani or Ketan Mehta are not enough to get even the government-backed National Film Development Corporation to look at a project.

The high investment on stars has brought about another pernicious trend in the industry, that of producers 'discovering' and promoting star children. Among the stars in the film industry today — Rishi Kapoor, Sunny Deol, Anil Kapur, Sanjay Dutt, Aamir Khan, Salman Khan, Ajay Devgan, Pooja Bhatt, Saif Ali Khan, Karishma Kapoor, Raveena Tandon, Twinkle Khanna, Bobby Deol, Tabbu, Sanjay Kapoor

— are all industry relatives.

It is very difficult for an outsider to crash into the scene today. Mithun Chakraborty, Jackie Shroff and Shah Rukh Khan are the only top male stars who had no industry connections (females still have a chance, because of the reluctance of industry men to let their daughters act). Producers feel that if they are to spend money on grooming and introducing a new face, why not invest in their own children. This is happening in the South — Chiranjeevi, Venkatesh, Nagarjuna, Balkrishna are all industry brats. But once inside the magic gates, they have to slog as hard as anybody else.

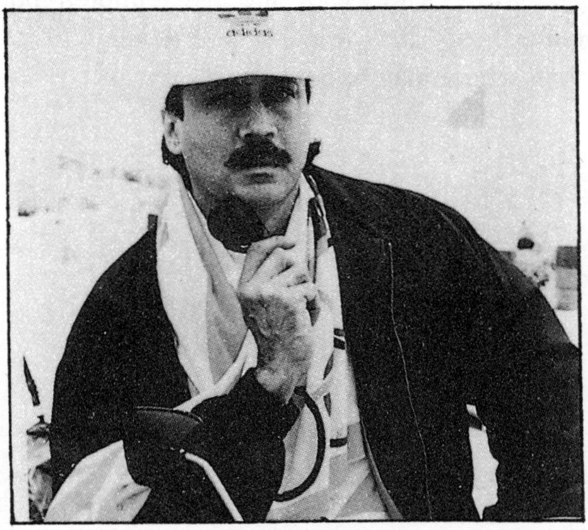

Jackie Shroff

For an aspiring actor, the road to success is paved with humiliation and heartbreak. Women have it worse than men. So if at all they make it big, they want to get their own back for all their past suffering. Rekha reportedly enjoyed harassing filmmakers with all sorts of pranks to avenge the pain of her struggling days.

To look at it from the star's point of view, the pressure to produce box-office hits is killing. Since so much money is invested on their mythical powers to make the box-office tick, stars are made and broken every Friday when a new film is released. One hit and a star is at the top, a flop and he is down in the dumps. Audiences are not loyal any more, career spans can be dangerously short. This constant teetering on the edge, the anxiety every time a new film comes up, and isolation from the real world makes stars lose their sense of equilibrium very soon. They gradually find themselves unable to react to people and events normally. They continue to live in the alternate reality that they have helped create. Waking up from this dream is a lethal shock. After paying a tough price for success, failure is all the more traumatic.

So while they are enjoying the fruits of stardom, they want to live it up, never mind if it is at the cost of a hapless producer. They want to enjoy the adulation of the masses, and savour the taste of unlimited power while it lasts. That makes them enjoy the sight of producers grovelling before them; makes them try to see how much they can demand and get away with. They are like children pulling out the wings from butterflies. They want to live several lives in one day. Because, for them, there may be no tomorrow.

19

To Be a Woman

— *Maithili Rao*

THE BUSINESS OF FILM is to create images. The more populist the image, the more potent its mythical, seemingly indestructible life. Women's response to popular cinema is a ceaseless love-hate thraldom because the film image ostensibly celebrates her eroticism while reducing her to a passive sex object. The space in which the screen woman is filmed, the way her body is fractured and is commodified into an object for the overwhelmingly male gaze, all thrust her even more irrevocably into depths of involuntary thraldom.

Critics — not all of them women — have recognised the all-pervasive male gaze which consumes this eroticised commodity. What is even more subversive to women's self-image is their own willing submission to this insidious, attractively packaged image. This is because even the crassest of populist cinema invokes the incantatory magic of ritualised iconography, the infiltrating potency of myth, the seduction of song and the sanction of societal approval. That is why women's response to this image resembles a nightmarish chase after a mirage that pretends to be a mirror. It is a mirror that also promises to educate and reward.

Popular cinema creates instant mythologies for uncritical consumption and not histories of credible people. This is truer of the heroine than the hero. Hindi cinema is so driven by its phallocentricity that its heroes inevitably acquire larger-than-life dimensions with archetypal overtones. You have the good-son-bad-son dichotomy, the lone warrior, the dispossessed son claiming his patriarchal inheritance, the avenging destroyer, the dutiful monogamous husband and the dark god of playful eroticism who scatters his seed. Not too many types, it's true, but varied enough. It is more potent when two or three elements are combined by enterprising scenarists.

The heroine is straight-jacketed into a chaste wife whose suffering can only make her more virtuous, the nurturing mother who denies her own self, an avenging Kali or a titillating strumpet. And yes, the eternal wronged victim, usually waiting for a male saviour. Hindi cinema in the '80s and '90s has really not progressed beyond these comfortable, easily identifiable stereotypes. The true archetypes of popular cinema are only two despite all the flurry of films flaunting female avenger *avatars* in the mid and late '80s. One is *Mother India's* matriarch who is the upholder of *dharma* and the true emotional centre of the hero's life. The second is *Pakeeza*, the romanticized apostrophe to woman as the pathetic, impossibly innocent Other to be rescued from the penumbra of social opprobrium. Every *tawaif* and her cousin is descended from *Pakeeza* and is a wan reflection of pale, derived poetic pathos. And every strong mother, sternly casting out her erring son, is *Mother India's* daughter. The only difference being that the Rakhee of *Khalnayak* is denied the moral stature and heartbreaking courage of Nargis. She cannot shoot down her erring son who has now graduated from village rebel to brainwashed terrorist, bent on destroying the nation.

The gradual decline in the moral authority of the mother was first visible in Amitabh Bachchan's angry heroics till she was reduced to a sentimental, ineffective figure. Yes, there have been exceptions when the mother regained her earlier stature as in *Agneepath.* It helped that Rohini Hattangadi still carried her Kasturba halo from *Gandhi*, readily invoked by dress and demeanour.

If the decline of the mother's authority was a reflection of the ongoing sociological reality — the disintegrating joint family — this authority was not immediately transferred to the wife in the emerging nuclear family. It only enhanced the hero's loneliness, umbilically severed from his Oepidal dependence. A few nostalgic family melodramas surfaced now and then, yearning for the uncomplicated patriarchal past. True to pattern, the educated young woman, who demanded that she come first in her husband's life, was the misguided destroyer of family harmony. Some films like *Ghar Ghar Ki Baat* regressed all the way back. Its beautiful, educated heroine was made to mouth how a woman finds *nirvana* in carrying out the meanest of household chores and wallows in servitude to the husband, exulting in total submission to a culture that makes India great (the heroine's words). She totally rejects the independent working woman as a wrecker of homes.

A curious variation of the mother-worship cult is *Beta*. It tells of a war where no weapon of subterfuge is taboo as the tough, modern young bride takes on the wily cunning of an evil step-mother-in-law. The setting is rural and the ambience rustic Nawabi. The hero is an uneducated simpleton who literally worships his conniving step-mother and will not brook any diminishing of her authority in a household where the rightful patriarch has been shut up as insane. Madhuri Dixit plays the determined middle-class girl whose marriage to the hero is brought about by circumstance rather than her volition. She is stern and seductive by turns...a Menaka tantalizingly dressed in saffron (baring a vast expanse of gyrating midriff) heaving to the 'Dhak dhak karne laga' beat and sending the hero (and the audience) into tumescent stupor. As the new bride, she matches wits with the older woman and wins hands down. The contrary messages of *Beta* are a semiotician's delight. The viper of a mother (is aptly named Nagmani) nearly devours her trusting son and yet, the deification of motherhood is so potent that it pierces her wicked heart so that mother and son are clasped in a late Oepidal embrace. The daughter-in-law fights the battle not to assert her rights but to restore the household to its proper patriarchal functioning. Madhuri is a shackled Savitri, owing more to the popular fictional heroine of *Swayamsidha* (and films based on this theme) than the awesome *Puranic* archetype, for Savitri has the courage to outwit Yama, the god of death.

New levels of permissiveness have obliterated the strictly enforced divide between the heroine and vamp. The rigid dress code disappeared as nubile heroines cavorted in itsy bitsy fluff, disported in diaphanous saris under waterfalls or studio-made rain, strutted in skin-tight dresses or undulated their navel-baring torsos in ethnic cabaret wear of sequinned, clingy figure-hugging saris. She danced with the seductive abandon of a houri as the camera routinely zoomed in on one body part or the other. Her titillating purpose done, she usually donned a demure sari towards the end as she attained the highly desirable wife status. It was Manu being updated all over again : westernised harlot before the wedding and chaste wife after. The autonomy, grace and dignity that popular cinema of the '40s and '50s had given its heroines was gone in the pursuit of the bitch goddess of box-office success.

Nothing personifies this frenzied, yet calculated, pursuit more than *Khalnayak* which trivializes not only the legacy of *Mother India* but diminishes the stature of the dissenting son into that of a gullible clown. For all its political posturing, and so-called contemporaneity, this over-long, uneven pseudo-epic dresses the eminently saleable charms of its heroine in the come-hither seduction of rustic raunch and the titillating suggestion that the pure heroine could be attracted to the disreputable villain. The knowing smirk behind 'Choli ke pichhe kya hai?', provocatively posed by the husky, put-on masculinity of the gypsy voice of Ila Arun is answered not so much by the innocuous lyrics but the collage of fragmented body parts an orgasmic camera puts together with such voyeuristic relish. The choreography plays with the juxtaposition of suggestive opposites: the all-enveloping veil followed by the bare skin under the backless choli. There is much heaving of thrusting breasts and wildly undulating midriffs. Sunjay Dutt's prominent eye patch draws attention to rivetted male gaze for whom Madhuri Dixit is displaying all her not-so discreetly veiled charms.

Khalnayak seeks to cast a pious halo of chastity on the heroine named Ganga, summoning up the mythological references to the purity of the sacred river as well as a Sita willing to risk voluntary exile and the charge of immorality, all to save her fiencé Ram's hitherto unbesmirched reputation for rectitude. Subhash Ghai also pays his tribute to Raj Kapoor's *Ram Teri Ganga Maili*, the trashy epitome of calculated hypocrisy which introduced bare breasts under a wet white sari, all in the name of bemoaning the desecration of India's noble heritage! *Khalnayak's* heroine Ganga is supposed to be a cop but the only scene showing her at work makes her a bad-tempered, cutely foul-mouthed, not too successful disciplinarian chiding her female charges for unruly behaviour. Whether it is with her fiencé Ram, or the villain she hopes to trap, Ganga's weapons are the old ones of feminine guile, sulks and seductive pouts when not dancing in wanton abandon.

A New Look

It was left to parallel cinema to give women their cinematic due. When not preoccupied with depiction of poverty or middle-class angst, or the pure joy of experimenting with cinematic language, sensitive filmmakers focused on the changing man-woman relationship in the flux of social turmoil. Basu Bhattacharya, Shyam Benegal, Kalpana Lajmi, Aparna Sen, Ketan Mehta and Kumar Shahani...all these filmmakers had their particular preoccupations and their own distinct approach to cinema. What is common to all is the sincerity of conviction and empathy for women, complex entities and not cardboard stereotypes, caught in the throes of a new morality.

Kumar Shahani's preoccupation with the epic mode made him see women as inheritors of archetypes. The Smita Patil of *Tarang* metamorphoses into the celestial Urvashi, from the earlier sentient being rooted in the working class and imbued with radical aspiration. The politics of radical ideology creates its own mythology and mints its new icons. In *Kasbah*, the female protagonist, played with swaggering grace and intelligence by Mita Vasisht, uses her sexuality to drive a hard bargain in the market place of familial relationships. Shahani's archetypal invocations are impalpable emanations of a highly complex narrative text. They seem to scorn the more immediate task of audience identification.

Tanuja and Sanjeev Kumar in
Anubhav, 1971, Basu Bhattacharya

Basu Bhattacharya and Shyam Benegal have brought palpable empathy and even tenderness on occasion to their female characters. Bhattacharya's lonely urban women coming to terms with their aspirations of clearly defined selfhood and yet desperately seeking the warmth of man-woman bond are, in a way, highly romanticized. Yet, the wife in *Anubhav* has a rare concreteness due as much to Tanuja's strong presence as the sympathetic script. *Panchvati* explores the undercurrents of forbidden sexual attraction in a joint family situation, where a sensitive painter is drawn to her husband's older brother, who is made of a finer grain than the crass young man she has married.

Panchvati is a far cry from Charulata's elegant perfection and intuitive understanding of a woman's loneliness. Yet, Deepti Naval's doe-eyed, fragile sensitivity captures the tragedy of marriage to the wrong man and celebrates the one memorable night which consummates the marriage of true minds. But instead of exploring the pain and fulfilment of this relationship, Bhattacharya loads his film with overt symbolism and laboured mythological references that fuse diverse epics most unsuccessfully.

Shyam Benegal has earlier used woman's sexual exploitation as a wider metaphor for the evils of feudalism which fought off the advent of modernity with a savagery born of the need to survive. *Mandi* was an uneven black comedy that missed a lot of its intended punches. But it had an unsentimental feel for the prostitutes who made their own separate bargains with respectability and approached their trade with matter-of-fact pragmatism. Shabana Azmi played the madame who really cares for her girls with a sort of gruff tenderness and yet can starve an unwilling novice into submission. Benegal imbues the first half of the film with the subtle nostalgia for a more elegant past when the *kotha* was a place of refined literary discourse and the *tawaifs* were keepers of courtly poetry. The frisson of latent lesbian yearnings — Shabana's protective tenderness for the virginally coquettish Smita (waiting for the highest bidder) — sits awkwardly like a stiff organdy frock on the sinuous silks the girls are draped in!

It is *Bhumika* that remains a true milestone. The Usha of *Bhumika* is a born rebel looking for a cause as well as a prisoner struggling against her circumstances. Usha's rebellion is against her sexual confinement and exploitation by her manipulative husband who sees her as a meal ticket for life. Her dilemma is highly ironic because she

Smita Patil in Shyam Benegal's *Bhumika*, 1977

is an actress doomed to play a variety of roles but confused about her own role in real life. She is exploited by the husband (who was also her mother's lover and we have the first intimation of near-incest) as well as the film industry which tries to mould her charms into saleable stereotypes for mass consumption. Usha's search for sexual fulfilment and emotional security drives her restlessly into the arms of many men who don't and can't measure up to her demands. Each of them is using her in his own way or forcing her into her yet another male-cast mould.

Usha's final lesson is to learn a bitter truth: like all complex individuals with a highly charged emotional drive, she must learn to live alone. After such knowledge, what forgiveness? Usha may not have found the road to forgiveness but she wrests a hardwon tranquillity after her rage is spent. Benegal bestows the combined aura of two mythological allusions on his actress-protagonist who is already subjected to the instant mythologies that popular cinema spawns. The heroine's given name is Usha and her screen name is Urvashi. In her are joined the Rig Vedic deity of dawn as well as the later legend of the Apsara Urvashi, in search of her human lover Pururavas. The fusion of two iconic image is validated by historian by D.D. Kosambi's observation that Urvashi is a later metamorphosis of Usha. These intimations of mythic immortality enrich *Bhumika* and add an ironic poignance to Usha's volatile vulnerability, born of her inchoate rage and restless passion.

Smita Patil's vibrant intensity and earthy yet frail sensuousness lit up a host of films, giving them a tragic afterglow. In Jabbar Patel's *Umbartha*, she paid the emotional price for her commitment to work. In Ketan Mehta's flamboyant *Mirch Masala,* her flaming defiance and challenging sensuality roused a whole village to rebellion. Even as she played the rebel, Smita Patil's sensuality was an integral part of the persona. She was never made to deny her sexuality as the cardboard rebels of commercial cinema were made to.

Recasting the Mould

It was in the '80s that Hindi cinema discovered the new angels of death in variations of the rape and revenge formula. Whether it was a clever response to the articulation of women's anger at increasing violence or a desperate clutch at novelty, filmmakers had frontranking stars clamouring to play the dacoit queen taking to a gun, or a female vigilante sworn to vengeance after the trauma of rape. Whatever the setting and whoever the star, this sub-genre immediately dictated its dress code to fit a new formula. Either the heroine or someone close to her is raped by a marauding dacoit or a gang of city goons. She discards overnight her coy village belle tricks, along with constricting *lehangas* and girlish braids embellished with tinsel tassels. She quickly finds a male mentor who could be surrogate father or well-meaning lover for initial guidance. Her seductive form is poured into skin-tight black leather jeans, high boots and even a whip to chastise the villain. Does she cater to our latent sado-masochistic longings, however western-inspired her image? This image teems with tantalizing, self-contradictory possibilities.

For instance, in *Sherni*, Sridevi's virginally braided locks are let loose in flowing abandon (when she is physically unpossessable) to tease and torment the collective male gaze. This complements her all-black, brass-studded leather outfit. A message of forbidding, alien sexuality that thaws into the familiar cosy warmth of the seductive *mujra* dancer, a disguise she dons to trap one of the villains. It is as if the unfamiliar image has to be periodically stripped of its alien accoutrements to reassure us of her docile Indianness and its promise of sexual submission to the patriarchal order. In only one film, *Khoon Baha Ganga Mein*, does the heroine switch to *dhotis* from her *lehangas*. And all the heroines must have names that invoke Kali, Durga and any other form of Shakti. Why, you even had Hema Malini astride a lion, posing as the deity in a temple, draped in flaming red sari and wielding the awesome trishul. This easy invocation of ready-made mythology is accompanied by the same bombastic rhetoric declaimed by the hero preliminary to destroying the villain-in-chief.

Among all these films, only two merit detailed examination for the subtext that negates the film's stated pro-woman stance. *Zakhmee Aurat* had an efficient, dedicated woman police officer for protagonist. Played by the stunningly beautiful Dimple Kapadia, the heroine is shown in her uniform, riding a phallic motorbike and her glorious hair bundled under a cap. Her zeal in capturing a few minor rapists ensures her gang rape at the quartet of villains with high connections. The rape sequence highlights the agony in her eyes as she stares at the ceiling fan from which dangle a pair of jeans. Her own or the rapists' is not clear. But earlier, they are shown clawing at her trousers as she runs to escape them. The visual reading of the sequence implies punishment for daring to flaunt male accoutrements of office.

Later, Dimple Kapadia is joined by other rape victims who lure the rapists till one of them, a doctor, castrates the men. This righteous anger is undercut by the usual game of exploitative obscenity, of gyrating sirens taunting castrated men. The heroine's boyfriend stands by her — unlike the first rape and revenge film *Insaf Ka Tararzu* a decade earlier — but his sermon is filmed under the calendar arty depiction of Krishna imparting the *Gita* to Arjuna. The rapists must be punished but the moral superiority of the "good" patriarchal order must prevail.

Pratighat had a non-glamorous protagonist who was depicted as the housewife next door till her public disrobing and subsequent humiliation rouse her to wrath. She walks out on her cowardly husband and aborts the child she has been carrying, not because she wants to assert her right over her body but to free herself for action. Earlier, the film establishes that the heroine defines her sexuality in terms of motherhood. What the film says in effect is that for a woman to be able to act in society and redress grievous wrongs, she must sacrifice her femininity. The heroine also uses the axe, usually a male weapon associated with a wrathful Parashuram, to behead the villain who has corrupted the body politic. It is revealing that even a matronly protagonist must voluntarily destroy her sexuality to be a free agent.

Two recent films have tried variations on the woman as rebel with varying degrees of success. Raj Kumar Santoshi's *Damini* aims to be a conscience-raising exercise of waking the middle-class out of its congenital apathy to injustice. The eponymous heroine is uncomfortably committed to speaking the truth even when this endangers the reputation of her rich in-laws. Damini has seen her loutish brother-in-law and his friends gang rape the maid during Holi. Her lower middle-class values subdue her conscience for a while as she gives in to the combined persuasions of her uppity in-laws and the dilemma that her husband, a really decent man, is caught in. But the script loads the dice against Damini and incarcerates her in a mental hospital where she is terrorised and certified insane. Tapping into the ready availability of mythological reference, the drums of Durga *puja* send Damini into a frenzied *tandav* and this shocks her out of a near-lobotomised lethargy.

The director, even as he valorises the heroine as the uncompromising fighter for justice, takes care to showcase her maidenly charms earlier on, inviting Meenakshi Seshadri to prance and preen, to rhythms folksy as well as the kitsch that passes for filmi classic. The real heart of the conflict — a traditionally brought up Indian woman's dilemma when her principles clash with family loyalty — does touch a responsive chord. It is this theme that rings true for ours in a society in a state of flux where old certitudes no longer exist and individuals have to find their own scale of values. *Damini* empowers a woman and celebrates her integrity even though the narrative is enveloped in the usual safety net of familiar assurances about Damini's earnest endeavour to be a

Damini, 1992, Raj Kumar Santoshi
with Meenakshi Seshadri and Rishi Kapoor

good daughter and good daughter-in-law. It is her in-laws, whose wickedness is enlarged to incredible proportions, who don't deserve her. Damini is, at any rate, a change from the usual brainless bimbettes let loose to satisfy collective voyeurism.

Khalnayika may be a calculated remake of a Hollywood horror-thriller (a genre alien to our soil in which sentimental piety thrives) and gratuitously inserts yet another, far more obscene choli song. For all that, this Sawankumar Tak film has enough significance (intended and otherwise) leaking into the text that it offers rich pickings to the interested viewer. The director can't really make up his mind as to what constitutes a heroine. Jaya (Jayaprada), for all that she looks like a well-preserved society matron, is soon reduced to the status of an anaemic and asthmatic mother of two. She might tempt an eminent gynaecologist into molestation— thus conforming to our society's deep-seated fears regarding male doctors examining women — but the anti-heroine Anu (Anu Agarwal) taunts her as a woman who can't satisfy her husband (naturally, a virile specimen whose desirability is not diminished by fatherhood!). Even Anu's deviously plotted and near-perfectly executed vendetta springs from an unshakeable conviction in her husband's innocence. The seemingly loving nanny who plans to kill her charges may look like a western import but we have the *Putana* image to validate the fear of an evil mother who would poison the baby she suckles.

The director wants to make her an ambiguous anti-heroine whose vengeance springs from a perfectly valid Hindu virtue — blind faith in her husband — and yet hint at sexual straying to finally put her beyond the moral pale. Twice the film suggests that the demure governess (with severely braided hair and draped in simple saris) is attracted to the master of the house and fantasies about him. Before the character turns irredeemably evil, you see Anu chastely enveloped in saris but when she turns killer, Anu Agarwal steps out of the pages of *Vogue* in black suit and red tie. From devious femininity, she is transformed into androgynous killer. Tak creates a similar dress code for the third woman in the film. Varsha is a chain-smoking, flirtatious journalist always dressed in western clothes except for the infamous "choli" number where she plays the harlot in midriff-baring ethnic chic. No wonder she is easily dispensable and becomes the killer's first victim. *Khalnayika* might have flopped for the very obvious absence of a simpering romantic heroine the audience could fantasise about. The heroine has to be desirable, yes. But she must also be non-threatening and demure.

No one exemplifies this more than Juhi Chawla in *Hum Hain Rahi Pyar Ke*. This charmingly juvenile remake of a more mature Hollywood hit mints the new bright image of the heroine as the nation's sweetheart. She must be an overgrown schoolgirl adorned with beribboned pigtails and dressed in pinafores. Of course, when the time comes she turns gutsy enough to fight for her man and put the scheming rich girl in her place. But for all her stubbornness and spunk in running away from home, Vyjayanti (Juhi Chawla) is Daddy's little cutiepie and the beloved of an equally sweetiepie male charmer. There is obviously no room for older and mature women. The trend is to go back to schoolgirlish giggles and gym slips.

Aaina was another film that departed from the normal surfeit of violence and titillation. Honey Irani is fast emerging as the professional matchmaker between the shallow wishfulfilment of Mills & Boon and the sacred cows of our sanctimonious morality. Irani's scripts transplant the formulaic fantasies of pulp romance into fertile *desi* soil. She did it in *Lamhe* — a bewitching ward wins the older man who is also her guardian — and now successfully adapts the formula of two sisters fighting over the same man, on a less lavish scale than *Lamhe*.

Aaina pits the shy, congenitally self-sacrificing younger sister Reema (the forever sweet and submissive Juhi Chawla), against the ambitious, selfish and glamorous Roma (Amrita Singh, our imperious gal par excellence). Though it is the younger Reema who first sets eyes on the stylish tycoon Ravi (Jackie Shroff) and promptly falls in love, the hero naturally is besotted with the regally glacial Roma. Men don't fall in love with girls who wear glasses and moreover put oodles of oil in their long tresses! Roma is ambitious enough to run away from home to pursue a glamorous career in modelling and films on the eve of her wedding and the chagrined groom marries the docile Reema to keep up appearances. The script also hints that Ravi has all along admired the younger girl's patience, forgiving nature etc. etc. All the qualities desirable in a suitable, submissive wife.

The selfish big sister returns just when the hitherto platonic relationship is about to be consummated. After the devious tortures of deceit and misunderstandings, true love triumphs and the ambitious Roma comes to grief. Reema flaunts her Mangalsutra and the sanctity of *saat pheras* while Roma struts her sexual wares and seductive wiles. The script sketches in scenes of sibling rivalry dating back to schooldays and you hear the wise Dadima exhorting the mother to teach the elder one how to lose and the younger girl to fight for what is hers. But *Aaina* must needs package this bit of pop psychology in the *Pativrata* norms of yore. Ambition in women is to be punished, because even the most indulgent of fathers throws the prodigal daughter out.

Girls who warble on about the joys of the husband's home, 'Meri saari duniya hai tera angana,' are rewarded for their patience. *Aaina* was much lauded for its negative virtues— the absence of physical violence — but the condoning of psychic violence done to women went largely unnoticed. Meekness and patience are rewarded whereas the ambitious woman's attempt to exploit her sexuality for personal fame was condemned as morally reprehensible. The camera paid tribute to Juhi Chawla's demure charm while it played voyeur to Amrita Singh's aggressive sexuality, confident of its power. That power was shown to be manipulative even as the camera manipulated Amrita Singh's persona and milked it of every possible iota of titillation. Talk of paradoxes and double standards that rule commercial cinema!

The Woman's Gaze

Women filmmakers have sought to restore women's confidence and pride in their sexuality. Kalpana Lajmi's first film *Ek Pal* had conformed to textbook feminism, like Aparna Sen's *Paroma*, to articulate a woman's right to her selfhood and sexuality. The protagonists in both films have extramarital affairs and both are made to announce a lack of guilt even though the filmic circumstance is to the contrary.

Lajmi's new film *Rudali* is a departure from feminist rhetoric which can be almost as tyrannical in its stereotyping as the old feminine variety. Lajmi brings an operatic flourish to a resonant narrative that details the arid life and dried up dreams of a Mother Courage figure. Sanichari's (Dimple Kapadia) life is so full of sorrows, betrayals and partings that she cannot cry ... even when she rejects the promised fulfilment of the unattainable love of her life. A deep commitment to her wastrel husband and vagabond son is as much a part of her psyche as is gritty sand part of the desert's harsh beauty. The son she so dotes on succumbs to his wanderlust and abandons her. It is the grief of losing the one friend, the visiting professional mourner, that burst the dam of Sanichari's grief. Poetic revenge lies in the fact that the dispossessed woman sells her tears to the feudal oppressors.

Lajmi contrasts two kinds of female sexuality — Rakhee's lush beauty and practised display of feminine wiles against Dimple's unadorned austerity that also hints at suppressed passion — to good effect. There is an underlying play on existential binaries — the lure of nomadic existence and the rootedness in one's own soil — and in a way, *Rudali* is a ballad that mourns the tragic outcome of these contrary impulses. Lajmi reveals that the woman who had abandoned home and child for the love of a wandering actor is the mother whom Sanichari knows only as a dear friend. It is wanderlust that takes away loved ones from a woman rooted in her own patch of soil. The poignancy of a barren earth mother runs like a lyrical undercurrent through *Rudali.*

Illusion as in *Maya*

Is a woman's dream of autonomy and fulfilment of sexual fantasies doomed to be an illusion? Ketan Mehta's *Maya Memsaab* isn't content to be a self-conscious Indianisation of Flaubert's *Madame Bovary.* Mehta aims at more than that and transcends the events of Maya's life to suggest the fleeting illusory quality of all striving, however passionately self-destructive it is. Among all the possible names for an Indian Emma Bovary, it is significant that Mehta chooses Maya, a brilliantly transcendental name that mocks physicality even as it celebrates it so exultantly. Deepa Sahi's Maya doesn't readily invite identification from the "intelligent modern Indian woman" thirsting for liberation from centuries of subjugation. This Maya has an inherent playfulness about her, setting off an unexpectedly playful response from the stolid doctor who comes a-wooing hesitantly. Maya is capricious, craving for the fulfilment of wayward fantasies which keep changing at a bewildering pace. Maya is not a realistic portrayal of a

Deepa Sahi as Maya in
Ketan Mehta's *Maya Memsaab*

woman's quest for meaning but non-judgmental plumbing of her deepest fantasies. Mehta suggests that a woman as sensitive as Maya could be drawn to the coarse, decadent machismo of the cowardly aristocrat played by Raj Babbar. Boredom with her unimaginative husband (who seems to have lost whatever playfulness he had earlier on) sends Maya hurtling into at capricious excess of heady consumerism and self-indulgence.

The point of *Maya Memsaab* is not to work at easy identification but to take Maya out of the mundane plane of existence all together. Death becomes her as does the passionate gratification of her rioting senses. The magical surrealism of Maya's death bestows a fabulous quality to a life lived with intensity. Is total freedom an existential mirage, an illusory chase after *Maya*? No other film has even dared to dream this philosophical vision and with such deliciously beautiful images and resonant words. You don't fully understand Maya. Nor can you forget her.

It is tempting to read in this illusory *Maya* an epitaph and an apostrophe to the essential mystery and unknowability of the Indian woman as she is sought to be captured in image and sound. Film is the shattered mirror of *Maya* in which a million fragmentary images collide and coalesce. Each fragment distorts the social reality out of which the imprisoned image seeks to escape. Escape where? Into yet another shard of splintered existence?

20

Narrativity

— *Kumar Shahani*

NARRATIVE IS MOST INTRICATELY woven with ethics. It is narrative which determines the involvement and the alienation of the spectator-director. It invites him to participate or to distance himself to change or to accept reality and its interpretation. It can free him from his own ideology and that of the ruling class, simultaneously: or imprison him in both.

The cinema, which is being discussed for the most part by Metz and others, is one subservient to ideology, not concerned with ethics but the pathology of pleasure. The ethical person cannot go to such spectacles, far less make them. His aim is to integrate himself, not to suture the wounds of his own identity and that of his mother.

In fact, ethics is interaction. The conflicting forces that act upon us through our natural and cultural being and, often, as we have noticed, by the confusion of the two, produce a response which looks at the manifest either as epiphany or as tragedy. Or better still, knows the presence of the one in the other. Both are propelled by action upon knowledge.

Narrative proceeds through action. The action of the narrator, author and maker, through his mode of address shapes the world to an end that he considers to be worthwhile in itself. The interpreter, bringing his history into play, enriches it with his own experience. The spectator carries it back into life, elevating the repetition of desire, to affirm the realisation of being which assumes self-determination.

The four ends of man are simultaneous in sequence. *Dharma*, *artha*, *kama* and *moksha* are not unconnected with the pursuit of happiness in honour, wealth, pleasure and contemplation which Aristotle takes as nodal points of discussion in his work on ethics.

The problem of narrativity in our times has been the replacement of God by mechanical causation. The structural rigidity of a framework which underlies concepts that reduce acts to invariance excludes the participant-observer. To compound the loss of agency with the illusion of reality, inexorably led by its 'scientific' natural laws, threw the spectator out into the cold, deprived of his passion, incapable of ecstasy or pathos, or any form of awakening to self-awareness.

While science initially liberated us by a complete submission to the law, it can only realise itself out of its present impasse in the life-sciences by admitting the presence of individual agencies that wish to cross the threshold from the subject to the self.

A group of cells may have the same code but the object of their action is to individuate themselves.

The reason that there is yet no anarchy is that the action is affirmative and not negative.

A reductive, definitional and functional understanding tends to end up with essences which give birth to other essences or, at worst, their corruption. One goes to the origins to clarify, not to muddy our thoughts, to view in them that glorious act which annihilated the given code in favour of virtue, wealth, beauty, truth.

One aspires to that improvisation which includes the excluded, having known that even nature abounds in redundancies.

The blank screen can be the most closed or the most open form of narrative. In the horror of the vacuum that it provokes, one may fill up the space with projectiles of a passive subject whose identity is manufactured in impotency; desire reduced pathologically repetitive; the object fractured into fragments; the morality of a system beyond him imposed through illusionistic means confusing the moral with the natural law, the central equation being that of private property.

The foundation of the great republics, it is true, has been laid upon the institution of private property. But this institution has been itself built upon the disappropriation of the majority by means of war, trade and the enunciation.

It is the enunciation which seems to have determined the group's identity of itself; having found through it that inner space-time by which it first became the other, the group used its enunciation in outer space-time towards disintegration of whatever it confronted itself against, treating the other as still-life or barbaric, who as long as he had another tongue or colour, was destined to be *nature morte*.

In that sense, Christianity is right in giving the same weight to thought, word and deed, if *only* not linked to original sin. The question is to free desire from guilt. Self-awareness will then not be a series of voyeuristic acts fragmenting infinitely the subject and the object, just so as to be able to create a self-image. The integration of the 'psycho-soma' can only proceed if while distinguishing different functions, we acknowledge the source as common to both sensuous and mental functions. It is their objectification that fills us with awe and wonder with what we make of ourselves.

The modernist debate as well as art practice, having inherited a closed system of cause and effect, "the sins of the father having visited the children", has tried to contain itself through a minimalism that frees forms of their specificity, history of its events. In this way, Freud's Oedipus Complex is assimilated into variations upon a myth; psychoanalysis itself as a system and not practice. The conflicting and converging aims of man when viewed from a metapsychological and linguistic perspective, embedded norms into natural law and deprive the spectator both of his voluntary and his transcendental act.

He is first denied the status of subjectivity by the doctrine of individualism, by the positing of an absolutely knowable-consumable objective reality. The rarefied and fetishistic parts of an indestructible structure are offered as constructs of his desire.

If God doesn't exist, collage does. Preceded by poetry, art, cinema and of course the experience that generated these superstructural fragments of figuration, present-day criticism is developing the same capacity and anarchy of a passive subject.

In the 'Third World', the reflection of this loss of faith — for, what else can we call it? — is demonstrated through fundamentalism, fanned by the totally transparent literal terms of discourse that develop finally into opacity in any dialogue. Praful Bidwai's excellent analysis of the modern-day Kulturkampf in our 'different' world from the first and second reveals to us the violence of intellectual passivity. It is through all our differences that we will increase the richness of the surface of a collage being stuck on elsewhere.

As the fortuitous is condensed into vacant metaphors, the absence of organicity forces an organisation of symmetries. The novel form, in trying to criticise that iron law of the market-become-nature introduced the full-blown subjectivities, whose energies were released by that very turn of history. The accident, too, came into its grasp, with its simultaneous presence in the organised event. Unpredictable mutations became part of the historical praxis of its times. Through its own critical structure, it came upon the loss of significance and the absence of life in its metaphor.

It has had more than one way open to it since about the time that the cinema has placed itself parallel to it. It could restore itself by a movement towards myth, presenting and naming it as such, while transforming it through its descriptive passage of time. It could enlarge and deepen the metaphor by permitting the word to enter unknown recesses of the mind. It could enter into a formal equilibrium with itself.

The safest method, of course, is the last one. And, by and large, the modernist solution has been content — in all the arts — with finding an equilibrium which is, at least, not false.

This step has to be the very first towards re-integration. Before we can ask, "where do we go from here?", we have to know exactly where we stand.

The fictional form may then appear as a long-drawn out algebraic equation in descriptive language to describe a state of events that had neither the blood nor the sweat of things past. It seems to approach the symmetry of verse, while poetry itself withdraws into collage, assymetries that yield meaning only in and through their disproportion. Films, likewise, that thus break away from the dead and arid main-stream are unable to water the banks that meander about them.

There is obviously a crying need for restoration. The cannibalisation that has taken place will have nothing more left for it to feed on, not even its own body which it construes as its own image....

The beginning will have to be made with the gaze itself. The gaze that fixes itself in aggression or lowers itself to find the same fetishistic pleasure would have to lean to be attentive instead.

To see through the intermediary of a "machine that does not see what you see" and yet to build the bonds that beings and things are waiting for in order to live, it will need the profound look of the reverie. It is that caress, at once intimate and distant, that holds together the flaying limbs. The groping hand, the exasperated breath, legs that strike air instead of water or earth, all contained by the look. The voice comes later, filling up her absence.

The words fill up the sounds; the images, the words. The body, the images. Invocations of breath in the body, of life which returns it to life, music, enchantment.

These are magical happenings which we all encounter and observe, extra-ordinary in their everydayness. They are the propulsions to knowledge, not in contradiction to it as those who wish to mystify might wish to proclaim. But, of necessity, they are the frontiers, rather than strictly within the scope. Narrativity in film obviously has to transform this enchantment of musical elements into a space-time axis that includes the visual, the auditory and the historical.

Our articulation of these functions has been, hitherto, separate, forming traditions within single homogeneous cultures which develop with the suppression of parallel possibilities not only within the sense-continuums referred to but also mental systems of organisation. Thus melody might develop at the expense of harmony; it may also demand that units may not be separate from one another and brought together in a perspectival combination. Instead, the combination, the harmonic, may be contained in the unit from the overtones of which a sequence is developed. Inevitably, the historical can be viewed as being inherent in a situation, action as being. The reverse would be true in a predominantly harmonic system. Action would be seen as being. However, in both cases, the simultaneity of the two would be established.

As indeed would be, in every case, the placement of the individual in the sequence with the intervals that he will fill up with such significance, mental-emotive-physiological-semsory that carry itself over into the passage of time, not only within the work of art but outside it.

The cinematographic sequence has destroyed the old condensation of drama and the evocatory description of the novel. On the other hand, by providing the visual concreteness of 'events' and 'characters', it has given a privileged position to their relationships as they constantly redefine themselves. It is the music of history, as it is of colour and form that the cinematographic event brings out where earlier the historical had articulated itself in arbitrary signs (often reducing ethics to a culture-specific morality proclaiming itself as absolute). Simultaneously, the visual in its earlier incarnation had to overcome its representational 'thereness' by appeals to magical-decorative function or to mythical condensation. With the opening out of the sciences of perception (which inevitably have to look upon every presence only within a scale to make any sense of it) and the cinema which assimilates and grows out of these sciences, all art has been given a new lease of life since it brings to the foreground, again, not the existence of things and ideas separated, distinguished and understood but held together, grasped, lived and restored. Or, at least, that is what the cinema, like all art, is capable of, when left to itself.

Yet, it is hardly ever left to itself. The strategies for the exploration of the self have to contend not only with the profit motive and the propaganda machine, obviously present as controlling forces, but also with the resistance of modes of thought that persist even if they no longer serve the dominant ideologies.

At a formal level, the difficulty lies in transpositions. From myth to music, from the articulated series penetrating to an unconscious to the permeation of the entire body and mind with the rhythms and self-created world, with all the immortality of time.

The visual distinctiveness of phenomena is transposed to the aural or intellectual, moving towards the opposite directions of poverty of matter. It is as if the logic of systems constructed by us leaves us all the time in partial realisations that militate against each other. Each art and each tradition of the art, linking itself to history and to nature, tries in despair to break itself down to re-integrate the whole of existence.

Compounded with the modern empiricist's total fragmentation, these transpositions are themselves rendered, both in theory and in practice, into mere transliterations from one discipline into another, referring to little else beyond the narrow 'terminologies' and techniques that were crafted to contain ineffable intimations of immortality.

Evidently, the impulse was spiritual, the breathtaking experience psycho-somatic, the forms social. The spectator too must enter, find the points of entry into this inner world extending into space-time, simultaneously, in his social-psychological, the personal as universal being.

The gift that one makes to nature in return for being gratuitously part of it has to be renewed constantly. In the renewal, the epiphany may turn into tragedy, yet will uplift the pathos to such heights that those blinded by it will weep more of their wisdom, less of their sorrow.

I think that as we pass from a world governed by law to that where a sense of play and the joy of re-creation will be made real, as full and eternal in its transitory reality, we will discover the narrativity that cinema has to offer, the ethics of weaving a language with which you may wrap and unwrap yourself in sensuous ease; not to shroud existence with a will of prophecy, but to facet experience with the brilliance of a thousand suns.

It is at this catastrophic hour that we may wonder how we have survived our tale. Like Yudhisthir, we may assign reasons for the fall of those who did not survive and were believed. Like Yudhisthir, we may overcome the ultimate ambivalence of the many religions and societies to affirm our faith in the dog.

We may, at the end of a millenium, be weary of the world. Let not the world be weary of itself.

Part IV

21

Directors' Perspective

A NUMBER OF DIRECTORS WERE asked the same set of five questions. Some, like Mani Kaul, Buddhadeb Dasgupta, Kumar Shahani, Adoor Gopalakrishnan, B. Narsing Rao, wrote down their answers themselves; Aribam Syam Sharma's answers were terse — and pithy; some did not respond. The others, in Bombay, were interviewed by Shoma A. Chatterjee who transcribed and sent in the answers.

The questons posed were the following:

1. What is it about the cinema as a medium of expression that attracts you?
2. Do you have an Indian or an international audience in mind when you make a film? Is there a difference at all? Do you find you have to make a choice in the matter?
3. Given the fact that ours is a developing country, do you feel that the creative artist in general, and the filmmaker in particular, should play a direct social role — as did, for instance, Eisenstein and his colleagues in Russia? Or do you feel that we are now at a stage where the filmmaker should be able to pursue his own inclinations and tastes?
4. How do you see the future of cinema? How would you like it develop under the present circumstances — generally and in India?
5. How do you think the government can play a constructive role?

Subhash Ghai

1. It is the magic of cinema and the impact of sound and visuals which can make people sit in an auditorium for three hours reacting to every emotion and humour of my play which I find attractive about cinema.
2. Whenever you make a film, you make it for a certain society and the people and characters on screen belong to that society. So, when I am making an Indian film, I am making it for an Indian audience. I have to make a choice and understand the difference between the national and international audience.
3. In a country like ours, we, film-makers, cannot play a direct social role because of the cultural mix. For Eisenstein, it was one Russia, one theory and he was one man. We have many theories. In a multicultural country, we cannot play a direct social role. A film-maker should be allowed to be a democratic and a secular person himself so that his inclinations and his tastes match with the tastes and inclinations of society.
4. New technology will always offer tough competition to current technology. But as I visualise the future of cinema, I feel it will always exist and will exist grandly, as it is existing at the present time in America. It will continue to exist because of its unique magic impact inside a darkened theatre. To really concentrate and develop the high points of cine technology like the 70 mm screen, stereo, the Dolby system, the panoramic screen are needed as inputs in our country. So far as outputs go, cinema should be taken more seriously. One way of doing this is to have good and sophisticated cinema halls for which a revolutionary change in the exhibiting system is called for.
5. The government, on its part, should do the following for cinema:

   (a) Creation of more talent for cinema by setting up more film institutes and cultural centres. India needs a minimum of 150 regular film institutes teaching mass communications and cinema techniques.

   (b) Developing the entire infrastructure of cinema halls by giving the exhibitors all kinds of subsidies, a better environment and, above all, giving cinema theatres the same importance that it gives to cultural institutions. What mainstream cinema lacks today is respect from the government. The Government, therefore, should begin to treat cinema with respect. Every theatre should be institutionalised as a cultural centre, like a public park or a place of entertainment for the masses.

Gulzar

1. Anybody who reacts to art in all its forms and is aware of it, and wants to share it with others, gets the urge to express it. One may express it through music, painting, poetry, literature, or any other form of art. The desire is to capture the essence of life and share it with others, to beautify this mother earth, the planet that we know. The urge to share may extend to the rest of the Universe too, as and when we extend our contact.

   I express myself through poetry, literature and films. Film imbibes many other forms of art. It expresses itself through photography, architecture, acting, music, other than my own medium of expression. This helps me to extend my contact with other forms of art and thus enrich my own knowledge, my own person and my extensive contacts with people. Hence, I find cinema to be the most satisfying in terms of creative effort.
2. Cinema is the most modern form of expression and offers extensive contacts with people. It crosses the barriers of language and can be shared internationally with much less an effort than other forms of art. Filmmaking is not just one art of expression. It is an assembly of arts. It is this complex form that makes it more fascinating than other forms of expression and, perhaps, that is good enough a reason for me to make films.
3. Every film, even if it is a medium of expression for its maker, in fact any form of art has the responsibility of promoting aesthetics and social values and to keep a critical eye on society. To study and improve human relationships is the role of any creative artist through any medium — nationally and internationally. Cinema is no exception.
4. The character of cinema remains the same, never mind the outlet or the form. It is a visual art. It has just crossed its infancy and is growing. So it is bound to grow. I would like cinema to develop a greater sense of responsibility towards society, particularly, in our

country, to educate through entertainment. In the distant past, this role was played very effectively by our great epics. Cinema should adopt the same with respect and dignity.

5. Government should expand its exhibiting outlets by making small art theatres, particularly in the field of children's films, animation films all of which should get encouragement from the government. Every state should have a cinema complex like West Bengal has, Nandan in Calcutta.

   And so far as censorship goes, it is conspicuous by its absence. One must understand that censorship is something that cannot be imposed from above. A man should censor his own conscience rather than censor his films. Censorship is something that should come from within.

Saeed Mirza

1. What attracts me to cinema is its images and the fact that one does not have to rely on words to bring out ideas. Actually, the possibility of reaching into the subliminal, both for oneself and for the audience, is also important. At another level, the possibility of juxtaposing the word to the image, at times in contradiction, at times in a complementary manner, and at times as rhetoric is what underscores the magic of the medium. In the process of dialogue, it helps me personally to clear my own thought processes and I find cinema a great ground for experimentation for myself.
2. I don't realy have any specific audience in mind when I am making a film. I do know that whatever I want to express, the entire experience, the entire stream of events, conditions, situations, are rooted and reflect my own country automatically. I nevertheless hope that there is a kind of universality in what I say which also reflects an international perspective. Images have a kind of universality. But situations, emotions, events are mainly rooted, though I believe that by their very nature they can also go beyond their roots. Rootedness does not necessarily make you colloquial. The very fact that you can relate to Bertrand Russell, to Balazc, to Tolstoy, to Che Guevara, means that in your soul, you are international.
3. At one point of time, I believed that cinema can also be a tool for political comment and, perhaps, change. I no longer do so because

I think it simultaneously requires other socio-political changes. Cinema is just one part of this social structure. Even so, it need not always be directed at social comment. For cinema to play a direct social role, the motivation has to be spontaneous, not designed, not manipulated.

4. Cinema seems to be going towards more technological changes. Technology can be used with a lot of grace like some people have done. Take, for example, people like Robert Altman, Francis Ford Coppola, who have used not only technology but other inputs as well. It is the very structure of the medium consisting of lights, events, incidents, characters, themes, sound, camera, music, where technology and aesthetics go hand in hand. You have to compartmentalise your mind and try to strike a delicate balance between poetry and mathematics.
5. There are so many things that the government should and can do : (a) building smaller theatres, (b) increasing distribution outlets, (c) telecast art films side by side with mainstream films on television so that viewers are exposed to more than one kind of cinema, and (d) some kind of ethical guidelines for the Censor Board to follow because censorship today is archaic on paper and practically non-existent in reality. A government body like the NFDC should have vision and compassion for humanity. Institutions which exist for specific purposes, be it the NFDC or be it any other organisation, are singularly lacking in vision.

Ketan Mehta

1. It is a process that you get in terms of dreams. And dreams are the most fascinating aspects of life and living. Cinema comes closest to human dreams. It excites the entire being, from the subconscious to the totally conscious relationship, inviting hyper-reality as a way of living. It evokes electrifying energy from within.
2. I am primarily an Indian, there is a direct link between my being Indian and my films but the audience is not limited. It is both universal and simultaneously rooted in India. When I make a film, I just have a fascinating script that I have in mind. "Audience" is too generic a term for the heterogenous group of people who, at times, have to project themselves as one. Audiences are arbitrary categories which are not valid. You don't have an audience till

you have made a film. We are all aware that even in India, the audience is a very, very heterogenous group. I cannot really dictate audience behaviour so my choice remains confined to the film that I want to make. I can only dictate my own behaviour in terms of the film I am making.

3. This divide between the socialist-realist cinema and the author-backed cinema was created in the 1930s and 1940s. Cinema is now a 100-year-old medium and, therefore, there is scope for making every kind of film and for every kind of filmmaker. To bracket any filmmaker into this or the other role amounts to actually clipping his wings. A human being's mind is not divided into categories. And to my mind, social reasoning and self-expression are not necessarliy mutually exclusive happenings.
4. Cinema as a celluloid medium is a product of the mechanical age and it is bound to go out by the end of the century to be replaced by newer technologies. But cinema as a collective, larger-than-life experience will survive because the need for this form will remain irrespective of anything and everything that is happening in the world of technology or entertainment. A filmmaker is not a linear happening, he grows and changes in different directions. It is a continuous process of self-exploration. Personally, the next few films I would like to make are a sciene fiction, a historical epic, a musical fantasy — which I am now making. I have still not explored the various genres that already exist in cinema. I am looking for new experiences so each film has to be a totally new experience for me.
5. India, though it is the largest film-producing country in the world, does not recognise cinema as an industry. The industry is burdened with the most oppressive tax structure by the government which is killing, and the government should do something about this. The attitude of the government is not media-friendly. The government should allow new technology, recognise cinema as a proper industry and subsidise the establishment of new theatres.

Govind Nihalani

1. Basically, it is the magical quality of the medium which has rich potential in terms of dreams, in terms of nightmares, in terms of poetry, visions, and, of course, in terms of creating a very intense

view of reality. The possibilities of the medium excite me the most. And then, there is the tremendous amount of creative satisfaction one gets when one sees one's work on the screen. It is like creating a complete world in itself, something which you have yourself created.

2. My ideal audience is myself. Apart from that, I have my own society as my audience because all my subjects are responses to the reality around me and reflect my ability to relate to my own people. This is the starting point. I have noticed that if your work has a certain honesty, authenticity and depth, in terms of aspects relating to the human condition that is expressed through your work, then it acquires a kind of universality and audiences from different linguistic and cultural backgrounds from all over the world can relate to it and respond to it. I also believe that, as a filmmaker, one must proceed from the particular to the general and when I say 'particular', I mean the film must have roots in the soil that I, as a filmmaker, have roots in. I cannot make a film for a hypothetical, international audience. What is an international audience? Is it French? It is American? Italian? I'd rather make a film for an audience I know. But this does not preclude the possibility of my working with another medium if I know the medium. Right now, the choice to make or not to make a film for an international audience is not in my hands. It is for another country to ask me to make a film for that kind of audience which has a broader base than my own roots.

3. A filmmaker is usually quite aware of the potential of cinema to create an awareness among his viewers about issues that are dealt with in a film. One canot forget one's social responsibility while handling cinema, which has the strong potential of arousing consciousness. There is no such thing as pure entertainment. A filmmaker's attitude comes through even in the films which he may not intend to be socially relevant. Beyond that, it is left entirely to the filmmaker to choose the role his/her films should play in the process of change, social, political, cultural, whatever. I am not in favour of creating a definite code of conduct for filmmakers but a filmmaker as an artist must be allowed full freedom of expression and the freedom to grow as an artist, which includes a total and complete change of viewpoint from time to

time.

4. Cinema as an art form has grown along with the scientific and the industrial development of the 19th century. Its evolution has been deeply related to advances in technology. The electronic media, satellite transmissions, home video system, cable are all part of the technology that employ image and sound and to a great extent, even the grammar of cinema. A filmmaker should look upon these technological development as something one should make the best use of for one's own creative expression. Whether all these invasions are a threat to the future of cinema or not is a matter of perception. Television or the electronic media should provide you with the possibilities of making a film free from box-office pressures. I look upon the future of cinema as bright since television, with some degree of persuasion and patience, can become a medium for a certain amount of experimental work which can make a film for the small screen and also for the larger one, like Kièslowski's short film series or some films by Fellini. A film can have a longer life through the electronic media of television than it ever had before.
5. Government has a responsibility towards culture, and cinema, to me, is a part of culture. It is not just a pure commercial activity. The government can do a lot with the rules and regulations prevalent in the country in terms of import of equipment, availability of raw stock, incentives which directly affect the industry. The government, at another level, should clean up its censorship act in the sense that if it thinks that the Censors are necessary, it should ensure that certain undesirable elements do not creep into films right from sex, vulgarity, obscenity, to the hurting of religious sentiments, feelings etc. Finally, I think that the government has the responsibility to ensure the growth of a stream of cinema which is not entirely controlled by market forces. A certain amount of experimentation in form, theme, content must occur for the healthy growth of culture of which cinema is an integral part.

Yash Chopra

1. The most fascinating thing about cinema is that it deals with all aspects of what you call art — with human emotions too. You don't have to be a cinematographer or an actor, but you must

know all these fields in order to define the exact shade and shape you wish to give to a film. As a director you deal with different situations, with different levels of human relationships which, to my mind, are the most unpredictable things about cinema.

2. We always have an Indian audience in mind because, though our films run abroad, they mainly run to an Indian audience. Sometimes, I do have to make a choice. For example, I am releasing *Lamhe* in the international circuit, completely dubbed in English, also edited to suit the demands of an international audience.
3. A filmmaker has to play a social role. But then, it all depends on what you mean by the phrase 'social role'. I think I have done it through my films. *Dhool ka Phool* dealt with illegitimacy, *Dharmputra* explored national integration, *Aadmi aur Insaan* underlined corruption, *Waqt* dwelt upon the ironies of fate, *Daag* probed into the dilemma of a man circumstantially placed between two wives. In *Lamhe,* too, I tried to break a few conventional barriers but it did not seem to click with the Indian audience. You cannot, however, use cinema as a pedagogic platform from which you deliver lectures on social change. You have to put things across very subtly. And therein lies the craftsmanship and the creativity of a filmmaker.
4. The future of cinema is very bright. Because, today a lot of avenues are opening up. Cinema as entertainment has a very bright future.
5. The government must play an important role. It has not legalised cable TV today. It has not been able to cut out video piracy. It could drastically revolutionise the entertainment tax structure and scrap it or give it back to the producer for his next project. NFDC, for example, should have more finance at their disposal, some to encourage new talent, some to mainstream cinema.

Ramesh Sippy

1. Cinema is certainly a big, audio-visual screen where you have an almost captive audience in a dark auditorium and you can bring out gentle nuances on a very large screen. You can make people laugh and cry with you, take them on a joyride, thrill them, psyche them. These audio-visuals are at your command and it is how you present this material that will determine the results. You can play with sound and pictures the way you want, within given parameters.

2. I have an Indian audience in mind when I make a film with the average Indian psyche in mind. Cinema has a language of its own, so, in a way, it is international because there are certain feelings, emotions, etc. which are international. All people love, hate, envy, fight, universally. On the other hand, certain cultures, norms and acceptances, beliefs may be localised. But if you are catering to an Indian audience, you do not have a choice. You must be clear in your mind about the audience you are dealing with. We are moving towards a time when you will be able to reach out to an international audience. But the success of duality is yet to be tested.
3. I am not rigid about the theory that a filmmaker must convey a social message. It is equally wrong for a filmmaker to decide once and for all that a film should never convey a social message. In my opinion, through an entertainment medium like cinema, if you can convey a social message, you should do so.
4. As a filmmaker myself, I have only positive things to say about the future of cinema. I would like to see cinema grow and flourish.
5. The government should play a significant role in the growth and development of cinema in our country in many ways:
   (a) Its attitude should be commercially helpful.
   (b) It should help in the control of video piracy.
   (c) The available infrastructure should be reinforced and enlarged instead of allowing it to dwindle.
   (d) Alongwith help from the corporate sector, studios and cinema theatres should be built in keeping with the changing needs of the changing times such as building multiple cinema halls alongwith shopping malls, restaurants, etc as in the West.
   (e) Existing cinemas should be updated with better seating, proper air-conditioning, etc. in order to meet the challenge of the satellite invasion which is keeping people away from cinema halls.

Shyam Benegal

1. Cinema uses elements from practically all the different arts — literature, music, painting, photography, dance, mime, movement, poetry. This is what I feel extremely attractive about cinema. It allows you to explore all the arts while you are actually making a

film, or, while you are working towards making a film.

2. When you are making a film, the primary audience of the film is no one else but you. At that point of time, therefore, you do not think in terms of an international audience. A film is complete only when the audience sees it. If you are thinking of an audience before you make a film, you are commodising it. You are seeing it as a product which will bring along with it its own compulsions. I don't particularly care for the kind of film which manipulates my creative expression by market factors.

   There is certainly a difference between an Indian and an international audience. There are cultural differences, linguistic differences, differences in body language, the manner in which people communicate with each other is different. Semiotcis, signs and symbols differ from one culture to another. But at another level, there is a cinema that creates a uniformity in communication which can be understood by all at that level. Hollywood has acquired the ability to communicate to a world audience. So Hollywood films have a world market.

   However, I believe that the essential source of creativity and of art lies in the specificity of the culture it is born into and belongs to. Creative artistic expression tends to be culture-specific. But exceptions are there — Charlie Chaplin, Kurasawa, Ray, who, through their films, could communicate with their heart and soul with everybody. I believe standardisation and uniformity militate against true artistic expression.

3. Whether creative people play a social role or not depends on the kind of compulsions society forces on them. Under certain social conditions, you, as a filmmaker, find yourself reacting to those conditions whether you like to react to them or not. Artistic inclinations sometimes have to do with individual compulsions, sometimes with social compulsions, sometimes with historical compulsions. Lenin thought and believed cinema to have an important revolutionary role to play. All early Soviet filmmakers like Eisenstein used cinema as a means of social and militant transformation as a given part of thinking of Soviet Communism itself. In Brazil, on the other hand, the new cinema used cinema as a means of destroying the Establishment. Finally, a filmmaker acts according to what his compulsions are. He is not just a reactive

individual. Being creative is more than being just a reactive person.

4. Cinema is now at the crossroads in the sense that TV is becoming the mass medium. So, the role of cinema as a mass medium of entertainment no longer exists. This gives us, filmmakers, the opportunity to redefine the space that cinema can occupy. In what manner are people going to enjoy cinema now? Would they go to the large-screen theatres, to small cinema halls, or would they watch it at home? All these possibilities have opened up. This solves the question of the greater accessibility of cinema for the masses. The factors that have made cinema more accessible are also allowing us to distinguish clearly between that cinema which is a genuine artistic creation and that cinema which is not. Cinema now, therefore, is seen in a role that goes beyond that of a simple means of mass entertainment. We can never work towards a serious, aesthetic kind of cinema.
5. Anything that is artistic needs support. It cannot be left to the marketplace. Government has a responsibility towards culture. Its constructive role would be to support, protect, preserve and help develop works of cultural significance. What is a civilisation worth without its culture?

Jahnu Barua

1. I could have been a musician or a painter. I have always been attracted to the arts and enjoy composing music or designing a poster. But cinema, for me, is the ultimate art form. This is because it combines in one medium so many creative facets. And technical craft as well. First you conceptualise the film, then you work out the screenplay using both imagination and writing skill. Then, while directing, you are composing your shots in collaboration with your cameraman, using a painter's eye. Coordinating and motivating actors, interacting with the technical crew, I become a sort of theatre person activating all individuals under my command towards a single aesthetic goal that has been dreamt of at the scripting stage....All this excites me tremendously because all my creative faculties are being utilised at the same time. In addition, I have to use a certain media instinct to make sure that I am communicating with my audience. Cinema makes me feel like a Renaissance artist at work.

2. There are two aspects to this question: the specific and the general. When I make a film, I am inspired by the subject, which, in the films I have made so far, refers to matters concerned with the heart and mind of the Assamese people. So, obviously, I have this audience in mind. But on the general level, whatever film I make is created with the attempt to universalise a specific problem. And if I succeed in my execution, then, automatically, I am reaching out to an international audience that can relate that particular Assamese problem to their own world. Therefore, I see my audience as an abstract, universal concept.
3. Firstly, I want to say that a filmmaker is always an indirect social commentator whether in the West or in the developing world. There is no real difference here. Where the difference occurs, in my view, is in the social responsibility of the filmmaker. In the West, a filmmaker who is an 'exploitation' artist, in the sense that he makes films exploiting violence or sex or something else, he is dealing with an audience which understands that it is watching a brand of 'exploitation' in the guise of entertainment. But such filmmakers are more dangerous in the developing nations because of the socio-economic vulnerability of the audience. That is why I feel that a filmmaker in India must feel responsible towards society for every film he is making without playing a direct social role. Also speaking directly to the audience on an issue tends to work as propaganda and inflame the sentiments of the people. A filmmaker anywhere in the world, I feel, must not attempt direct social activism. He must not forget that he is a commentator and not a participator.
4. From what I see around me, I see a great future for cinema as business. But not as an art form. But I must emphasise that cinema as an art form cannot be wiped out completely, because its need will always arise at some point or the other. It will struggle through a process of self-generation.
5. The government can play a constructive role by having organisations like the NFDC, but different from the present set-up. These organisations should emphasise the creative output more than the monetary profit on a balance sheet. A good film must be seen by the government as a cultural investment for which there may be no quick economic returns.

Adoor Gopalakrishnan

1. In a way it is the realisation that the medium still lends itself to further explorations. And then there is the great thrill in reaching out to a multitudinous audience at home as well as everywhere else on this earth and sharing with them the perception of a world according to you.
2. My films are primarily addressed to a home audience, what you call a regional audience. The nuances and subtleties of the languages, customs and culture as expressed in these films would be best understood and appreciated by a Malayali, if he really cares. This is not to preclude the cultivated audiences outside the region in the country.

   It has been my observation, maybe a partial one, that an international audience unfamiliar with life lived in India often fails to grasp our genuine works of cinema as there is a lot of resistance to accepting things that do not conform to their idea of how the third world carries on. And when they pick up crass imitations and commonplace works in acceptance and at times for adulation, one is left wondering how vague value judgement can be. This is not to say there are no welcome exceptions. The reality of international receptivity being so, the real challenge of a filmmaker is to remain true to himself and to his art.
3. I would rather leave it to the artist. An artist's role in society, which is always self-assumed, is to remain an artist and to fiercely preserve his integrity. And this the society should savour and nourish for its own health and well-being. Poor art even when it preaches social messages fails to affect society.
4. It is likely that all predictions about the future of cinema may go wrong. The technology is bound to change, but will the communal and magical experience of being under the spell of larger-than-life images in the darkened halls of cinema ever be substituted? I am doubtful. In fact, an alternative, intermediate technology needs to be encouraged. We need to develop a technology which would save the filmmaker from the vagaries and variations of the chemistry of film processing and the callous handling of films at every stage of production and projection.
5. It is becoming fashionable these days to talk and write about

commercial cinema with an air of seriousness and reverence although the makers hardly pay that kind of attention to those efforts. The Government also seems to take the populist line. Look at the national awards for instance. They were originally instituted to encourage production of films with high aesthetic and technical excellence, and social relevance. Every year juries are set up to evaluate these qualities in our films. But do we get the right juries who have the professional knowledge and integrity and the passion and commitment for good cinema? One gets the sad impression that year after year awards are partitioned on the basis of sheer numerical strength of members from a particular region or language. Governmental promotion being what it is, it is high time we started preserving and promoting a minority cinema which like the best of literature and art addresses itself to the intelligent and the discerning. We have a sizeable population of them large enough to sustain a movement. But this audience is scattered all over the country. They are not concentrated in one city or region. The answer is to have small cinemas devoted exclusively to the screening of these films in every big city of the country.

This is an area where we have so far not made any effort or progress save seminars and resolutions. Maybe it is up to some crazy enterprising individual to set up a chain of such cinemas and disprove the fears of financial loss.

Maybe I am day-dreaming.

Buddhadeb Dasgupta

1. It gives me the freedom of expressing the experiences of visits to my second world where I always wanted to live.
2. I care no less than any other filmmaker about my audience here and abroad, especially the audience of my country as my cinema has to be meaningful to them first. But it is cinema that becomes more significant than my audience while I make my film. The audience can grow with time rejecting and re-accepting many things in between shots. There is always a chance that a filmmaker will be understood one day if he has not knowingly faulted to speak in living images to give his impressions of truth.
3. It is almost next to impossible to be in a creative process like cinema without commenting on anything about the society around

one because it operates within reality. A filmmaker extends this reality, sometimes unconditionally, to read out pages from his second world, but even that can be a hypothesis of the structure of social reality.

4. With the constant threat of electronic media cinema might one day lose the mystery of images, and that can happen anywhere. But I don't want to last till that time. But if I have to, I shall better keep myself away from it for the sake of my writings.
5. For the government cinema has lost all its importance. So one had better not to expect anything from the government.

B. Narsing Rao

1. Basically, I took to cinema because of its audio-visual format that embodies several arts. To me cinema provided a fountainhead for my own creativity.
2. I make films in Telugu. Obviously I think in that idiom while shaping my scripts. Though my films may be restricted to a province, their themes are of universal appeal and are easily accessible to the rest of the world as well.
3. I believe that any film reflects the inner self of the filmmaker. It is itself his or her social statement. But there is no question of any ordinance that all filmmakers should fall in a particular mould.
4. I don't see any great impediments to the development of the cinema in our country. As an art form, cinema is flying high. We must enable the audience to appreciate and imbibe the art of cinema.
5. No comment

Aribam Syam Sharma

1. -
2. No.
3. No. The filmmaker should be free to pursue his own inclinations.
4. In India, confusing.
5. By establishing an academy of film, an autonomous body, at he centre.

Mani Kaul

1. The fact that cinema permits a conception of feeling without any

given code! You may begin with small interventions, even deviations in the norm and enlarge/discover a new whole — a new becoming. The creative procedures of the cinematograph, therefore, stand diametrically opposite to those of pre-industrial and traditional forms.

2. If you are not selling anything you need not keep any audience in mind, Indian or international. Marketing surveys or political campaigns need to keep specific targets in mind when making a choice in regard to regions. But cinema must learn to above all respect its prospective audience, accept as made up of feeling and thinking individuals, capable of making individual association, evoking different world. It is another matter that at this moment of time films aiming to exploit or brainwash an audience have incapacitated the spectator of his power to fantasise. The audience is repeatedly made to respond to a multitude of 'types'.
3. When a filmmaker, working as an artist, pursues his own inclinations and tastes, he is already playing a direct social role. The Russian experiment was not born in the heads of a few filmmakers — it was a deeply specific and particular flowering of the Bolshevik upsurge. In the dominant consumerist universe in our age (carried to the edge by the fundamentalists who force a divide between the sensuous and spiritual domains) the work of an artist anywhere in the world must be understood in a new light.
4. It is absolutely a responsibility of the government to discover ways of mobilising a new culture, to initiate artistic experiments and protect the interests of the artists.
5. -

Kumar Shahani

1. The cinema is divinity rendered palpable, profane, true.
2. I think that I have every individual that I have ever seen or heard or sensed in mind when I make a film, as an *individual* where the group constructs dissolve or are seen in embryonic forms.
3. All creative artists anywhere do play a social role, even if they are not aware of it. The difference with Eisenstein was that (a) he was intensely self-conscious, and (b) that when the 'social' role became prescriptive (directed by the State or the market, it is the same), he was virtually unable to make films.

4. If people want to preserve and develop what the 20th century has to offer, to work on it, or realise its aspirations, the cinema will help them discover themselves. If, on the other hand, people want to obliterate history, consume it, the cinema will have to face the same regression into craft that the other arts will face.
5. Free it from the market as it frees it from its own control.

Sai Paranjpye

Its potency, directness, reach, pliability above all. This medium is putty in the hands of a creative person. It holds up a mirror to life; can be larger than life; or quite simply turn its back on life and escape into the nether world. Cinema is the ultimate tool of one-way communication for the egoist. An expensive outlet for self expression — multifaceted and challenging.

Frankly, I am the audience when I make a film. Once you stop to wonder whether a certain thing is too subtle of too gross — too abstract or too simplistic for a certain section of the audience — you are in trouble. You cannot make films on a computer. I try to keep one step ahead of what I do. It usually works.

I don't believe that a creative person — a filmmaker in particular — should take it on himself to play the keeper of the nation's conscience. A piece of exquisitely created whimsy is every bit as valid as a film laden with a contemporary social message. The choice of subject is the prerogative and the privilege of the creator. His obligation is primarily to his art; and through his art to society. My film *Disha* was built around a very deep malaise of our times: the exodus of able-bodied youth from villages into cities. A socially relevant film! I made it because the dramatic contradictions and scope of the subject matter appealed to me as a filmmaker. My earlier film *Chashme Buddoor* was pure fun. A giddy comedy with no claim to social relevance, other than making you laugh for two hours. To my mind both these films have their place in the scheme of things, despite the vast difference in their premises.

The NDFC has given the nation a spate of very meaningful and worthy films. It is the Indian government's parallel channel of film production. A viable distribution network has to be set up and put into action; to match it. Making great film is a self-defeating activity if these films do not reach their audience.

Contributors

1. **RAFIQUE BAGHDADI**: Film critic and writer in Bombay. Has been writing regularly and extensively on cinema, books and urban history in major newspapers and magazines for many years. Currently working with *Business India*.

2. **VINOD BHARDWAJ**: Journalist, film critic and Hindi poet. Publications include collections on poetry, two books on Indian art and books on cinema: *Naya Cinema* (New Cinema) and *Samaye aur Cinema* (Time and Cinema). Has written scripts for television serials, including a twelve-part story of Indian painting. Is currently media and cultural correspondent of *Navbharat Times*, New Delhi.

3. **SUDHIR BOSE**: Reader in English at the University of Delhi. British Council scholar in the early '70s. Winner of the National Award for Best Film Critic of 1992. Writes film criticism regularly for national newspapers and periodicals. Contributing editor of *Cinemaya*.

4. **PARTHA CHATTERJEE**: Filmmaker/critic. Directed *B.C. Sanyal,* a documentary on the noted Indian painter. Produced a forty-minute documentary on Tribal Medicine. Has written regularly on cinema and culturally related matters for the last decade. Contributing editor of *Cinemaya.*

5. **SHOMA A. CHATTERJEE**: Bombay-based free-lance journalist and author, specialising in cinema, television, women's issues and culture. Winner of the National Award for Best Film Critic of 1990, she is the author of three books- *An Indian Woman's Search for an Identity, Yes, and Other Stories,* and *The Indian Woman in Perspective.*

6. **CHIDANANDA DAS GUPTA**: Author of *Talking about Films, The Cinema of Satyajit Ray* and *The Painted Face,* he has written extensively on cinema and literature. Along with Satyajit Ray, co-founder of the Calcutta Film Society in 1948. Has made a number of documentary films including the exquisite *Ananda Coomaraswamy.* Directed the feature *Bilet Pherat* in 1974. Currently directing his second feature film, *Amodini,* a black comedy.

7. **RASHMI DORAISWAMY** : Film critic and theoretician. Her doctoral thesis was on Mikhail Bakhtin, the Russian philosopher. Teaches Russian at Jamia Milia Islamia, Delhi. Writes on cinema for leading publications in India and abroad. Deputy editor of *Cinemaya.*

8. **AMRIT GANGAR**: Bombay-based film critic in English and Gujarati, is the head of Screen Unit, one of the leading film societies of the country. He has edited many books on cinema, including *Andheri Tarkovsky: A Homage, Rigours of Austerity: Robert Bresson,* books on Luis Bunuel and Joris Ivens, *Genres of Indian Cinema,* etc, received the award for outstanding performance in the film society movement by the International Federation of Film Clubs in Germany, 1989.

9. **B.D. GARGA**: Veteran film historian, critic and long-time documentary filmmaker. Grew up with the rise of the Indian talkies as well as with the coming of the documentary and chronicled the fortunes of both with precision and affection. Pioneer of the film society movement in India. Played an active role in setting up the National Film Archive in Pune.

10. **DEEPA GEHLOT**: Free-lance film and theatre critic in Bombay. She has scripted documentaries and done various programmes for radio and television. Currently she is consulting editor of *Plus Newsbank,* a features syndicate, and is working on a series of film biographies.

11. **S. KRISHNASWAMY**: With a Ph.D from Columbia University, New York, Dr. Krishnaswamy is a noted filmmaker and film historian. His book *Indian Film*, co-authored with Eric Barnouw, is a standard text for film students. He has won national and

international awards for his short films which include the four-hour documentary *Indus Valley to Indira Gandhi*, and the Tamil serial *Thalaimurai Ezhuchi* on the freedom struggle. His Hindi TV *Upasana*, based on the ancient Tamil twin-epics, is to be telecast in 1995.

12. **K. HARIHARAN** : Graduated in direction from the Film and Television Insitute of India, Pune, in 1976 and has since made a number of award-winning feature films, documentaries and films for children. Currently he is concentrating on series for television. He is also an incisive writer on Tamil cinema.

13. **IQBAL MASUD**: Retired senior government official, has been writing on cinema, literature and related subjects for many years. Regular film critic of the *Indian Express*. In an era of fiercely partisan criticism he continues to hold his own through eminently fair, balanced and astute writings.

14. **TAMAKI MATSUOKA-KANDA**: With a B.A. in Hindi Literature from Tokyo University of Foreign Studies, she started to introduce and promote Indian films in Japan from 1975 onwards and with a group of friends publishes a monthly magazine, *Indian Newsletter*. Received a Toyota Foundation grant to conduct research on "Cultural Exchange through Films in 20th Century Asia" and is currently completing a book based on her research.

15. **P K NAIR** : Film scholar and former Director of the National Film Archive, Pune. Has contributed extensively to film education in India including the training of filmmakers at the Film and Television Institute, Pune.

16. **KIRONMOY RAHA** : Film and theatre critic. Has been associated with the Calcutta Film Society from its inception in 1948. Has written two books — *Bengali Theatre* and *Bengali Cinema*. Has written extensively for national and international publications.

17. **MAITHILI RAO**: Former lecturer with a Masters in English Literature, she has been a freelance film critic and writer since 1981. Has been a regular film critic, TV critic and columnist for *The Sunday Observer*, the *Independent* Bombay Magazine and

Eve's Weekly in addition to writing for other leading newspapers and journals. Has subtitled films from Hindi, Telugu and Kannada into English. Lives in Bombay.

18. **MADAN GOPAL SINGH**: His doctoral thesis was "A Semiotic Study of Indian Cinema". Reader in English at University of Delhi. Has contributed articles and papers on film theory to leading journals on the subject. Has lectured on cinema in India and abroad. Contributing editor of *Cinemaya* and executive editor of *Journal of Arts and Ideas*.

18. **KUMAR SHAHANI**: Leading director of the Indian avant-garde. Has directed memorable features like Maya Darpan, Tarang and Kasba and the documentaries *Fire in Belly*, *A Ship Aground* and *Bhavantarana*. Awarded the Bhabha Fellowship to study the Epic form. Has recently been given the Nehru fellowship. Scholar and theoretician; has written for prestigious journals and lectured and conducted workshops in London and Geneva.

Landmarks

— Compiled by Rafique Baghdadi

1895 The Lumière Brothers launch the 'Cinématographe' on December 28 at the Grand Café in Paris

1896 The operators of Lumière Brothers bring the 'Cinématographe' to India in the months of June-July, and give shows at Watson's Hotel, Bombay. First show at the Novelty Theatre, Bombay, on July 14, 1896, by Maurice Sestier, en route to Australia. Touring conjurors on all continents include short films in their 'magic' acts. The types of subjects shown on the screen are: *Arrival of Train, Sea Bathers, Parade of the Guards, Stormy Seas,* and so on.

1897 Maharashtrian photographer Harishchandra Sakharam Bhatvadekar imports a motion picture camera and begins filming Indian 'topicals'.

1898 Short films shown at Indian theatres include such items as *Poona Races '98* and *Train Arriving at Bombay Station.*

1899 In Calcutta, Hiralal Sen films excerpts from plays at the Classic Theatre and shows them in conjunction with stage performances.

1901 First Indian newsreel shot by Bhatvadekar, *Return of Wrangler Paranjpye,* based on the life of the mathematician and Indian scholar.

1902 In Calcutta, J.F. Madan launches regular 'bioscope' showings in a tent on the Maidan.

1903 The Coronation Durbar for Edward VII is filmed by Bhatvadekar and many others.

1904 Films begin coming into India from French, American, Italian, British, German, and Danish sources, with French films dominant.

1906 'Picture palaces' become a feature of major cities in India.

1907 J.F. Madan of Calcutta launches a cinema chain, starting with the Elphinstone Picture Palace. Regular cinema shows are established in the country when Charles Pathé opens a branch of his company for the production of films and projection equipment at Bombay. Messrs Colonello and Cornaglia of the Excelsior Cinema and P.B. Mehta of America-Indian give regular shows in their tents on the Maidan in Bombay.

1908 'Films d'Art' featuring stage stars, dominate imports from Europe, with 'comics' also a growing attraction.

1909 The Madan cinema chain grows to more than thirty cinemas.

1910 Dadasaheb Phalke, scholar and fine printer, sees the film *Life of Christ* at the America-India Cinema in Bombay and determines to bring Lord Krishna to the screen.

1911 Phalke travels to England for equipment and technical instruction. *The Delhi Durbar* is filmed in colour by Charles Urban of the Kinema Color Company, New York. It is the first time that a foreign producer comes to India to shoot.

1912 Phalke makes *The Growth of a Pea,* a film in time lapse photography in order to secure backing for his first feature.

1913 *Raja Harishchandra:* First Indian film, produced and directed by D.G.Phalke and released at Coronation Cinema, Sandhurst Road, Bombay; length 3,700 feet. The film's theme is inspired by Hindu mythology. Through the choice of the subject, Phalke offered the audiences a story that they were familiar with, and created a genre specific to Indian cinema: the mythological film. In *Raja Harishchandra,* the role of the queen is played by a young man as it was considered a social taboo for a woman to act on the stage or on the screen during that period. The early silent films were nearly all inspired by Hindu mythology.

1914 Esoofally and partners take over the Alexandra Theatre in Bombay.

1916 Universal Pictures becomes the first American company to establish an agent in India.

1917 The Hindustan Film Company is formed by Phalke and financial backers. To educate audiences, Phalke releases a documentary entitled *How Films Are Made. Satyawadi Raja Harishchandra :* First film made in Bengal directed by J.F. Madan. *Nala Damayanti* : Produced by J. F. Madan of the Elphinstone Bioscope Company featured Italian artistes Signor and Signora Manelli.

1918 The Indian Cinematograph Act establishing a censorship and cinema licensing system is passed. It gives legal recognition to the industry. All provocation to crime, scenes of nudity, and love scenes including kissing are forbidden. From a Censor Board operating in different regions, a Central Board of Censors is established in the '50s.

1919 *Keechaka Vadham* : First film made in South Indian Madras. Directed by Nataraj Mudaliar.

1920s The first topical short, produced by the Oriental Film Manufacturing Company, Bombay, on the cremation of Lokmanya B.G. Tilak.

1921 Dhiren Ganguly's comedy *England Returned*, satirizing Indians imitating British ways, is a triumph in Calcutta.

1922 Ganguly forms the Lotus Film Company in Hyderabad, finds the Nizam of Hyderabad cooperative, and opens two cinemas.

1923 Cinemas in India now number more than 150, of which a third belong to the Madan chain.

1925 In Bombay, Chandulal Shah produces *Gun Sundari* that gives rise to the 'social film'.

The Light of Asia, inspired by the life of the Buddha, is produced by the Great Eastern Film Corporation in collaboration with Germany's Emelka Film Co., Munich. Directed by Himansu Rai and Franz Osten with technicians and capital mostly European, it is the first 'Indian' film to be released abroad. It has its London premiere at the Philharmonic Hall in 1926 where it runs for ten months. The *Daily Express* opinion poll ranks it the third best picture of that year.

1927 Indian Cinematograph Committee (Rangachariar Committee) is appointed to study the cinema in India, and the feasibility of furthering 'Empire Films' to counter American dominance.

1928 The six-man Rangachariar Committee makes a report recommending support of Indian films, but the three British members issue a dissenting statement.

1929 Universal's *Melody of Love* inaugurates the sound-film era in India at Madan's Elphinstone Picture Palace, Calcutta. Universal negotiates for the purchase of the Madan chain. The Wall Street crash ends the Universal-Madan negotiations, bringing widespread depression, unemployment, and unrest. Many Indian silent film companies collapse.

1930 The studio system, which dominated the film industry until the '40s is launched. Prabhat Film Company is founded in Kolhapur. New Theatres created in Calcutta taking on important directors like Debaki Bose and P.C.Barua. The Ranjit Film Company is based in Bombay, and Bombay Talkies is founded by Himansu Rai and Devika Rani. Film themes of the '30s move away from mythologicals and start reflecting social issues. *Achhut Kanya* (1936) deals with problems faced by the untouchables; *Devdas* (1935) with marriages arranged against the will of those concerned; V. Shantaram's *Duniya Na Mane* (1937) with the liberation of women. These are early examples of what is known as the 'social film'. The films of the '30s, however, tend towards a romantic interpretation of problems rather than examining their causes.

1931 *Alam Ara* : First Indian talkie produced by Imperial Film Company, Bombay, in Hindi, with several songs featuring Master Vithal and Zubeida, directed by Ardeshir M. Irani, is released at the Majestic Cinema, Bombay on March 14, 1931. From the very first sound film, Indian productions take on a musical form. According to ancient Sanskrit theatre, no separation is made between drama, music and dance. Other film historians believe that Indian sound films were inspired by the Parsee theatre of the '30s. Sound films gave a boost to regional cinema. However, as the majority of films at that time were produced in the North and a vast majority of the population understood Hindi or Hindustani (a mixture of Hindi and Urdu), Hindi became the dominant language used in films that still enjoy a nationwide distribution. *Jamai Sasthi* : first Indian talkie made in a regional language (Bengali). J.F.Madan and brothers launch sound production activity, but then decide to liquidate the Madan film empire.

1932 The Motion Picture Society of India is formed. Prabhat's *Ayodhyecha Raja*, in Marathi, featuring Durga Khote, signals increasing acceptance of film by people from 'good families'.

1933 25 Hindi films are produced, all with songs and dances. The Prabhat Film Company moves to Poona and develops a large studio complex. Wadia Movietone is founded and begins to specialize in 'stunt films'.

1934 Himansu Rai's *Karma*, first English-language film made in India featuring Devika Rani, opens in Bombay and leads to the formation of Bombay Talkies. *Amrit Manthan,* produced by the Prabhat Film Company, Bombay, is sent to the Venice Exhibition.

1935 P.C. Barua's *Devdas*, in a Bengali version and then a Hindi version starring K.L. Saigal, produced by New Theatres, Calcutta, creates a sensation and popularizes the theme of the doomed hero, and sets a high standard of film production. The playback singer becomes a fixture in Indian film production.

1936 Modern Theatres Ltd. is formed in Salem by T.R. Sundaram. Madras United Artistes Corporation is formed in Madras by K. Subrahmanyam.

The Tamil film, *Balyogini,* features a Brahmin widow, flouting ancient taboos.

The Bengal Motion Picture Association is established in Calcutta.

The Indian Motion Picture Producers Association is established in Bombay.

First All India Motion Picture Convention in Bombay;

Founding of Bombay Motion Picture Convention in Bombay;

Participation of Prabhat's *Amar Jyoti* in the Fourth International Film Festival in Venice;

Formation of Bengal Motion Picture Association;

Bombay-ki Billi, produced by the Imperial Film Company and starring Sulochna, establishes the star system in India.

1937 Prabhat's *Sant Tukaram* (Marathi), by Y. Damle and S. Fatehlal, becomes the first Indian film to win a Venice Festival Award.

Phalke makes his last film, *Gangavataran.*

Sulemani Shetranji : Produced by Wadia Movietone, is the first attempt to synchronise Indian songs and dances with the American silent film *Thief of Baghdad* starring Douglas Fairbanks, Sr.

Kisan Kanya : Produced by the Imperial Film Company, Bombay, starring Padmadevi, Zillu, Gulam Mahomed and Nisar, directed by Moti B. Gidwani, and photographed by Rustom M. Irani is the first Indian film to be produced in colour.

1938 Formation of South Indian Film Chamber of Commerce in Madras and Indian Motion Picture Distributors' Association in Bombay.

1939 Vauhini Pictures is formed in Madras by B.N. Reddi.

1941 *The Court Dancer*, produced by Wadia Movietone, directed by Modhu Bose and starring Sadhona Bose and Prithviraj is first film to be made with English dialogue. It was sent to the USA, but was released only in a few unimportant towns.

Minerva Movietone's *Sikandar*, depicting Alexander the Great's expedition to and retreat from India is banned from cantonment areas.

Independent production begins to undermine the major Indian studios.

1942 Portraits of Gandhi and Nehru, as well as Congress songs and symbols, are excised by censors from feature films.

1943 Establishment of Information Films of India and Indian News Parade : Factual films produced by the Government of India for the promotion of the war effort. Showing of newsreels of Indian News Parade and documentaries of Information Films of India is made compulsory, with theatres obliged to pay a rental fee. *Tree of Wealth*, a documentary film produced by the Government of India and directed by A. Bhaskar Rao, is among the films considered for the coveted annual award for the best production in this field given by the American Academy of Motion Pictures Arts and Sciences. Though it does not get the prize, it is highly commended and appreciated.

Kismet, directed by Gyan Mukherjee, starring Ashok Kumar,

breaks box-office records and runs for more than three years in the same cinema hall in Calcutta.

1944 D.G. Phalke dies, forgotten and destitute.

1945 Removal of restriction on the distribution of raw film stock which started in 1940 and limited films to a length of 11,000 ft.

The '40s see a decline of the studios. Black market money made during World War II finds its way into film production. Financiers, realizing that the success of a film was often due to its stars, offer large amounts to stars in order to entice them away from contracts with studios. This results in the rise of the star system that takes on incredible proportions through the years and remains today the dominant factor in popular cinema.

A parallel economy becomes an integral part of film financing too.

Dr. Kotnis Ki Amar Kahani, produced by Rajkamal Kalamandir, directed by V. Shantaram and starring Jayashree and Shantaram is approved as a 'war effort' film. The end of the war brings renewed pressure for India's independence.

1946 Indian News Parade comes to an end, and Information Films of India is dissolved.

The Story of Dr Kotnis, is sent to the USA for exhibition. *Neecha Nagar,* produced by Chetan Anand, is awarded a prize at the International Film Festival held at Cannes in France in October 1946.

1947 Independence of India, Partition of India and Pakistan;

Satyajit Ray, Chidananda Das Gupta and others form the Calcutta Film Society.

Ram Rajya, Shah Jehan and *The Story of Dr Kotnis* (English version) are selected by the Government of India for exhibition at the Canadian National Exhibition, Toronto, held in August 1947.

The Story of Dr Kotnis is also sent to the International Cinematographic Art Exhibition held at Venice in August-September 1947.

Sindoor : Produced by Filmistan Ltd., directed by Kishore Sahu and starring Kishore Sahu and Shamim awarded an

'Oscar' by the 'CIMPA' Award Committee for the best picture of 1947.

Production of IMPPA's Film *Azadi ka Utsav* in celebration of India's Independence.

Indian independence arouses vast hopes in the film industry but brings new taxes and crises.

Shantaram's *Shakuntala* becomes the first Indian feature shown in a United States theatre.

1948 Mahatma Gandhi assassinated.

Government creates Films Division, the state organization that produces documentaries and newsreels on the pattern of Information Films of India.

Shakuntalala : produced by V. Shantaram and starring Jayashree, is released at the Art Theatre, New York, in January 1948. It runs for two weeks and is acclaimed by the press and the public.

Romeo and Juliet : Produced by Nargis Art Concern, directed by Anwar Hussain and starring Nargis and Sapru, a creditable attempt to put Shakespeare on the Indian screen. A rather unsuccessful effort had been made by the Stage Film Company in 1935 to put across a crude rendering of *Hamlet* under the title of *Khoon ka Khoon* by Sohrab Modi. *Kalpana*, produced and directed by Uday Shankar, starring Uday Shankar and Amala Shankar, is the first feature-length dance fantasy. Its unique theme and setting made it an outstanding film in spite of its many faults. It reportedly shared a prize for 'Exceptional qualities' with some films from the U.S.A. at the Second World War Festival of Films & Fine Arts, Belgium, June-July 1949.

Mother, Child and *Community* : Three documentary films, directed by Paul Zils and sponsored by the UNO. These films are the first of a world series planned by the UNO.

Baghdad ka Chor : Western India Theatres' Hindustani dubbed version of Alexander Korda's *Thief of Baghdad,* starring Sabu, Maria Montez and Jon Hall, released at Excelsior and Minerva, Bombay, on August 6, marks another attempt to dub foreign films in Hindi; a great box-office success.

Censor Codes formulated in Bombay and Madras.

Gemini's *Chandralekha* sets a new record in box-office collections.

1949 In protest over taxes, the film industry stages an all-India protest day.

The Government stirs hopes with the formation of another Film Enquiry Committee (Patil Committee).

K.A. Abbas' *Dharti ke Lal* becomes the first Indian feature shown in Moscow.

The Indian Cinematograph (Amendment) Act, passed on May 1, makes provision for granting 'A' and 'U' certificates. *Meera,* produced by T. Sadasivam, directed by Ellis R Duncan and featuring M. S. Subhalakshmi is selected by the Government of India for screening at the Fourth International Film Festival at Prague, Czechoslavakia in August, at the Tenth International Exhibition of Cinematographic Art, Venice in August-September and at the Canadian National Exhibition, Toronto.

Chandralekha : A film of grand spectace produced by S. S. Vasan on the lines of Cecil B. de Mille's epics, is also selected by the Government of India for exhibition at Prague.

Chhota Bhai : Produced by New Theatres Ltd., Calcutta, selected for screening at the Canadian National Exhibition, Toronto.

Ajit : Produced and directed by M. Bhavnani and released on December 16; India's second colour film photographed on Kodachrome 16 mm film, blown up to standard size by the Ansco process in the USA. Though its theme is all too familiar on the Indian screen, the novelty of colour attracts attention.

1950 The rise of the Dravidian Forward Movement (DMK) is closely linked to Tamil film interest and the opposition to Hindi as a national language.

Conference of film trade organisations for the formation of Film Federation of India;

1951 Establishment of Central Board of Film Censors with B. N. Sircar on the Board. Launching of Film Federation of India under the presidentship of Chandulal J. Shah. Formation of SIMPSA in Madras and CCA in Bhusaval. *Aan* produced by Mehboob in colour 16 mm and blown up to 35 mm (in London).

Awara, produced and directed by Raj Kapoor, establishes him as leading director of Bombay. *Awara* remains tremendously popular in the Soviet Union, Middle East and China.

Report of the Film Enquiry Committee urges creation of a Film Finance Corporation, an Institute of Film Art as a training school, and an Export Corporation to promote Indian films in markets.

Films Division's documentary, *Jaipur,* wins an award at the Venice festival.

1952 India's First International Film Festival held in Bombay, Madras, Delhi and Calcutta.

All India Film Conference in Bombay.

Cinematograph Act 1952 passed.

M. P. Production *Babla* wins a prize for 'Struggle for Social Progress' at the Czechoslovak International Film Festival.

Mineva Movietone makes *Jhansi ki Rani,* India's first technicolor film.

Bombay Talkies ceases production.

Aan produced and directed by Mehboob Khan is widely distributed throughout the Third World where it becomes an all-time favourite under the title *Mangala, Fille des Indes.*

1953 FILMFARE, a leading film magazine starts annual awards in various categories of filmmaking.

State Awards also initiated by the Government of India.

Prabhat Film Company ceases production, virtually ending the big-studio era in India.

Cavalcade of Indian Films, organised by FFI, to acquaint Members of Parliament with Indian films. S. S. Vasan accorded public reception for his classic film *Avvaiyar* (Tamil).

1954 Government publishes its decision on Patil Committee recommendations; Introduction of National Awards for films; P. K. Atre's *Shyamchi Aye* (Marathi) wins President's Gold Medal as India's best feature film of 1953; Bimal Roy's *Do Bigha Zamin* receives special mention at Cannes Film Festival, & Karlovy Vary Opening of Indian Film Festival in USSR.

K. A. Abbas's *Munna,* the first Hindi feature without songs or dances, wins kudos at the Edinburgh festival but fails financially in India.

Raj Kapoor's *Awara* is a smash hit in the Soviet Union.
Film Seminar, organised by Sangeet Natak Akademi, in New Delhi; Indian Festival in China;
First Indian Film Festival held in London at the Scala Theatre, organized by the Asian Film Society. The festival encouraged regular screenings of Indian films in the UK.

1956 Formation of Supreme Council of Film Producers.
Satyajit Ray's *Pather Panchali* wins prize at Cannes film festival as the 'best human document';
Raj Kapoor's *Jagte Raho* wins Crystal Globe at Karlovy Vary International Film Festival.

1957 Satyajit Ray's *Aparajito* wins the Golden Lion at Venice.
Pardesi, made by K.A. Abbas in collaboration with Mosfilm, becomes the first India-USSR co-production.
Mother India directed by Mehboob Khan, wins for its leading lady, Nargis, the Best Actress Award at Karlovy Vary International Film Festival and the film is nominated for an Oscar (1958).
Jaldeep wins Certificate of Merit at the IX International Exhibition for Children in Venice.

1959 V. Shantaram's *Do Ankhen Bara Haath* wins a Silver Bear at Berlin Festival, Samuel Goldwyn International Film Award and the 'best foreign language film award' from the Hollywood Foreign Press Association; M.G. Ramachandran's *Nadodi Mannan* links heroic melodrama with Dravidian symbolism.
Television is started as an experiment in Delhi.
Sagar Sangame (Bengali) by Devaki Bose wins Special Award from Karlovy Vary International Film Festival; Satyajit Ray's *Jalsaghar* wins Silver Medal at Moscow Festival.

1960 *Heera Moti* earns special mention at Karlovy Vary International Film Festival; Satyajit Ray's *Teen Kanya* wins Grand Prix at Melbourne Film Festival, and the Selznik Golden Laurel Award for 'international understanding'.

1961 Dilip Kumar wins Diploma of Special Honour from Czechoslovak Academy of Arts, Prague, for his role in *Ganga Jamna.* This film also wins the Silver Bowl at Boston Festival.
New Delhi hosts the Second International Film Festival of India.

1962 Film Societies win partial exemption from censorship.

1963 The Indian Motion Picture Export Corporation is established. Suchitra Sen wins 'Best Actress' award for her performance in *Sat Pake Bandha* (Bengali) at Moscow Festival; K. A. Abbas' *Munna* wins a special award for photography at the Fourth International Festival of Documentary and Experimental Films, Uruguay.

K. A. Abbas' *Shehar Aur Sapna* wins Special Award at Karlovy Vary.

1964 Film Society exemption from censorship is strengthened through arrangements negotiated by the Federation of Film Societies of India.

1965 New Delhi hosts the Third International Film Festival of India, with additional screenings in Bombay, Calcutta, and Madras. *Arohi* wins a Silver Medal at Locarno Film Festival, Satyajit Ray wins Best Director Award for *Charulata* at Berlin Film Festival; *Hamara Ghar* wins Special Jury prize at the Festival of Children's Films, Gottvaldov, Czechoslovakia; Waheeda Rehman wins Best Actress Award for her role in *Guide* at Chicago Film Festival.

1966 Satyajit Ray wins Special Award of Honour at Berlin Film Festival for *Nayak.* Prithviraj Kapoor wins a Special Award for *Aasman Mahal* at Karlovy Vary.

The Dadasaheb Phalke award is introduced to honour Indian film pioneers.

1967 Devika Rani receives the first Dadasaheb Phalke award. Sunil Dutt's *Yaadein* wins Grand Prix at Asian Film Festival, Frankfurt; *Daak Ghar* wins Golden Plaque at Chicago Film Festival.

1968 Tapan Sinha's *Hatey Bazare* (Bengali) wins Silver Trophy at Pnom Penh Festival. K. A. Abbas's *A Tale of Four Cities* precipitates a censorship struggle at the Supreme Court level. Firstever Retrospective of Indian cinema in Paris.

1969 The Fourth International Film Festival of India is held in New Delhi.

Mrinal Sen's *Bhuvan Shome,* financed by the Film Finance Corporation, wins multiple awards and commercial success. *Gopi Gyne Bagha Byne* directed by Satyajit Ray wins Silver

Award for Best Direction at Adelaide and Auckland Festivals.

1970 From the early '70s two kinds of cinema become vaguely defined; 'new' and 'popular' cinema. The new cinema is produced in several regions and in different languages with an emphasis on regional cultural identity. Despite acute problems of distribution within India, the new cinema filmmakers continue in their determination to evolve another kind of film. The importance of the movement lies in the explosion of themes new in the cinematic context of India.

The popular cinema in Bombay had evolved in such a way that a single film included many kinds of film genres unlike the early days of Indian cinema when the mythological film was central to film production.

In the '70s Bombay films become more diverse and many excelled at the box-office, creating new classics, like *Sholay* (1975), *Deewar* (1975), *Amar, Akbar, Anthony* (1977). The themes in the films often centred on action, crime, revenge, the lost-and-found family member etc. The Hindi cinema no longer included a few leading stars but went in for a parade of box-office names, with many stars in the same film. These films known as the 'Multi-Starrers' were dominant during this period. Amitabh Bachchan reached unimaginable heights of popularity and has begun to be called the 'one-man industry'.

The Phalke birth centennial is celebrated as Bombay names a street after him.

Mrinal Sen's *Bhuvan Shome* wins Gold Medal at the Venice Film Festival; *Kunku* (Gujrati) wins a special Award at Chicago Film Festival.

1972 Film imports from the United States stopped as a result of breakdown in negotiations with American film interests.

Directorate of Film Festivals set up in Delhi under the Ministry of Information & Broadcasting.

1974 *Ankur,* the first film by Shyam Banegal, becomes a major success.

The International Film Festival of India becomes an annual event.

1975 Films from the United States again enter the Indian market.

Emergency proclamation brings tightened censorship and other government controls.

1976 Ritwik Ghatak, stormy petrel of Indian cinema, passes away.

1977 Lifting of Emergency brings a gradual easing of governmental controls over the film industry.

Film Star M. G. Ramachandran becomes Chief Minister of Tamil Nadu but announces continuation of his film career.

1980 The National Film Development Corporation (NFDC) is created, merging the Film Finance Corporation with the Indian Motion Pictures Exports Co., takes over the Directorate of Film Festivals from the Ministry of Information & Broadcasting. NFDC's briefs is to encourage new filmmakers and plan the construction of film theatres. It is supposed also to encourage production in 16 mm films in India.

1980s The explosion of video technology drastically damages the export market for Indian films. Piracy flourishes.

1981 Govind Nihalani's *Aakrosh* shares Best Film Award at 8th International Film Festival of India.

Mrinal Sen's *Akaaler Sandhane* wins the Silver Bear at the Berlin Film Festival.

K. A. Abbas's *The Naxalites* wins a gold medal at Bergamo Film Festival in March; Rabindra Dharmaraj's *Chakra* wins the Golden Leopard at Locarno Film Festival in July/August. K. Viswanath's *Sankarabharanam* (Telugu) wins 'Prize of the Public' at Basançon's Special Festival of Choreography and Music in November; in December at the Nantes Festival of Three Continents, *Akriet* (Marathi), directed by Amol Palekar wins a Special Mention and Ketan Mehta's *Bhavni Bhavai* (Gujarati) wins the UNESCO Club Award.

1982 At Manila's First International Film Festival in January, Aparna Sen's *36 Chowringhee Lane* (English) wins the 'Golden Eagle'. At the International Film Festival in Kuala Lumpur, P. Padmarajan's *Oridathu Oru Phayalvaan* (Malayalam) gets the Best Film and Best Screenplay awards; Ashok Ahuja's *Aadharshila* gets a cash prize and Filmdukaten at the Mannheim Film Festival in October. In November at Nantes Aribam Syam Sharma's *Imagi Ningthem* (Manipuri) gets the Best Film prize. In London Adoor Gopalakrishnan receives the British Film Institute Award for *Elippathayam* (Malayalam).

1983 *Kharij* directed by Mrinal Sen in Bengali wins the Special Jury Prize at Cannes Film Festival.

Bhanu Athaiya wins an Oscar for Best Costume Design in *Gandhi,* directed by Richard Attenborough, the first Indian to win this prestigious award.

1984 *My Dear Kuttichathan* directed by Jijo in Malayalam, India's First Film 3-D.

1989 *Piravi* (directed by Shahji N. Karun) in Malayalam wins more than 20 international awards, including the Chaplin Award at Edinburgh, and the Silver Leopard at Locarno.

1990 Legion d' Honour presented to Satyajit Ray in Calcutta by President François Mitterand of France.

1991 Satyajit Ray directed his last feature *Aguntuk* (The Stranger).

1992 Special Oscar awarded to Satyajit Ray by the American Academy of Motion Picture Art and Science.

Satyajit Ray passes away on 22nd April.

Indian Panorama Films 1978-95

Compiled by Sudhir Bose

Directors	1978*	1979	1980	1981	1982	1983	1984	1985	1986	1987	1988	1989	1990	1991	1992	1993	1994	1995
Shyam Benegal	Bhumika (Hindi)	Junoon (Hindi/Urdu) Anugraham (Telugu)			Kalyug (Hindi)	Arohan (Hindi)	Mandi (Hindi)		Trikal (Hindi)	Susman (Hindi)							Suraj ka Satwan Ghoda (Hindi)	Mammo (Hindi)
Basu Chatterji	Swami (Hindi)	Khatta Meetha (Hindi)	Jeena Yahan (Hindi)															
Girish Karnad & B.V. Karanth	Godhuli (Hindi & Kannada)																	
M.S. Sathyu	Kanneshwara Rama (Kannada)	Chitegu Chinte (Kannada)			Bara (Kannada)													
Mrinal Sen	Oka Oorie Katha (Telugu)	Parasuram (Bengali)	Ekdin Pratidin (Bengali)	Akaler Sandhane (Bengali)	Chaalchitra (Bengali)	Kharij (Bengali)	Khandhar (Hindi)						Ek Din Achanak (Hindi)		Mahaprithibi (Bengali)		Antareen (Bengali)	
Yukt	Ghashiram Kotwal (Marathi)																	
Bhabendra Nath Saikia	Sandhyarag (Assamese)								Agnisnaan (Assamese)			Kolahal (Assamese)			Sarothi (Assamese)		Abartan (Assamese)	
Bhimsain	Gharaonda (Hindi)																	
Aruna-Vikas	Shaque (Hindi)																	
P. Lankesh	Pallavi (Kannada)																	
Girish Kasaravalli	Ghata-shraddha (Kannada)		Akramana (Kannada)								Tabarana Kathe (Kannada)			Mane (Kannada)				
Sridhar Kshirsagar	Kanakambara (Kannada)			The Great Indian Film Bazaar (English)														

* There is no list of films of the first Panorama package in the handbook (called *Indian Cinemas '77/78*) for the Madras Filmotsav in 1978. The above list of 1978 films is, thus, based on the material contained in the handbook.

Directors	1978	1979	1980	1981	1982	1983	1984	1985	1986	1987	1988	1989	1990	1991	1992	1993	1994	1995
Balu Mahendra	Kokila (Kannada)		Azhiyatha Kolangal (Tamil)									Veedu (Tamil)		Sandhiya Ragam (Tamil)				
C.R. Simha	Kakankote (Kannada)																	
V.R.K. Prasad	Rishyashringa (Kannada)																	
T.S. Ranga	Geejagana Goodu (Kannada)		Savithri (Kannada)															
Chandrashekhar	Huli Bantu Huli (Kannada)																	
G. Aravindan	Kanchana Sita (Malayalam)	Thampu (Malayalam)	Kummatty (Malayalam)	Esthappan (Malayalam)	Pokkuveyil (Malayalam)				Chidam-baram (Malayalam)	Oridathu (Malayalam)					Vasthuhara (Malayalam)			
P.A. Backer	Manimu-zhakkam (Malayalam)	Chuvanna Vithukal (Malayalam)	Sanghaganam (Malayalam)															
Adoor Gopalakrishnan	Kodiyettam (Malayalam)					Elippathayam (Malayalam)		Mukha-mukham (Malayalam)			Anantaram (Malayalam)		Mathilukal (Malayalam)				Vidheyan (Malayalam)	
Jabbar Patel	Jait Re Jait (Marathi)			Simhasan (Marathi)		Umbartha (Marathi)										Ek Hota Vidushak (Marathi)		Mukta (Marathi)
K. Balachander	Avargal (Tamil)				Thaneer Thaneer (Tamil)			Achamillai Achamillai (Tamil)										
Devaraj & Mohan	Annakili (Tamil)																	

Directors	1978	1979	1980	1981	1982	1983	1984	1985	1986	1987	1988	1989	1990	1991	1992	1993	1994	1995
A.Bhimsingh	Sila Nerangalil Sila Manithargal (Tamil)	Oru Nadigai Natakam Parkiral (Tamil)																
Eranki Sarma	Chilakamma Cheppindi (Telugu)																	
Singitam Srinivasa Rao	Taram Marindi (Telugu)								Mayuri (Telugu)			Pushpaka Vimana (no dialogues)						
Muzaffar Ali		Gaman (Hindi)			Umrao Jaan (Hindi)					Anjuman (Hindi)								
Grish Karnad		Ondanondu Kaladalli (Kannada)						Utsav (Hindi)								Cheluvi (Hindi)		
C. Radhakrishnan		Agni (Malayalam)												Ottayadippathakal (Malayalam)				
John Abraham		Agraharathil Kazhuthai (Tamil)								Amma Ariyan (Malayalam)								
Saeed Akhtar Mirza		Arvind Desai ki Ajeeb Dastaan (Hindi)		Albert Pinto ko Gussa Kyon Aata Hai (Hindi)				Mohan Joshi Haazir Ho! (Hindi)					Salim Langde Pe Mat Ro (Hindi)					
Inder Sen		Chameli Memsaheb (Bengali)																
Raj Dutt		Davaki Nandan Gopala (Marathi)																
Buddhadeb Dasgupta		Dooratwa (Bengali)				Grihajuddha (Bengali)		Andhi Gali (Hindi)			Phera (Bengali)		Bagh Bahadur (Hindi)		Tahader Katha (Bengali)			Charachar (Bengali)
Tarun Majumdar		Ganadevata (Bengali)	Ganadevata* (Bengali)	Dadar Kirti (Bengali)														

* *Ganadevata* was listed in both years.

Directors	1978	1979	1980	1981	1982	1983	1984	1985	1986	1987	1988	1989	1990	1991	1992	1993	1994	1995
Chandrasekhar Kambar		Kaadu Kudre (Kannada)																
Atul Bardoloi		Kallol (Assamese)																
K.G. George		Mannu (Malayalam)		Kolangal (Malayalam)		Yavanika (Malayalam)	Lekhayude Maranam – Oru Flashback (Malayalam)	Adaminte Variyellu (Malayalam)		Irakal (Malayalam)								
J. Mahendran		Mullum Malarum (Tamil)	Utharipokal (Tamil)		Nenjathai Killathe (Tamil)													
Nirmal Mitter		Parichaya (Bengali)																
B. G. Bharathan		Rathi Nirvedam (Malayalam)		Lorry (Malayalam)		Ormakkai (Malayalam)	Marmaram (Malayalam)	Kattathe Kilikkoodu (Malayalam)				Oru Minna-minunginte Nurungu Vettom (Malayalam)		Thazhavaram (Malayalam)				
Satyajit Ray		Shatranj ke Khilari (Hindi)	Joi Baba Felunath (Bengali)	Hirak Rajar Deshe (Bengali)	Pikoo (Bengali) Sadgati (Hindi)			Ghare-Baire (Bengali)					Ganashatru (Bengali)	Shakha-Proshakha (Bengali)	Agantuk (Bengali)			
K.R. Mohanan			Ashwathama (Malayalam)								Purushartham (Malayalam)					Swaroopam (Malayalam)		
Vinod Pande			Ek Baar Phir (Hindi)															
T.S. Naga-bharana			Grahana (Kannada)				Banker Margayya (Kannada)								Mysoora Mallige (Kannada)		Chinnari Mutha (Kannada)	
Basu Bhattacharya			Grihapravesh (Hindi)							Panchvati (Hindi)								
Utpal Dutt			Jhor (Bengali)		Baisakhi Megh (Bengali)													

Directors	1978	1979	1980	1981	1982	1983	1984	1985	1986	1987	1988	1989	1990	1991	1992	1993	1994	1995
Bimal Dutt			Kasturi (Hindi)															
Goutam Ghose			Ma Bhoomi (Telugu)		Dakhal (Bengali)			Paar (Hindi)				Antarjali Yatra (Bengali)				Padma Nadir Majhi (Bengali)	Patang (Hindi)	
B.S. Narayana			Nimajjanam (Telugu)															
P.Padmarajan			Peruvazhi-ambalam (Malayalam)		Oridathu Oru Phayalvaan (Malayalam)		Koodevide? (Malayalam)		Thinkalazcha Nalla Divasam (Malayalam)									
Ramdas Phutane			Sarvasakshi (Marathi)															
Nachiket & Jayoo Patwardhan			22nd June, 1897 (Marathi)						Anantyatra (Hindi)									
Govind Nihalani				Aakrosh (Hindi)			Ardh Satya (Hindi)	Party (Hindi)	Aghaat (Hindi)			Tamas (Hindi)	Jazeere (Hindi)	Drishti (Hindi)				Drohkaal (Hindi)
Tapan Sinha				Bancharamer Bagan (Bengali)	Adalat O Ekti Meye (Bengali)				Aadmi Aur Aurat (Hindi)	Atanka (Bengali)	Aaj ka Robin Hood (Hindi)			Ek Doctor Ki Maut (Hindi)				Wheel Chair (Bengali)
Ketan Mehta				Bhavni Bhavai (Gujarati)				Holi (Hindi)		Mirch Masala (Hindi)						Maya Memsaab (Hindi)		Sardar (Hindi)
Rabindra Dharmaraj				Chakra (Hindi)														
K. Vijayan				Doorathu Idi Muzhakkam (Tamil)														
V.R. Gopinath				Greeshmam (Malayalam)							Oru Mayma-sappulariyil (Malayalam)							

Directors	1978	1979	1980	1981	1982	1983	1984	1985	1986	1987	1988	1989	1990	1991	1992	1993	1994	1995
V. Jagannath				Kadige Hodavaru (Kannada)														
Bharathi Rajaa				Nizhalgal (Tamil)		Seethakoka Chilaka (Telugu)			Mudhal Mariyadhai (Tamil)			Vedham Puthithu (Tamil)						
K. Viswanath				Shankara-bharanam (Telugu)			Sagara Sangamam (Telugu)					Swarna Kamalam (Telugu)				Swathi Kiranam (Telugu)		
Mani Kaul				Satah se Uthata Aadmi (Hindi)						Mati Manas (Hindi)				Nazar (Hindi)				
Biplab Ray Chaudhuri				Shodh (Hindi)														Aranya Rodana (Oriya)
Sai Paranjpye				Sparsh (Hindi)		Katha (Hindi)								Disha (Hindi)				
Ashok Ahuja					Aadharshila (Hindi)													
Nabyendu Chatterjee					Aaj-Kal-Parshur Galpa (Bengali)				Chopper (Bengali)		Sarisreep (Bengali)		Parasuramer Kuthar (Bengali)		Atmaja (Bengali)		Shilpi (Bengali)	
Amol Palekar					Akriet (Marathi)			Ankahee (Hindi)						Thodasa Roomani Ho Jayen (Hindi)				
Victor Banerjee					An August Requiem (English)													
Aribam Syam Sharma					Imagi Ningthem (Manipuri)									Ishanou (Manipuri)				
K.S. Sethu-madhavan					Oppol (Malayalam)										Marupakkam (Tamil)			

Directors	1978	1979	1980	1981	1982	1983	1984	1985	1986	1987	1988	1989	1990	1991	1992	1993	1994	1995
Bapu					Thyagayya (Telugu)													
T. Hariharan					Valarthu Mrugangal (Malayalam)					Panchagni (Malayalam)			Oru Vadakkan Veeragatha (Malayalam)					Parinayam (Malayalam)
Aparna Sen					36 Chowrin-ghee Lane (English)				Parama (Hindi/Bengali				Sati (Bengali)					
Dilip Roy						Amrita Kumbher Sandhaney (Bengali)												
Jahnu Barua						Aparoopa (Assamese)				Papori (Assamese)	Halodhia Choraye Baodhan Khai (Assamese)		Banani (Assamese)		Firingoti (Assamese)			
Utpalendu Chakraborty						Chokh (Bengali)				Debshishu (Hindi)			Chhandaneer (Bengali)					
Saikat Bhattacharya						Dulia (Bengali)												
H. Hariharan						Ezhavathu Manithan (Tamil)												
M. Mohan						Ilakkangal (Malayalam)	Rachna (Malayalam)											
Shekhar Kapur						Masoom (Hindi)												
Dasari Narayan Rao						Megha Sandesam (Telugu)										Surigadu (Telugu)		
Prema Karanth						Phaniyamma (Kannada)												

Directors	1978	1979	1980	1981	1982	1983	1984	1985	1986	1987	1988	1989	1990	1991	1992	1993	1994	1995
Vinay Shukla						Sameera (Hindi)												
Manmohan Mahapatra						Seeta Raati (Oriya)		Neeraba Jhada (Oriya)	Klanta Aparanha (Oriya)		Majhi Pahacha (Oriya)							
Ambili						Veena Poovu (Malayalam)												
G.V. Iyer							Adi Shanka-racharya (Sanskrit)			Madhavacharya (Kannada)							Bhagwad Gita (Sanskrit)	
K.N. Sasi-dharan							Akkare (Malayalam)											
Saghir Ahmad							Dhaare Aalua (Oriya)											
Fazil							Ente Mama-ttukkuttiya-mmaikku (Malayalam)		Nokketha Dhoorathu Kannum Nattu (Malayalam)									
Kundan Shah							Jaane Bhi Do Yaaro (Hindi)										Kabhi Haan Kabhi Naa (Hindi)	
Nirad Mohapatra							Maya Miriga (Oriya)											
Nitesh Mukherjee							Nayan-Shyama (Bengali)											
Komal Swaminathan							Oru Indhiya Kanavu (Tamil)											
Sandip Ray							Phatik Chand (Bengali)								Goopy Bagha Phiray Elo (Bengali)		Uttoran (Bengali)	

Directors	1978	1979	1980	1981	1982	1983	1984	1985	1986	1987	1988	1989	1990	1991	1992	1993	1994	1995
B. Narsing Rao							Rangula Kala (Telugu)						Dasi (Telugu)	Matti Manushulu (Telugu)				
M.A. Singh							Sanakeithel (Manipuri)											
Vijaya Mehta							Smriti Chitre (Marathi)			Rao Saheb (Hindi)		Pestonjee (Hindi)						
Prakash Jha								Hip Hip Hurray (Hindi)	Damul (Hindi)									
I.V.Sasi								Kana Marayathu (Malayalam)				1921 (Malayalam)						
Saroj De								Kony (Bengali)										
P.N. Menon								Malamuka-lilae Daivam (Malayalam)										
Ardhendu Bhattacharya								Manik Raitong (Khasi)										
Mahesh Bhatt								Saaransh (Hindi)	Janam (Hindi)									
Vamsy								Sitara (Telugu)										
T. Kranthi Kumar								Swathi (Telugu)							Seethara-mayyagari Manavaralu (Telugu)			
Kumar Shahani								Tarang (Hindi)					Khayal Gatha (Hindi)	Kasba (Hindi)				
Shankar Nag									Accident (Kannada)		Swamy (Hindi)							

Directors	1978	1979	1980	1981	1982	1983	1984	1985	1986	1987	1988	1989	1990	1991	1992	1993	1994	1995
N.Lakshmi-narayan									Bettada Hoovu (Kannada)									
Raghavan									Kilippatt (Malayalam)									
Ramesh Sharma									New Delhi Times (Hindi)									
John C. San-karmangalam									Samaandaram (Malayalam)									
Ketan Anand									Shart (Hindi)									
Kalpana Lajmi										Ek Pal (Hindi)						Rudali (Hindi)		
Pradip Krishen										Massey Saheb (Hindi)			In Which Annie Gives It Those Ones (English)					
Mani Ratnam										Mouna Ragam (Tamil)		Nayakan (Tamil)			Anjali (Tamil)		Roja (Tamil)	
Lenin Rajendran										Meenamasathille Sooryan (Malayalam)	Swathi Thirunal (Malayalam)						Deivathinte Vikruthikal (Malayalam)	
G.S. Panicker										Pandavapuram (Malayalam)								
Pavithran										Uppu (Malayalam)								
Sudhir Mishra										Yeh Woh Manzil To Nahin (Hindi)						Dharavi (Hindi)		

Directors	1978	1979	1980	1981	1982	1983	1984	1985	1986	1987	1988	1989	1990	1991	1992	1993	1994	1995
Kishan Kartha											Amshini (Hindi)							
Krishna Masadi											Avasthe (Kannada)							
Raja Mitra											Ekti Jiban (Bengali)							
Prathap Pothan											Hrithubhedam (Malayalam)							
Gulzar											Ijaazat (Hindi)			Lekin (Hindi)	Libaas (Hindi)			
Tanvir Ahmed											Su-raaj (Hindi)							
Joseph Madapally											Thoranam (Malayalam)							
P. Sreekumar												Asthikal Pookkunnu (Malayalam)						
Rajeev Nath												Kadaltheerathu (Malayalam)						
Aditya Bhattacharya												Raakh (Hindi)						
Mira Nair												Salaam Bombay! (Hindi)						
Nabendu Ghosh												Trishagni (Hindi)						
T.V. Chandran													Alicinte Anweshanam (Malayalam)					Ponthan Mada (Malayalam)

Directors	1978	1979	1980	1981	1982	1983	1984	1985	1986	1987	1988	1989	1990	1991	1992	1993	1994	1995
Sadanand Survarna													Kubi Mattu Iyala (Kannnada)					
Surinder Singh													Marhi da Deeva (Punjabi)					
Pervez Merwanji													Percy (Gujarati)					
Shaji N. Karun													Piravi (Malayalam)					Swaham (Malayalam)
Gaganvihari Borate													Suryodaya (Marathi)					
Jayaa-bharathy													Uchchi Veyil (Tamil)					
Madan Bawaria														Ankur, Maina Aur Kabootar (Hindi)				
M.P. Sukuma-ran Nair														Aparahnam (Malayalam)				
Sivaprasad														Vembanad (Malayalam)			Gowri (Malayalam)	
Gautam Bora														Wosobipo (Karbi)				
Sivan															Abhayam (Malayalam)			
A.K. Bir															Adi Mimansa (Oriya)		Lavanya Preeti (Oriya)	Aranyaka (Hindi)
B.C. Mouli															Ashwini (Telugu)			

Directors	1978	1979	1980	1981	1982	1983	1984	1985	1986	1987	1988	1989	1990	1991	1992	1993	1994	1995
Sibi Malayil															Bharatham (Malayalam)			
Sanjay Surkar															Chaukat Raja (Marathi)			
Arun Kaul															Diksha (Hindi)			
Ujjal Chatterji															Gondi (Bengali)			
M.T. Vasu-devan Nair															Kadavu. (Malayalam)			
P. Sambasiva Rao															Mrigatrishna (Telugu)			
Ajayan															Perumthachan (Malayalam)			
Sanjeev Hazorika																Haladhar (Assamese)		Meemanxa (Assamese)
Pamela Rooks																Miss Beatty's Children (English)		
Sanjiv Shah																Hun Hunshi Hunshilal (Gujarati)		
Mansoor Hussain Khan																Jo Jeeta Wohi Sikandar (Hindi)		
Gopi Desai																Mujhse Dosti Karoge? (Hindi)		
Nana Patekar																Prahaar (Hindi)		

Directors	1978	1979	1980	1981	1982	1983	1984	1985	1986	1987	1988	1989	1990	1991	1992	1993	1994	1995
B. Sundar Krishna Urs																Sangya Balya (Kannada)		
Kamal																Ulladakkam (Malayalam)		
Oken Amakcham																Khonthang (Manipuri)		
K.P. Sasi																	Ilayum Mullum (Malayalam)	
P.T. Kunhi-mohammed																	Magrib (Malayalam)	
K. Ibohal Sharma																	Sambal Wangma (Manipuri)	
Ashoke Viswanathan																	Sunya Theke Suru (Bengali)	
Subhankar Ghosh																	Woh Chokri (Hindi)	
Bappa Ray																		Ek Thi Goonja ... (Hindi)
James Joseph																		Galileo (Malayalam)
Vidhu Vinod Chopra																		1942: A Love Story (Hindi)
C.P. Padma-kumar																		Sammohanam (Malayalam)
K. Bikram Singh																		Tarpan (Hindi)

INDEX

Aakrosh (1980), 94
Aankhen (1992), 175
Aasmaan (1952), 55
Aag (1948), 38
Aar Paar (1954), 34
Abbas, K.A., 21
Abartan (1993), 98
Achhut Kanya (1936), 24
Admi (1939), 21-21
Adoor Gopalakrishnan, 84, 92, 280-281
Agantuk (1991), 90
Agnisnaan (1985), 98
Ajantrik (Bengali, 1958), 75
Akaler Sandhane (1979), 91
Akhtar, Jan Nissar, 64
Alam Ara (1931), 18
Albert Pinto Ko Gussa Kyon Ata Hai (1980), 94
Al Hilal (1935), 22
Amarjyoti (1936), 20
Amar, Akbar, Anthony (1978), 173
Amrit Manthan (1934), 20
Anantaram (1987), 91
Anarkali (1935), 19
Andhi Gali (1984), 97
Anjali (1990), 99
Ankur (1974), 89
Antarjali Yatra (1987), 96
Aparoopa (1982), 97
Ardh Satya (1983), 94
Aravindan, G., 92-93, 206
Art Direction, 131-133
Arvind Desai ki Ajeeb Dastan (1978), 94
A Time to Rise (1981), 163
Aurat, 22, 30-31
Avvaiyar, 28
Awara (1951), 38-39
Ayodhya Ka Raja (1932), 20
Azmi, Shabana, 93

Badayuni, Shakeel, 64
Bagh Bahadur (1989), 92
Baishey Sravan (Bengali, 1960), 76
Baran, Timir, 25, 53
Barua, Jahnu, 97, 278-279
Banani (1989), 97
Barua, P.C., 23, 25, 26
Bazigar (1993), 171
Benegal, Shyam, 93, 246, 276-277
Bhakta Prahalad (1926), 9
Bhakta Pundalik (1912), 4
Bhattacharya, Timir Baran, 53
Bhatwadekar, S.H., 4
Bhavni Bhavai (1980), 95
Bhonsle, Asha, 60-61
Bhumika (1977), 93
Bhuvan Shome (1969), 76, 89
Biswas, Anil, 53, 62
Bobby (1973), 81
Boral, Raichand, 25, 53
Bose, Debaki, 25-26
Bose, Mukul, 25
Bose, Nitin, 25-26
Brahmachari (1938), 22
Brandi Ki Botal (1939), 22
Burman, S.D., 62

C.I.D. (1956), 34
Camerawork, 121-124
Central Cinema Department, 15
Chandidas (1932), 25-26

Chhandaneer (1989), 100
Chaudhvi ka Chand, 37
Chidambaram (1985), 93
Chhinnamul (Bengali, 1951), 71
Chintamani (Tamil, 1937), 44
Chokh (1982), 99
Chopra, Yash, 274-275
Cinema
in Bengal, 69-78
in Bombay, 19
in Calcutta, 24
in early days, 220-221
in Madras, 27
Cinta (1948), 45
Clockwork Orange (1973), 82
Composers, 62
Co-productions, 12

Daag (1953), 61
Dakhal (1981), 96
Darr (1993), 171
Dasgupta, Buddhadeb, 96-97, 281-282
Debashishu (1985), 100
Deewar (1975), 173
Desai, Vasant, 53
Devdas, (Barua's 1955), 208
Devdas, 23
Devolution Act of 1920, 14
Dharmatma (1935), 20
Dhartiputra (1993), 174
Diamond Queen (1940), 19
Divyashakti (1993), 177
Do Bigha Zamin, 32, 207
Dooratwa (1978), 97
Drishti (1990), 94
Dunia Na Mane (1937), 21
Dutt, Guru, 33-37, 210

Editing, 129-130
Ek Hota Vidushak (1992), 96
Ek Hi Rasta, 22
Elippathayam (1981), 91-92
England Returned (1921), 11
Entertainment Tax, 13

Firingoti (1991), 97

Ganesan, Sivaji, 195
Gangavataram (1937), 103
Ganguly, Dhiren, 11, 49
Gardish (1993), 174
Ghai, Subhash, 268-269
Ghatak, Ritwik, 71-72, 75, 77, 90, 111, 206
Ghatashraddha (1977), 96
Ghose, Goutam, 96
Gokhale, Kamalabai, 7
Government and Cinema, 13
Grihadada (1936), 26
Grihjuddha (1982), 97
Gulzar, 269-270
Gumasthavin Penn (Tamil, 1941), 47

Haider, Ghulam, 55
Halodhia Choraye Baodhan Khai (1987), 97
Hang Tuah (1956), 48
Heroines and Singers, 57-60
Hindustan Film Co., 8
Hirak Rajar Deshe (1980), 90
Holi (1984), 95
How Films are Prepared (1913), 6
Hunterwali (1934), 19
Husain, Sajjad, 63
Hum Hain Rahi Pyar Ke (1993), 175

Imagi Ningthem (1981), 98

Imam Farosh (1937), 45
Imperial Film Co., 19
Indian Cinematograph Committee, 13
completion of report by, 15
evidence of, 14
report of, 14-15
setting up of, 13
Indira, M.A. (1934), 19
Irani, Ardeshir, 18
Ishanou (1990), 98

Jagga Daku (1940), 45
Jagirdar, 22
Jait Re Jait (1977), 96
Jai Baba Felunath (1978), 90
Jawani ki Hawa (1935), 24
Jayalalitha, 228
Junoon (1978), 93

Kadhalan (1994), 191-192
Kagaz Ke Phool, 35, 37, 211
Kalpana (1948), 71
Kalidas (Tamil, 1931), 27
Kalia Mardan (1919), 7, 9
Kala Bazar (1960), 211
Kalyug (1981), 93
Kamalabai, 7
Kangan (1939), 24
Kanniyin Kathali (1949), 45
Kapoor, Raj, 38-40
Karanth, Prema, 100
Karun, Shaji N, 100
Kasba (1990), 94
Karuthamma, 193-194
Kasaravalli, Girish, 96
Kati Patang (1971), 172
Kaul, Mani, 93-94, 113, 282-283
Keechka Vadham (1916), 10
Khandhar (1983), 91
Khan, Mehboob, 19, 22, 30-32
Khayal Gatha (1989), 94
Khazanchi (1941), 55
Khoon ka Khoon, 23
Khursheed, 58
Kimti Qurbani (1933), 47
Kismet, 35
Kolahal (1988), 98
Krishna Bhakti (1948), 45
Krishnan, L, 46-47

Laila Majnu (1931), 24
Laila Majnun (1933), 43
Lajmi, Kalpana, 101
Lanka Dahan (1917), 7
Life of Christ (1911), 4
Light of Asia (1925), 12, 23
Ludhianavi, Sahir, 64
Ma Bhoomi (1979), 96
Madan, Jamshedji Framji, 9
Madhuri (1932), 19
Mahanadhi, 192
Majumdar, Phani, 43, 48
Mammo (1994), 93
Mandi (1983), 93
Mangeshkar, Lata, 56-57
Mane (1989), 96
Manzil (1936), 26
Marthandavarma (1931), 13
Mathilukal (1989), 91
Mati Manas (1985), 93
Maya Memsaab (1992), 95
Maya Miriga (1983), 100
Meetha Zahar (1938), 23
Mehmood, Talat, 60-62
Megha Dhake Tara (Bengali), 75
Mehta, Ketan, 95, 271-272
Melody of Love (1929), 18
Mera Naam Joker, 39
Mirch Masala (1986), 95
Mirza, Saeed Akhtar, 94-95, 270-271
Miss Frontier Mail (1936), 19
Mistry, Baburao K., 10

Modi, Sohrab, 19, 22-23
Mohammad, Ghulam, 62
Mohan, Madan, 62
Mohan Joshi Hazir Ho! (1984), 94
Mohini Bhamasur (1914), 7
Mother India (1957), 22, 30-32
Mouna Ragam (1986), 99
Mr and Mrs 55, 34-35, 211
Mouz Magazine, 5
Mudaliar, R.N. 10
Mukesh, 62
Mukhamukham (1984), 91
Mukti (1937), 26
Mullick, Pankaj, 25, 54
My Son (1945), 45

Nagarik (Bengali, 1952), 71
Narayanan, Anathanarayana, 10
Nargis, 39
Narrative Dispersals, 174-175
National Film Development Corporation, 83
  achievement of, 85
  formation of, 83
  role played by, 83
  number of films produced by, 85
  publication of, 87
Nayakan (1987), 99, 193
Nayyar, O. P., 55, 59, 64, 215
Nazar (1990), 94
Nihalani, Govind, 94, 272-274
1942-A Love Story (1995), 117
New Audio-Visual Ecology, 133-134
New Cinema, 107
Noorjahan, 58

Oka Oorie Katha (1977), 91
Oridathu (1986), 93
Osten, Franz, 19, 23

Pakeezah (1972), 212
Paar (1984), 96
Padma Nadir Majhi (1992), 96-97
Paranjpye, Sai, 101, 284
Paranjpye, Wrangler, 4
Party (1984), 94
Patang (1993), 97
Patànkar, S.N., 10
Pather Panchali (Bengali, 1955), 72-74, 100
Patwardhan, Anand, 162-164
Phalke, Dhundiraj Govind, 3-8, 10, 14, 103-105
Phalke, Mandakini, 7
Phaniyamma (1982), 100
Phera (1986), 97
Pikoo (1980), 90
Politics of Songs, 180-182
Pontianak (1957), 48
Post-Sacred World, 185
Pre-Cinema Efforts, 3-4
President (1937), 27
Prisoners of Conscience (1978), 163
Pukar (1939), 23
Pune Film Institute, 84
Punjab Mail (1939), 19
Puran Bhakta (1933), 25
Puri, Amrish, 175
Pyaasa (1957), 35-36

Rafi, Mohammad, 60-62
Rai, Himanshu, 12
Raja Babu (1994), 171
Raja Harishchandra (1913), 3-6
Rajhans, B.S., 45
Ram Banwas (1918), 10
Ramachandran, M.G., 222-224
Ramanathan, S., 44
Rama Rao, N.T. 224-225
Ram Ke Naam (1992), 163
Ram Teri Ganga Maili, 39

Ramlee, P., 44-46
Rao, B. Narsingh, 47, 282
Rao, P.V., 13
Rao, B. N., 47
Ratnam, Mani, 99
Rawal, Paresh, 174
Ray, Satyajit, 72-74, 90
Regional Expansion, 10
Rehman, A.R., 192
Rise and Dominance of Bombay, 19
Rojik, Omar, 49
Roja (1992), 99
Roti, 30
Roy, Bimal, 25, 32-33

Sadgati (1981), 90
Sahib, Bibi aur Ghulam, 37
Said-e-Havas (King John), 23
Saigal, K.L., 26, 53-54
Saikia, Bhabendra Nath, 98
Sairandhari (1920), 10
Salim Langde Pe Mat Ro (1989), 94
Samadhi (1950), 55
Sandhyarag (1977), 98
Sant Eknath (1926), 9
Sant Namdev (1922), 9
Sant Tukaram (Dada Saheb Phalke's) (1921), 9, 145-154
Sarothi (1991), 98
Satah se Uthata Admi (1980), 93
Satyam, Shivam, Sundaram, 38
Satyavadi Raja Harishchandra (1917), 7
Satyavan Savitri (1914), 7
Savkari Pash (1925), 11
Seeta, 26
Sen, Aparna, 78
Sen, Hiralal, 4
Sen, Mrinal, 76-77, 85, 90
Sethumadhavan, 191-193
Shahani, Kumar, 93, 113-114, 283-284
Shailendra, 64-65
Shakha-Proshaka (1990), 90
Shanker-Jaikishan, 62
Shantaram, V., 11, 19, 21
Sharma, Aribam Syam, 98, 282
Sharma, Kidar, 49
Shatranj ke Khilari (1977), 90
Shaw, Sir Run Run, 43-45
Shiraz (1928), 12, 23
Shirin Farhad (1931), 24
Sholay (1975), 172
Shree 420 (1955), 38-39
Shri Krishna Janma (1918), 7
Signs of Villainy, 175
Silent films, 15
    number of, 15
Simhasan (1979), 96
Singh, Sehjo, 163
Sippy, Ramesh, 275-276
Sircar, B.N., 27
Social Codes, 111
Sound Recording, 125-128
Stage Designing, 131-133
Sujata, 32-33
Sulong, Jamil, 49
Sultanpuri, Majrooh, 64
Swayamvaram (1972), 91
Suraj ka Satvan Ghoda (1992), 93

Tabarana Kathe (1986), 96
Tahader Katha (1992), 97
Takdir Ilahi (1950), 46
Talaq (1938), 23
Tamas (1987), 94
Tarang (1984), 94
Thampu (1978), 93
36 Chowringhee Lane (1981), 100
The Birth of a Pea Plant (1912), 5
The Idiot (1992), 113
The Woman Betrayed (1993), 162
Throw of Dice (1930), 12, 23

Tiranga (1992), 174
Trikal (1985), 93
Tukaram (1935) (by Damle-Fatehlal), 22

Udayer Pathe (Bengali, 1944), 71
Uski Roti (1970), 93

Valli Thiru-Manam (1921), 10
Vasthuhara (1990), 93
Vidheyan (1993), 91
Vidyapati (1937), 25
Vinayak, Master, 19, 22

Wadia, J.B.H., 11
Watan, 22

Yaadon ki Barat (1972), 173

Zanjeer (1973), 81, 172